MONUMENT SCHOOL OF THE PEOPLE

A Sesquicentennial History of
St. Mary's College of Maryland,
1840–1990

by

J. Frederick Fausz

Associate Professor of History
St. Mary's College of Maryland

This book is dedicated to the students,
staff, and supporters of St. Mary's
College, past and present, who have
made this school so special.

Rich joy and love we got and gave,
Our hearts were merry as our desires.
Pile laurel wreaths upon our grave
Who did not gain, but were *success.*
—Joyce Kilmer,
as quoted in *The Castellan, 1949*

STATE OF MARYLAND

OFFICE OF THE GOVERNOR

WILLIAM DONALD SCHAEFER
GOVERNOR

All Marylanders have a reason to celebrate the 150th anniversary of St. Mary's College of Maryland. Founded in 1840 as a "living monument" to the birth of Maryland, the College has helped to preserve our first capital, St. Mary's City. Since its beginnings, the College has advanced the principles of tolerance that made Maryland so important in American history. Today, as in 1840, St. Mary's is an affordable public institution serving a diverse student population with the highest standards of excellence.

The story of St. Mary's, recounted so well in this book, is the story of individual Marylanders who repeatedly saved the school when it was threatened by economic crisis, natural disaster, or changing state policies. Their efforts are a heroic lesson in citizenship. They show how men and women, acting not for self-gain but for intellectual ideals, can make a lasting contribution to the state. Their struggles testify, as well, to the profound way in which St. Mary's has inspired every generation of Marylanders.

Today, St. Mary's College of Maryland continues to inspire us. We treasure its close links with our history, its campus of rare beauty and charm, and its national reputation for academic excellence. As the Governor of the State of Maryland, I feel privileged to congratulate the College on this happy occasion. May the "monument school" continue to thrive, enriching our state's collective heritage as it offers future generations the gift of knowledge.

William Donald Schaefer

William Donald Schaefer

GMI

TABLE OF CONTENTS

*Whatever one person's path to the past, once there it is
an intriguing place to spend time. And the only self-
respecting way back to the present leaves each of us
with the responsibility of fashioning our own route out.*
—James Davidson and Mark Lytle, *After the Fact: The Art
of Historical Detection*

PREFACE

In writing this first book-length history of St. Mary's College, I have belatedly fulfilled a century-old directive of the Board of Trustees. Meeting on Thursday, 8 September 1887, the school's trustees unanimously passed a resolution that instructed Board Secretary John A. Camalier to "prepare an authentic history of this Institution from its inception, [to include] . . . all matters of interest connected with its progress from the origin thereof to the present time." There is no evidence that Camalier's history, like so many others that were proposed over the past 150 years, was ever written. In December 1911, Trustee Daniel C. Hammett did write the first known account "of the origin and conduct of the School," but it was brief enough to be read in its entirety at the June 1912 commencement. Presidents M. Adele France and A. May Russell mined a wealth of historical information in producing the school's notable pageants from the early 1920s to the late 1950s, but their main contribution was to leave behind the archival raw material without which this book could not have been written.

While it might seem odd that the state's Monument School, founded to memorialize the rich legacy of historic St. Mary's City, has never had a comprehensive history of itself, this institution has successfully imparted an abiding appreciation of its heritage even without a written text. Five generations of students have lived among the landmarks and artifacts of Maryland's colonial past on the St. Mary's campus, and after one has felt the presence of dead ancestors and their living ideals, no book can do justice to the experience. While all colleges have a history, St. Mary's is unique as a living memorial *to* history. This special site of notable firsts in American history is truly a place *where the past is present for the future,* and no single volume can possibly encompass or evoke all of its significance.

Aware of that daunting challenge, I conceived this book as a basic source that would explain institutional development and as an introduction to the social history of the school, representing the individual dreams and dramas that bestow vitality and meaning to institutions. Although the many rare photographs and eyewitness accounts that appear in this volume help the reader empathize with former generations, I am well aware of the limitations of time and of traditional documentary research for imparting what literary critic Lionel Trilling described as the "huge, unrecorded hum of implication [which] was once there and left no trace." I beg the indulgence of alumni and friends of St. Mary's whose memories, insights, and contributions are omitted from this book, for my interpretations are designed as an initial contribution to a long, ongoing process of historical recovery and recollection. If this first history stimulates the formation of richer and more diverse archives because of its errors of omission or commission, then the project will have been a most fitting memorial for the sesquicentennial anniversary of St. Mary's College.

Acknowledgments
Monument School of the People was written over the course of two hectic academic years, sandwiched into an already tight schedule of teaching, research, and administrative responsibilities, and it could not have been completed without the patient support of my students, colleagues, and family. I am particularly grateful to Ted Lewis for giving me the opportunity to write this first history (every historian's dream), and I hope his confidence is rewarded by the result. The alumni and community supporters of St. Mary's College came through like they always have, providing important documents and rare photographs that immensely improved the final product. Sharing my sense of excitement as those contributions arrived were the members of the Sesquicentennial Book Advisory Committee: Christine C.

Cihlar, Director of Public Affairs, a constant supporter with a keen appreciation of the school's history; Dr. M. Starr Costello '80, Director of College Advancement, who oversaw the administrative details of the project; Dr. Dana K. Greene, Professor of History, who vastly improved the manuscript with her perceptive readings; and Daniel Laskin, formerly Director of Grants and Publications, who copyedited the book with great skill. Librarian Joe Storey, Head of Technical Services, was most helpful in placing archival materials at my disposal and in working with Melissa Worthington '88 and Betsy Keisman, my indispensable student research assistants. Dr. Beth L. Truebell, Director of Grants and Publications, Ann E. Cruse, Coordinator of Publications, and Marybeth Burke, the indexer, provided talent and support in equal measure. Finally, I must thank my wife, Jeanette Fox Fausz '81, and my three-year-old son, John, for their patience in tolerating my obsession with this project. After enduring the night-long clattering of my printer for months on end, they consistently gave the kind of warm, familial support that made me feel less alone amid the distant centuries.

Fred Fausz
Calvert Hall 17
November 1989

ST. MARY'S
COLLEGE
OF MARYLAND
FOUNDED 1840
150 YEARS

The past remains integral to us all, individually and collectively. We must concede the ancients their place . . . {but} their place is not simply back there, in a separate and foreign country; it is assimilated in ourselves, and resurrected into an ever-changing present.
—David Lowenthal, *The Past is a Foreign Country*

INTRODUCTION
Where the Past is Present for the Future

Anniversaries are always occasions for retrospective glimpses into the forgotten, often forbidding, "foreign country" that is the Past, and this sesquicentennial observance gives us a unique opportunity to consider the special character, charm, and significance of St. Mary's College of Maryland, an institution so dear to so many. The sesquicentennial is all the more meaningful because St. Mary's has survived—indeed thrived—despite much adversity and against incredible odds. This 20-year-old college with 150-year-old roots as a female seminary is regarded today as the premier undergraduate institution in the Maryland state system of higher education—a fitting testament to five generations of human inspiration, dedication, and perseverance.

For most of its century-and-a-half, St. Mary's has been the best kept secret in Maryland, a school too poor, too small, and too isolated to take seriously. Recently, however, it has received national attention as an affordable alternative in liberal arts education to elite private colleges. St. Mary's was ranked first among "regional liberal-arts colleges" in the northeast by the *U.S. News and World Report* "1990 College Guide" issue of 16 October 1989, and the young college with the venerable heritage enters its sesquicentennial anniversary after six years of unparalleled progress, popularity, and favorable publicity. All Marylanders should know about St. Mary's College, not only because they financially support it and benefit from its rise to prominence, but because it is the state's living memorial to the colonial founders and their enduring principles. This Monument School of the People—Maryland's oldest state-owned institution of higher education, its first public boarding school for females, its first junior college, and its only liberal arts college in the state system —marks 150 years of service to the citizens of Maryland still committed to innovation inspired by tradition.

Since its founding in 1840, St. Mary's College has had but one campus—a beautiful riverside landscape of quiet charm on the sacred site of Maryland's first settlement and seventeenth-century capital. This region of Southern Maryland, nurtured by warming winds and the rich resources of the Chesapeake Bay, has supported human habitation for more than ten thousand years, from a Stone Age of flint chips to a Space Age of computer chips. Since the arrival of the first Maryland colonists in 1634, the St. Mary's River has attracted people of diverse backgrounds and beliefs and educated them in the lifeways and world views of one another. Native peoples from every continent have found the area alive with potential for abundant living, spiritual renewal, and an enriching knowledge evolved from adaptation to new challenges and opportunities.

It is significant that the campus of St. Mary's College was the setting for so much human inspiration and creative adaptation two hundred years before the school existed. The remarkable early pioneers—of ideas and ideals as well as territory—were the first Americans to embrace our values of human freedom, values that were then considered radical or heretical everywhere else in the English-speaking world. Maryland was Great Britain's first overseas settlement dedicated to the principle—*and practice*—of religious toleration; the first to foster demands for women's suffrage and equal political participation; the first to establish long-term cooperative relations with a large neighboring Indian population; and the first to integrate Africans and continental Europeans, Catholics, Protestants, and Jews into the social, economic, and political mainstream of colonial life.

St. Mary's City was unique among British colonial capitals in having both Jesuit priests and an English baron in extended residence, and in establishing official nonsectarianism as well as English Catholicism along the shores of the New World.

The progressive liberalism of St. Mary's City spawned an impressive pluralism that is typically American. By the last quarter of the seventeenth century, the thriving, cosmopolitan capital city of a prosperous province welcomed visitors or immigrants from most of Western Europe, many shires of England, all the neighborhoods of London, the townships of Massachusetts, the river plantations of Tidewater Virginia, and the tribal territories of Algonquian and Iroquoian Indians. This pluralism of culture, creed, color, and condition created a new, hybrid society with a uniquely pragmatic perspective on accommodating diversity and adapting to rapidly changing circumstances. The acceptance of change and innovation in all phases of life quickly emerged as Maryland's—and ultimately America's—enduring tradition in a land of endless immigrants and limitless frontiers. The vast promise of life here, of opportunity perceived and realized, prevented England's rigid class system from taking root in this soil.

Founded to commemorate those significant colonial achievements, St. Mary's College has relied upon both tradition and innovation, continuity and change, to accomplish its mission as the Monument School of the People. The history of the school has in many ways mirrored the history of early Maryland in the trials faced and tragedies surmounted. Like the indomitable phoenix of mythology, St. Mary's College has been reborn many times, ever rising from ashes, both figurative and literal, and each time, the school has rebounded with new energy and innovation. Changing in size, form, and function to better serve the educational needs of each new generation of Marylanders, St. Mary's has nonetheless retained a unique identity for 150 years. True to the founding ideals and original purposes of its creators, the school has retained its significant campus, despite criticisms of rural isolation, and kept its name, despite persistent, and at times detrimental, confusion that it is a private religious institution. From the beginning, St. Mary's has consistently been a state-owned, independently administered, nonsectarian public institution, providing an excellent education in the liberal arts at a reasonable cost.

The pioneering origins of the College as Maryland's only state-owned boarding school for young women and its mandated identification with revolutionary principles of the New World experience have allowed it to embrace innovations as integral to its traditions. Nurturing each new generation's quest of the "what-might-be" through an appreciation of the "what-once-was," St. Mary's—as female seminary, high school, junior college, and senior college—has used the rich, varied wisdom of the traditional liberal arts as the basis for evaluating the past and preparing for ever new futures. If this special school is today regarded as an innovative model for collegiate education in the twenty-first century, it is because it has stayed forever young by embracing a heritage that kept alive the optimistic dreams of those first Maryland pioneers, who forged a bright future with the spirit of daring, confident, youthful adventure.

FREEDOM
OF CONSCIENCE

ERECTED BY
THE COUNTIES OF MARYLAND

There was a wind over England and it blew.
There was a wind through the nations and it blew.
Strong, resistless the wind of the western star,
The wind from the coasts of hope, from the barely-known,
And, under its blowing, Plymouth and Jamestown sink
To the small, old towns, the towns of the oldest graves,
Notable, remembered, but not the same.
—Stephen Vincent Benet, *Western Star*

ST. MARY'S CITY, HAVEN OF HOPE:
The Seventeenth Century as Prologue

CHAPTER I

Strong bonds of place and principle link St. Mary's College to the first Maryland settlement and capital at St. Mary's City. The seed of the present College, St. Mary's Female Seminary, was founded in 1840 to "cherish the remembrance of great events and sacred places . . . connected with the early history of our ancestors," and the legislature required that this Monument School be built on the very spot "where [European] civilization and Christianity were first introduced into our State." Maryland's original capital had begun its precipitous decline exactly 150 years before the creation of the Seminary and had long since disappeared by the time the school was built in 1845. It was the Monument School that brought new life to St. Mary's City and reawakened interest in the long-obscured legacy of the Calverts. Considering the timeless bonds that connect the young College to the ancient capital, it is essential that this sesquicentennial history begin with the significant seventeenth-century heritage of St. Mary's City.

In the "Beginning"
Although Southern Maryland had been visited by Indian bands and farmed by native villagers for thousands of years prior to English settlement, the wider world

first learned of the region through the experiences of Captain Henry Fleet (1600–1660). Raised near the Thames River in Chatham, Kent, a London suburb famous for its royal dockyards and the overseas adventures of Sir Francis Drake and Sir John Hawkins, young Fleet came to the Chesapeake in 1621 with his second cousin, Virginia Governor Sir Francis Wyatt. Just six months after his arrival at Jamestown, the Powhatan Indian Uprising of 22 March 1622 nearly destroyed England's only Southern colony, and the following year, Fleet was captured by other Algonquians while exploring the Potomac River. He spent the next four years living and learning among the Nacotchtank tribe along the Anacostia River and quickly became an expert in the Indian dialects and customs of the Southern Maryland area.

Captain Fleet was the first known Englishman to reside at the future site of St. Mary's City, for his quest for beaver pelts between 1627 and 1632 frequently brought him to the villages of the Yoacomacoes, nestled along both banks of the St. Mary's River at Horseshoe Bay. Fleet's knowledge of England's insatiable demand for furs and of the Indians' growing desire for European products made him the earliest intermediary between the boardrooms of London financiers and the beaver-dams of the Chesapeake. Long before there was a Maryland or a Monument School, education was an important activity in this region, bridging cultural frontiers on the site of St. Mary's City. The Yoacomacoes taught Fleet the delicate etiquette of native trading, while he taught these traditional "deer Indians," who ate beaver

---

Freedom of Conscience Monument, St. Mary's College. Designed by sculptor Hans Schuler, this statue was erected for Maryland's Tercentenary in 1934 to commemorate the first practice of religious toleration in America.

but discarded the thick pelts as useless in a warm climate, how to preserve those furs for the lucrative hat markets of Europe.

Having gained the trust of skillful native trappers, Captain Fleet and his three brothers were soon prospering in mercantile activities that took them to far-flung ports of call from the Canaries to the Caribbean. Transporting Chesapeake maize to Boston, North Atlantic fish to Virginia, beaver pelts to London, and European products to Potomac River Indians, Henry Fleet enjoyed the kind of commercial success that breeds jealousy. In 1632, his fellow Kentishman, Captain William Claiborne, Secretary of State of Virginia and Commander of Kent Island (a rival trading base for beaver pelts established the year before), used his considerable political influence among Jamestown officials to disrupt Fleet's Potomac River enterprise. Only with the arrival of the first Maryland colonists two years later would Henry Fleet find the patronage and protection he needed to continue his entrepreneurial activities.

When the *Ark* and *Dove* brought the first 150 Maryland colonists into the Potomac River in early Spring 1634, Governor Leonard Calvert (1606–1647) immediately recognized Captain Fleet's invaluable frontier talents and hired him to find an appropriate site for settlement. No other English colony began with such an advantage, for Fleet ably instructed Governor Calvert in the intricacies of Algonquian diplomacy, served as his translator in negotiations with the Piscataway "emperor" and regional chieftains, and ultimately guided him to the Yoacomaco lands, where he had so often received hospitality. "Skillful in the tongue and well beloved of the natives," Fleet was the only Englishman who knew that this small Piscataway tribe was most anxious to abandon the future site of St. Mary's City in exchange for protection against the perennial, devastating raids of the powerful Susquehannocks–Claiborne's allies and trading partners from the head of the Bay.

One look at the Yoacomaco site convinced the Calvert colonists that this was an ideal location for the capital of their province. The Reverend Andrew White, S.J., described it as "a noble seat" with "as good ground as I suppose is in all Europe." Accessible to the Potomac, "the sweetest and greatest river" that Father White had ever seen, the waterfront site featured "two excellent bayes" that he predicted could "harbor 300 saile of 1000 tunne a peece with very great safete" and offered a high, defensible bluff that could easily be fortified to repulse intruders. Governor Calvert recognized a bargain when he saw one, and he quickly purchased "thirtie miles" of this "primest parcell" for "Hatchetts, Axes, Howes, and Clothes"–products that the Indians

had come to value thanks to the prior commercialization of the area by Fleet. According to traditional accounts, this first and most vital real estate transaction in Maryland history took place under the boughs of an imposing and now-famous mulberry tree, which remained standing until 1883.

On 27 March 1634, all of the Maryland colonists left their temporary lodgings on St. Clement's Island and disembarked at the new capital of St. Mary's City. Finding the "ayre wholesome and pleasant" along this "very bould shoare," they started their settlement under the best conditions of any English colony, for the Yaocomacoes left them rich fields already seeded with maize and bark-and-reed longhouses to protect them from the elements. In addition, those friendly, helpful Indians remained nearby, residing across the river at "Pagan Point," and continued to assist the settlers in their transition to a new American future. Father White believed the warm welcome extended by the Yoacomacoes was "miraculous," but Captain Fleet and Governor Calvert realized that the willingness of the colonists to "conforme . . . to the Customs of . . . [the] Countrey" and to treat the Indians fairly had provided this hopeful beginning in intercultural cooperation.

From its first days, the new Maryland colony actually *practiced* the liberal principles of interracial harmony that were just then being popularized by farsighted English intellectuals. In his 1624 *Encouragement to Colonies,* Sir William Alexander, a Scottish nobleman at the court of Charles I, admonished English colonists to "possesse" lands in America "without dispossessing . . . others," for the "ruine" of Indians "could give us neither glory nor benefit." A fellow courtier, Sir Francis Bacon, had advocated a similar policy in his essay "Of Plantations" (1625). Influenced by the brutal, wasteful Indian wars in Virginia, Bacon advised "plantation in a pure soil; that is, where people are not displanted . . . for else it is rather an extirpation than a plantation." Combining idealistic principles with practical concerns, the Calvert colonists became the first Englishmen to offer "kind and faire usage" to natives living in close proximity, for the Marylanders and the Piscataways could only survive as allies against their common, stronger enemies–the hostile Virginia Protestants and the fierce Susquehannocks.

Church and State in Early Maryland

While the Maryland pioneers enjoyed harmonious relations with their Indian neighbors, they faced almost constant hostility from their fellow countrymen in Virginia, who regarded them as religious deviants and economic competitors. The Calvert family knew only too well the harmful divisiveness and discrimination that religious differences engendered, for Sir George Calvert's conversion to Roman Catholicism in the mid-1620s had cost him his powerful position as Secretary of State and Privy Councillor to King James I. In a nation that had regarded heresy as treason and equated Catholicism with disloyalty since Henry VIII's break with Rome in the 1530s, neither Calvert's faithful service to James I nor his long friendship with Charles I could preserve his governmental offices against a suspicious Parliament and a hostile Protestant public. Retiring from court with the title of First Baron Baltimore, Calvert used his money and influence to establish a refuge where fellow English Catholics might live prosperously and worship peacefully. Before his death in April 1632, he conceived the unique charter that would create the proprietary province of Maryland as a haven of hope for oppressed Catholics.

The Second Baron Baltimore, Cecil Calvert (1605–1675), was granted the charter for Maryland on 20 June 1632 and began to turn his father's dreams into reality as the first lord proprietor of the province. Conspicuous in his own Catholicism as the heir of George Calvert and the son-in-law of Thomas, First Baron Arundell of Wardour, the young Lord Baltimore was determined to create a colony that would appeal to the principles of his friends and address the prejudices of his enemies. The near-regal powers of the proprietary charter allowed him to introduce English Catholicism to America through the immigration of Jesuits and to practice tolerant nonsectarianism by not establishing any denomination as the official faith of the province. Maryland thus began as a unique and radical experiment in the separation of church and state, for throughout the western world, governments had long assumed they could and should control the spiritual beliefs of their subjects.

"A Land-skip {landscape} of the Province of Mary Land," ca. 1666, published in George Alsop's A Character of the Province of Mary-Land *. . . (London, 1666); from the edition of the Maryland Historical Society, Fund Publication No. 15 (Baltimore, 1880). This rare, crude map shows the varieties of game animals that attracted Virginia fur traders like Henry Fleet and William Claiborne to the northern Chesapeake.*

Leonard Calvert Monument, Trinity Episcopal Churchyard, St. Mary's City. The 36-foot obelisk was erected by the State of Maryland in 1890, on the site of the "Old Mulberry Tree," to memorialize the founder of St. Mary's City and Maryland's first governor (1634–1647).

In declaring human conscience to be free from the coercion of politics, Cecil Calvert hoped to end a violent century of carnage that had produced "Fights, Frights, [and] Flights" in the name of religion.

Lord Baltimore's convictions were conveyed to his brother Leonard as the first Maryland expedition prepared to sail for the Chesapeake in late November 1633. Because Catholic settlers would be vastly outnumbered by Protestants in the cramped quarters of the *Ark,* Cecil Calvert thought it imperative that the endangered minority preserve "peace and unity" by "suffer[ing] no scandall or offence to be given" through proselytizing or public worship. His written "Instructions" to this effect explain why the colonists, who had been in the Potomac River for three weeks, did not celebrate a public Mass of thanksgiving until 25 March 1634. Even the most vehement antipapists could not object too strenuously to this commemoration of "Lady Day" (Feast of the Annunciation), which all English Christians then recognized as the first day of the new year.

Once the colonists had arrived at St. Mary's City, the Calverts sought to preserve interpersonal harmony and intracolonial unity through an official policy of nonsectarianism. They encouraged Catholics and Protestants to share a common chapel and denied special religious privileges and immunities to the Jesuits, even though they were major investors in the province. Thus, according to historian Henry Kamen, St. Mary's City became "the first colony in the New World, and indeed in the history of the Christian world, to be established on the foundation of complete religious liberty."

But enlightened principles of interracial and interdenominational cooperation could not alone control the destiny of the province. From the mid- to late-1630s, Lord Baltimore engaged Captain Claiborne in battles legal and lethal for control of Kent Island and the key beaver territories in the northern Chesapeake. Throughout the turbulent decades of the English Civil Wars (1642–1649) and the revolutionary Puritan Republic (1649–1660), military aggression and political oppression exacerbated the problems of the fledgling province and brought bloodshed to the once-hopeful shores of St. Mary's City. In 1642, Claiborne's Susquehannock allies raided settlements only seven miles from the capital and initiated a ten-year war with the Marylanders, during which the Virginia loyalists on Kent Island twice revolted against Lord Baltimore's authority. In February 1645, Captain Richard Ingle, piratical master of the ship, *Reformation,* invaded St. Mary's City in the name of the Puritan Parliament, intending to crush the alleged "tyrannical power" of the Calverts. During the "Plundering Time" of the next two years, his brigands and discontented Protestant servants vandalized Catholic homesteads throughout St. Mary's City. In late 1646, Governor Calvert finally returned to the capital and dispersed the invaders with the assistance of mercenaries from Virginia.

Leonard Calvert died in May 1647 before he could fully restore stable government, and with his passing, the province was plunged into still more crises. The presence of unpaid Protestant mercenaries encamped at St. Mary's City created a volatile situation, which was addressed by a most revolutionary proposal. On Friday, 21 January 1648, Mistress Margaret Brent (ca. 1601–ca. 1671), a wealthy resident of the capital and the executrix of Governor Calvert's estate, appeared before the General Assembly meeting at "St. John's," the home of John Lewger. On a spot that is today located behind the President's House on campus, she requested a seat in the Assembly "for her selfe and voyce also . . . as his

Lordships Attorney." When this shocking petition for equal political participation was denied, "Mistress Brent protested against all proceedings in this present Assembly, unlesse she may be present and have vote." Undeterred, this first American activist for female suffrage moved decisively to save the struggling colony. She sold cattle belonging to Leonard Calvert and Lord Baltimore in order to pay the mercenary troops and thus removed the "intollerable Yoke" of marauding troops. Although the assemblymen had denied her voice and vote because of her sex, they praised her leadership abilities, reporting to Lord Baltimore on 21 April 1649 "that it was better for the Collonys safety at that time [to be in her hands] then in any mans, . . . for the Soldiers would never have treated any other with that Civility and respect. . . . She rather deserved favour and thanks . . . then . . . bitter invectives . . . against her."

The Calverts survived the assaults on their sovereignty and property in the late 1640s, but the Province of Maryland changed greatly under crisis conditions. By the time the English Civil Wars ended with Charles I's defeat, imprisonment, and execution (1649), pro-Parliamentary Puritan emigres from Virginia had effectively taken control of Maryland's destiny. Escaping from the Anglican orthodoxy of Virginia, they established large communities along the Severn and Patuxent rivers, and this new immigration, combined with the flight of many original Catholic settlers—including Margaret Brent and her siblings—soon gave them a majority of Maryland's population. Seeking to preserve the interdenominational harmony that had generally existed within the colony since 1634, Lord Baltimore convinced a bipartisan Assembly to pass the famous "Act of Toleration" (officially called "An Act concerning Religion") on 21 April 1649. This significant statute was the first colonial law to guarantee freedom of religion for all Christians and the first document in American history to require a majority population to respect and protect the rights of an unpopular religious minority. Maryland was the only place in the English-speaking

---

The Feminist Challenge of Margaret Brent

Friday 21th Jan. 1647{8}
The Generall Assembly held att St. Johns.

. . .

Came Mistress Margarett Brent and requested to have vote in the howse for her selfe and voyce allso for that att the last Court 3d Jan: it was ordered that the said Mistress Brent was to be lookd uppon and received as his Lordships {Cecil Calvert's} Attorney. The Governor denyed that the said Mistress Brent should have any vote in the howse. And the said Mistress Brent protested against all proceedings in this present Assembly, unlesse shee may be present and have vote as aforesaid.

−Source: William Hand Browne, ed., *Archives of Maryland* (Baltimore, 1883), I, 215.

* * *

Margaret Brent was a remarkable woman. Arriving in Maryland in 1638, she and her sister Mary (two of the thirteen Brent siblings) patented seventy acres at "Sisters Freehold," along the river south of Governor's Field and the Chapel Lands. In addition to being rebuffed by the General Assembly in 1648 and praised by it in 1649, Margaret Brent patented nearly 1,100 acres and served as guardian for Mary Kittamaquund, the baptized "Empress of Piscataway." About 1650, the Brents left Maryland to settle in Virginia's Northern Neck, where Margaret died on her plantation, "Peace," about 1671. Historian Lois Green Carr has written that "her brief public career has more importance in the history of Maryland than in the history of women; nevertheless, the men who served with her evidently felt that it was not only her strength but also her womanliness that inspired 'Civility and respect' and saved the day."

−Source: Edward T. James, et al., eds., *Notable American Women, 1607–1950: A Biographical Dictionary* (Cambridge, Mass., 1971), 236–237.

Memorial to Margaret Brent, Governor's Field, Historic St. Mary's City. This commemorative bas relief of Mistress Brent before the Assembly was created by sculptor Mary dePakh of Avenue, Maryland, and is part of the gazebo-garden complex erected in 1984 by the statewide "Friends of Margaret Brent."

world where Catholics could worship openly without persecution, since even England's own "Act of Toleration" in 1689 only perpetuated discrimination against them for almost another two centuries.

Unfortunately, the liberal principles of Lord Baltimore faced determined opposition from power-brokers in London and Jamestown who were still hostile to the Maryland Catholics. On 26 March 1652, Cecil Calvert's old nemesis, William Claiborne, successfully invaded St. Mary's City with a Parliamentary fleet sent by Oliver Cromwell to "reduce all the plantations within the Bay of Chespiak to their due obedience" to England's Puritan regime. Claiborne replaced all officials loyal to the Calverts with former or present Virginia Puritans, and within a few weeks, his newest English supporters had negotiated an enlightened treaty with the Susquehan-

nocks, his oldest Indian allies. It was an ironic comment on the process of American acculturation that the Virginia invaders recognized the racially different "Nation and State of Sasquehanogh" after they had extinguished the legal rights of their fellow countrymen in Maryland. Claiborne's supporters soon voided the Toleration Act of 1649 and subjected Catholics and Anglicans to religious persecution and political disenfranchisement. In addition, Maryland's new Puritan government moved the capital of the province across the Patuxent River and expunged "popish" names from the map, transforming St. Mary's County into "Potomac" in the mid-1650s.

The repressive fanaticism of Maryland's Puritan majority produced a violent backlash. On Sunday, 25 March 1655, Lord Baltimore's deposed officials led their outnumbered Calvert loyalists against the forces of the anti-proprietary Puritans in the bloody Battle of the Severn. In this Sabbath-day slaughter on the feast day commemorating Christ's conception—the twenty-first anniversary of the first Mass in Maryland—several hundred well-armed colonists sought to resolve the issue of whom God favored in a most grotesque fashion. When the smoke of combat had cleared, the Puritans boasted about the heavy casualties inflicted on their Maryland neighbors and fellow Christians: "twenty slain, many wounded, and all the place strewed with Papist beads where they fled." After executing four prominent captives, the victorious Puritans reported that "thus God our Strength appeared for us; and the blood which they [the Calvert forces] thirsted after in others, was given to themselves to drink. . . . This is the Lord's doing; it may well be marvellous in our eyes."

These shocking atrocities helped quell the revolutionary passions of fanatical Puritans on both sides of the Atlantic. Following a thorough review of the decades-old Calvert-Claiborne struggle for control of Maryland, even Lord Protector Cromwell was convinced that Lord Baltimore's charter rights should be restored. Cecil Calvert signed a formal peace treaty with his Virginia adversaries on 30 November 1657, in which he guaranteed a blanket amnesty and the legalization of land titles for his rebellious Puritan subjects. Most significantly, Lord Baltimore reaffirmed the tolerant policies of 1649, "whereby all persons professing to beleeve in Jesus Christ have freedom of Conscience." This liberal reaffirmation of religious toleration ironically helped those who had once fought hardest to defeat it, for many leading Maryland Puritans had converted to Quakerism by 1660 and came to appreciate that the Calverts' province was the one place in the English-speaking world where Quakers were free "to be governed by Gods lawe & the

The "Act of Toleration," 21 April 1649

Forasmuch as in a well governed and Christian Common Wealth matters concerning Religion and the honor of God ought in the first place to bee taken into serious consideration and endeavoured to bee settled; Be it therefore ordered and enacted by the Right Honorable Cecilius Lord Baron of Baltemore absolute Lord and Proprietary of this Province with the Advise and consent of this Generall Assembly . . .

{T}hat whatsoever person or persons shall from henceforth uppon any occasion of Offence or otherwise in a reproachful manner or Way declare, call, or denominate any person or persons whatsoever . . . an heritick, Scismatick, Idolator, puritan, Independent, Presbiterian, popish priest, Jesuite, Jesuited papist, Lutheran, Calvenist, Anabaptist, Brownist, Antinomian, Barrowist, Roundhead, Separatist, or any other name or terme . . . relating to matter of Religion shall for every such Offence forfeit . . . tenne shillings sterling.

. . .

Be it Therefore also . . . Ordeyned and enacted . . . that noe person or persons whatsoever within this Province, . . . professing to beleive in Jesus Christ, shall from henceforth bee any waies troubled, Molested, or discountenanced for or in respect of his or her religion nor in the free exercise thereof . . . nor any way compelled to the beleife or exercise of any other Religion against his or her consent. . . .

[Confirmed by Cecil Calvert, Second Baron Baltimore, the Lord Proprietor of Maryland, on 26 August 1650]

—Source: William Hand Browne, ed., *Archives of Maryland,* (Baltimore, 1883), I, 244–247.

light within them" without fear of repression or execution.

The Golden Age of St. Mary's City

By 1660, when the Stuart dynasty was restored to England's throne and the Calverts reasserted their full authority in Maryland, the province had experienced two decades of terror and turmoil. Compared to those disheartening days, the next thirty years were to be a golden age of peace, progress, and prosperity for St. Mary's City—the first, and unfortunately the last, time in the colonial era when all of Maryland's citizens had the full opportunity to seek their fortunes in an atmosphere of freedom.

Although St. Mary's City never became the major port and population center envisioned by Lord Baltimore—due to the lure of good tobacco lands along the many distant creeks and rivers—the capital did experience a steady development after 1660 that reflected the province's new spirit of energy and enterprise. In 1642, when Maryland's English population was a mere 400, about a quarter of the settlers lived within the two square miles of fields and forests that were known as the St. Mary's "townlands." This 1,200-acre site at that time featured a mill, a forge, a chapel, and perhaps ten homes, but these frame dwellings were generally crude and impermanent, quickly rotting because of their post-in-ground "foundations" or often burning because of wooden chimneys and tarred roofs. Before 1660, the capital contained only two substantial structures, both dating to the first decade of settlement—the "Country's House" of Leonard Calvert (40 × 67 feet) and "St. John's," built by Secretary of State John Lewger (20 × 52 feet). But over the next thirty years, the growing

Reconstructed State House of 1676, Historic St. Mary's City, erected by the State of Maryland for its Tercentenary Celebration in 1934. The original building, the colony's capitol from 1676 to 1695, stood near Trinity Episcopal Church, which was built with its bricks in 1829.

influence and affluence of St. Mary's City resulted in the construction of more and better buildings. These included several inns, lawyers' offices, William Nuthead's printing shop, and four notable brick structures: a small prison (ca. 1676, located near today's College Boathouse), a massive Catholic chapel (ca. 1672), a substantial schoolhouse (ca. 1677), and the impressive State House (1676), erected at a cost of 330,000 pounds of tobacco.

From the early 1660s to the mid-1680s, Calvert "nobility" located their residences at the provincial capital, which contributed to an improved image of St. Mary's City. Philip Calvert (1626–1682), Cecil's young half-brother, came to Maryland in 1656 and for the next twenty-five years served in a variety of offices—governor, councillor, chancellor, chief justice of the Provincial Court, and mayor of St. Mary's City. He resided on the 100-acre Pope's Freehold (located at what is now the Route 5 entrance of St. Mary's College) until 1679, when construction was completed on his magnificent brick proto-Georgian "Great House" (54 × 54 feet) at St. Peter's Freehold. This regal residence, which apparently rivaled any contemporary structure in British America, was literally blown to bits in a 1695 explosion of gunpowder that was stored in its basement. Charles Calvert (1637–1715), Cecil's son and heir, followed his uncle to Maryland in 1661 and served as governor until he became Third Lord Baltimore and second lord proprietor upon his father's death in 1675. From that date until 1684, Charles Calvert was the first and only Baron Baltimore ever to live more than a few months in Maryland. During his tenure at St. Mary's City, he resided at St. John's from 1661 to 1667 and thereafter lived at Mattapany-Sewall, the "fair House of Brick and Timber" he built along the Patuxent River.

At the point of its maximum growth and greatest influence in the early 1680s, St. Mary's City was, according to archaeologist Henry Miller, "apparently the first example of a Baroque-designed community in the English-speaking world." Although the capital was still a small, compact village of fewer than twenty substantial structures, the placement of public buildings conformed to an innovative "Baroque Plan" of geometric design that emphasized symbolic significance. Recent archaeological research has revealed a symmetrical arrangement in which the bases of two equal triangles linked four important structures (the State House to the prison and the Catholic Chapel to the Jesuit schoolhouse), while the vertex of each triangle met in the town center, close to the present Brome-Howard House. Near the focus of the colonists' daily activities in St. Mary's City but *farthest apart from each other* were the Catholic Chapel (a cruciform building, 55 × 57 feet), standing on the City's highest hill, and the State House (a cruciform building, 45 × 61 feet), standing on the prominent bluff above Church Point exactly a half-mile away. Thus, this ingenious first example of Baroque town planning in British America sent a clear message that was consistent with Calvert principles: church and state were the most important influences in a civilized society, making equal claims on the loyalty of citizens, but they were to be separated and kept far apart for the benefit of both and the good of all. (The only other English Baroque towns in colonial America, Annapolis and Williamsburg, sent contrasting messages of church-state *connection*, as is evident in the former's State Circle and Church Circle.)

The Intellectual Life of the Early Colony

Because of the Calverts' early emphasis on recruiting wealthy Catholic gentlemen and their consistent efforts to encourage immigrants of diverse backgrounds to settle in Maryland, St. Mary's City was more cosmopolitan and intellectually sophisticated than its small size would imply. Several important colonists had graduated from Cecil Calvert's alma mater, Oxford University, including Fulke Brent, brother of Margaret Brent, and Robert Brooke, a major landowner and justice of the Provincial Court. Secretary of State Lewger obtained a B.A. from Trinity College, Oxford, where he taught before emigrating to Maryland. This trusted councillor and talented officeholder was successively ordained an Anglican minister and a Catholic priest in the course of a long career. Other early colonists received legal educations at London's Inns of Courts in Chancery Lane. The extensive libraries of some St. Mary's City residents also revealed broad intellectual interests, although the colleges they attended are not easily identified. Dr. Luke Barber, for instance, had a collection of eighty-two books in English, fifty in Latin, and forty-three in French in the mid-seventeenth century.

Although formal schooling was a rare luxury in a small, rural society of dispersed plantations, in which a majority of men and nearly all women were illiterate and trained only in manual occupations, the presence of Jesuit priests provided seventeenth-century Maryland with more intellectual stimulation and educational opportunities than other southern colonies. Father Andrew White, S.J. (1579–1656), called the "Apostle of Maryland," was one of the first four Jesuits to emigrate to the Calvert colony, and his impressive educational credentials prepared him to minister to both English and Indian populations. Born in London, he was educated at St. Alban's College, an English Catholic semi-

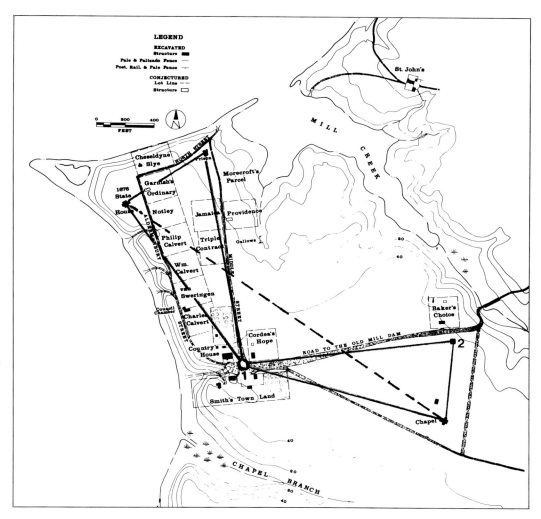

Map of St. Mary's City as a "Baroque City," ca. 1680, based on the research of Dr. Henry M. Miller, Senior Archaeologist of Historic St. Mary's City, and his staff. Originally published in a slightly different version in Henry M. Miller, "Baroque Cities in the Wilderness: Archaeology and Urban Development in the Colonial Chesapeake," Historical Archaeology, Vol. XXII, No. 2 (1988), p. 63, and reprinted with his permission. No. 1 on the map refers to the town center; No. 2 to the conjectured location of the brick school in Mill Field.

nary in Valladolid, Spain, and at the Jesuit novitiate of St. John in Louvain, France. After his ordination, Father White was a professor of theology, sacred scripture, Greek, and Hebrew at Louvain and Liege. Arriving in Maryland in 1634, he wrote important books about the early colony and translated several sacred texts into the Piscataway Algonquian dialect.

While Father White had great success in converting local Indians to Catholicism, other Jesuits served the needs of the colonial population. By 1650, the Reverend Lawrence Starkey, S.J., and Ralph Crouch were probably operating a privately endowed school at St. Inigoes or St. Mary's City, and seven years later, Crouch was teaching children of all faiths at Newtown Manor. Jesuits also ran a Latin grammar school at Newtown Manor—which sent its most promising students to the English seminary at St. Omer, Flanders—and a girls' academy in Port Tobacco, which sent its graduates to convents in France and Flanders. Of potentially greater significance was the large brick "School of the Humanities" at St. Mary's City. Archaeological evidence suggests that it was located in Mill Field, not far from the

Catholic Chapel and the present College campus, and that it was only the fourth brick building in the capital city. Jesuit priests probably conducted classes here until Catholic churches and schools were banned in 1704.

The Death of Old St. Mary's City

The golden age of the capital city ended abruptly after only three decades, aborted by the political jealousy and religious prejudice of a large Protestant underclass that did not share the ideals and prosperity of the Catholic elite. In 1689, some 22,000 whites lived in Maryland, triple the figure of 1660, and probably three-fourths of them were at least nominally Anglican (an estimated 13 percent were Roman Catholics and 13 percent Quakers). Vocal Anglican critics reported to the Bishop of London that Maryland was "becom[ing] a Sodom of uncleanness and a Pest house of iniquity," because the Calverts' persistent policy of allowing all faiths but funding none had, in effect, created a secular society that left the Protestant majority almost entirely unchurched and susceptible to "Popery, Quakerism or Phanaticisme." The "tyrannical yoake of papacy" was blamed for per-

Memorial to Mathias de Sousa, the first black legislator in the English-speaking world, Historic St. Mary's City. This plaque, with bas relief created by Mary dePakh of Avenue, Maryland, was erected in 1987 to commemorate the 350th anniversary of St. Mary's County.

verting politics in the province, because Cecil Calvert and Charles Calvert since 1660 had created a ruling oligarchy of wealthy, trusted Catholic friends and family members in an effort to prevent the destabilizing upheavals that had plagued Maryland in the 1640s and 1650s. Politically and religiously impotent, the large Anglican majority resented this monopoly of power and privilege and grew increasingly paranoid about an alleged alliance between Lord Baltimore, the Catholic King James II (son of Charles I), his patron, Louis XIV of France, and the many Jesuit-converted Indians in Maryland and French Canada.

When Lord Baltimore failed to declare Maryland's support of the Glorious Revolution (November 1688–February 1689), which had replaced James II with the Protestant William III and Mary II, discontented colonists John Coode, Nehemiah Blackistone, and Kenelm Cheseldyne led 700 armed and angry rebels into St. Mary's City on 27 July 1689 and toppled the Calvert government. This "Protestant Rebellion" brought the final political downfall of the Calverts and resulted in

the imposition of royal authority and the establishment of Anglicanism as the sole legal religion in Maryland. After the arrival of Royal Governor Sir Lionel Copley at St. Mary's City in 1692, no Catholic could vote or hold office, and every citizen was taxed for the support of the Anglican Church. In 1704, the all-Anglican Assembly passed the infamous "Act to Prevent the Growth of Popery," which forced Catholics to worship and conduct their schools in secret, just as their ancestors had done in Elizabethan England. That same year, Maryland legislators imposed an exorbitant tax "to prevent the importing of too great a number of Irish Papists into this Province." Truly, the Glorious Revolution was no victory for democratic liberalism in Maryland; only the American Revolution would restore the toleration and freedom that religious minorities had enjoyed in the province since 1634.

Although lax enforcement often lessened the impact of discriminatory laws in the latter eighteenth century, the Catholics of Southern Maryland suffered the ultimate indignity and greatest economic deprivation when the new royal government in 1694 decided to relocate the provincial capital to the "safer" Protestant area of Arundel Town, soon to be known as Annapolis. Despite pledges by St. Mary's City residents to make the "antient . . . Seate of Government" more convenient for the crowds that thronged here during the "Publick Times" of Assembly sessions, biased royal officials were determined to build a new capital from scratch along the Severn River, where anti-Catholicism had flourished since the days of Claiborne's Providence allies. Ruling that "the Citty of St Maries is very Unequally Rankt with London [and] Boston," Royal Governor Sir Francis Nicholson and his Council in 1695 relegated the once-prominent capital and the "Mother County of Maryland" to economic stagnation and political impotence. The government turned over the State House to the vestry of William and Mary Parish, and its subsequent use as an Anglican chapel truly symbolized the dangerous marriage of church and state that the Calverts had always opposed. In 1706, St. Mary's City even lost its status as the county seat, when the administrative offices of local government were moved to Leonardtown.

The Legacy of St. Mary's City

The sudden demise of St. Mary's City ironically ensured its modern fame. Because the old capital quickly reverted to sparsely settled fields and forests reminiscent of earlier Indian occupation, it survived as a unique time capsule, preserving the hidden archaeological treasures of an early, precious heritage unrivaled in

North America. In the 150 years since concerned citizens memorialized the site with the creation of St. Mary's Female Seminary, the seventeenth-century legacy of St. Mary's City has assumed an even greater significance. Increasingly, scholars and the general public have realized that the principle of toleration, extended beyond religious disputes to include all types of human rights, is as essential—and as controversial—in our late twentieth-century world as it ever was. Only since the 1960s, with the election of the first Catholic president and the successful campaigns against racial, cultural, and sexual discrimination, have Americans fully appreciated the innovative liberalism of St. Mary's City's first century.

Seventeenth-century Maryland was no paradise, with disease and deprivation on a rebellion-riddled frontier consigning all too many colonists to Hobbesian lives that were "solitary, poor, nasty, brutish, and short." However, frequent disruption and premature death contributed to upward social mobility for vast numbers of hopeful immigrants. Catholics, women, blacks, illiterate freemen, and poor servants got their first and only opportunities for economic success and political participation in this simple, crude, disaster-stalked society with a surplus of arable land and a shortage of available leaders. Margaret Brent's pioneering demands for equal political participation, while unique, overshadowed her success as a prosperous landowner and businesswoman—successes that other women also achieved in early Maryland. Similarly, the fame of Mathias de Sousa as the first black man to serve in an English-speaking legislature obscures the fact that other African-Americans enjoyed upward mobility in Maryland *not as property* but as *owners* of property.

The crudeness and newness of Maryland's first frontier offered abundant opportunities for large numbers of settlers. Cecil Calvert's dream of an aristocratic society dominated by manor lords could not be sustained in the land-rich province, where for much of the seventeenth century small farms predominated over large estates and many ex-servants attained the coveted status of freeholder. In contrast, the eighteenth-century "golden age" of huge plantations and beautiful brick mansions represented an end to frontier opportunity for all but a few wealthy, white, Anglo-Saxon male Protestants. This narrow gentry elite was responsible for the elegant planter culture that so captivates modern visitors to Annapolis and Williamsburg, but such a monopoly of affluence and influence came at a dreadful cost in abuse and intolerance. Indeed, what supported the "progress" of that "enlightened" century was racial, religious, cultural, and sexual discrimination. Rigid boundaries

of class, creed, and color by 1700 resulted in the dispossession of Indians, the disenfranchisement of Catholics, the debasement of women, the enslavement of Africans, and the exploitation of poor white laborers.

The American Revolution at least partially established an improved political system that could correct such abuses, and it is significant that the founders of our republic rediscovered many of the liberal policies that the Calverts had pioneered 140 years before. The innovative ideals of the old capital were brought to reality again by the new nation and are now accepted as the traditional values of the American heritage. From its founding to the present, St. Mary's College has reflected that complex connection between innovation and tradition, the past and the future. The Monument School has been a distinctive memorial to a unique place, and both the city and the college that were created at St. Mary's have shared an intangible bond of mutual inspiration across the several centuries.

Significant Firsts at St. Mary's City

America's first English proprietary colony, 27 March 1634

America's first large-scale settlement of English Catholics, 27 March 1634

America's first residence of English Jesuits, 27 March 1634

America's first English Catholic chapel, 1635

America's first practice of church and state separation, 27 March 1634

America's first law requiring religious toleration, 21 April 1649

America's first intercolonial, intercultural conference, June 1634

America's first black legislator (Mathias de Sousa), 23 March 1642

America's first woman seeking equal rights (Margaret Brent), 21 January 1648

America's first English Baroque city, 1670s

America's first example of Georgian architecture (St. Peter's), 1679

South's first printing press (William Nuthead), 1685

St. Mary's! St. Mary's! awake from thy slumbers,
For footsteps are crowding thy late lonely plain;
. . .
There rest on thy bosom no ruined old towers,
No relics of pride that have battled with time;
But the low simple hearths which the waving grass covers
Have beautiful mem'ries of virtues sublime.

For here breathed the spirit of ardent devotion,
With freedom of conscience, a priceless bequest;
Thy Calvert and pilgrims for this braved the ocean,
Then offered to others a haven of rest.
. . .
Then list thee, St. Mary's! thou art not forsaken,
Though long years have flown o'er thy sleep by the wave;
For patriots' hearts have now come to awaken
The glorious past from a hallowed grave.
New cities have risen, in grandeur and splendor,
In the beautiful land where thy dwellings first rose,
But dearer the mem'ry, more thrilling, more tender,
Of thee, on this spot of thy dreamless repose.

—An "Ode" by Mrs. Mary A. Ford of Philadelphia,
sung at the fourth commemoration of the
landing of the pilgrims of Maryland, St. Mary's
City, 15 May 1855, and published by the Philodemic
Society of Georgetown College.

The St. Mary's River is very beautiful; and the choicest spot on its lovely banks is the site of its forgotten city. . . . {The} scenery is a picture of almost Italian beauty, and like the wizzard streams of that classic land, it is haunted by visions of the hoary past.
—Emily Regina Jones of Cross Manor, ca. 1865

EVER RISING FROM THE ASHES:
St. Mary's Female Seminary, 1840–1923

CHAPTER II

St. Mary's City is today filled with many monuments and memorials to its significant colonial accomplishments, but the one that has lasted the longest is not constructed of granite or marble. St. Mary's Female Seminary, the only school in America built on the founding site of any state as a living memorial to colonial forebears, retains both tangible and intangible links with the present and future after 150 years. As the seed of today's blossoming St. Mary's College, the Seminary in its formative years truly reflected the mixed legacy of Maryland's seventeenth century, sharing both its buoyant dreams and bitter disappointments. Ever rising from the ashes of near extinction, the Seminary resembled the mythical phoenix in its frequent flirtations with death and subsequent rebirths during a turbulent first century. But survive it did, remaining a state-owned, secondary boarding school for girls until June 1960, despite the addition of a coeducational junior college curriculum. "Female" remained in the name until 1949, and "Seminary" was retained until the institution was again reborn in 1964 as St. Mary's College of Maryland, on the verge of senior college status. This chapter will trace the Seminary seedling that imparted impressive values and an indomitable spirit that are still prominent.

Mrs. Theodora (nee Anderson) Norris, who attended St. Mary's Female Seminary in the early 1850s. Taken from a photographic memorial to the mother of Alice Norris (Mrs. Frank J.) Parran.

The Evolution of Public Education for Women

Formal education of any kind developed very gradually and grudgingly in Maryland's first two centuries, given the predominance of farm households and rural occupations, but the controversial concept of public education for women had an especially long gestation period. In a society dominated by plantation gentry, the first type of schooling to emerge in Maryland was private preparatory and collegiate education for male elites, followed much later by denominational schools for girls, and finally, with the founding of St. Mary's Female Seminary, state-sponsored secondary education for young women. Between 1750 and 1840, the elitism of the eighteenth-century Enlightenment universities gradually gave way to the egalitarianism of Jacksonian America; the principle of nonsectarianism competed with the interests of religious organizations; and individual states debated the priorities of providing advanced education for the male electorate versus schooling an entire population in the basics.

To understand the evolution of these conflicting perspectives, we must follow the development of education in eighteenth-century Maryland. During that century, the pioneering efforts of a handful of Jesuit priests in the 1600s were eclipsed by the full weight of the royalist church-state establishment that emerged after the "Protestant Rebellion" of 1689. Sir Francis Nicholson, who served as Virginia's royal governor both before and after his administration in Maryland, used his transatlantic political, religious, and commercial connections to establish King William's School at the new capital of

Annapolis in 1696. Created by royal charter, funded by the Maryland Assembly, administered by the rector of St. Anne's Parish, and adjoining the State House grounds, King William's School was a classical Anglican academy designed to prepare young gentlemen for advanced coursework at Williamsburg's new College of William and Mary and eventual ordination into the priesthood of the Church of England. For Governor Nicholson, who relocated the capitals of both Virginia and Maryland to new Baroque cities he designed, the patronage of the Annapolis academy and the Williamsburg college reflected his desire for closer ties between London's crown-and-church hierarchy and the maturing culture of the Chesapeake planters.

Revolutionary Thoughts on Education

I know that the elevation of the female mind, by means of moral, physical, and religious truth, is considered by some men as unfriendly to the domestic character of a woman. But this is the prejudice of little minds and springs from the same spirit which opposes the general diffusion of knowledge among the citizens of our republic. . . . It will be in your power, LADIES, to correct the mistakes . . . of our sex . . . by demonstrating that . . . the cultivation of reason in women is alike friendly to the order of nature and to private as well as public happiness.

Women . . . should be instructed in the principles of liberty and government, and the obligations of patriotism should be inculcated upon them. The opinions and conduct of men are often regulated by women in the most arduous enterprises of life, {and} . . . the first impressions upon the minds of children are generally derived from the women.

—Source: Dr. Benjamin Rush, *Thoughts Upon Female Education* (Boston, 1787) and *Thoughts upon the Mode of Education Proper in a Republic* (Philadelphia, 1786).

* * *

In providing the means of public education, . . . it ought to excite the state legislature to attend particularly to those who are most likely to be deprived of the advantage of such an institution. . . . The foundation of the system {exists} in the establishment of proper or suitable introductory seminaries, rather than in converting the greater part of the public support to the temporary advancement of one or two schools or colleges.

—Source: The Reverend Samuel Knox of Bladensburg, *An Essay on the Best Systems of Liberal Education . . . {and} An Address to the Legislature of Maryland on That Subject* (Baltimore, 1799).

In 1723 the Maryland Assembly sought to expand the influence of education throughout the province by passing the "Act for the Encouragement of Learning, and erecting Schools in the several Counties." This pioneering legislation set up twelve county boards of seven "Visitors" each (always to include an Anglican minister) and charged them with establishing one "free school" on the King William's model in their respective regions. Although the colony provided start-up expenses, these were in no way tuition-free public schools. Free only in the sense of "liberating" the minds of pupils through the disciplined study of the liberal arts, these county academies were generally limited to wealthy gentry sons who could afford to spend the money and take the time to study Greek, Latin, mathematics, "good Letters, and Manners."

The St. Mary's County Free School received one hundred acres of donated land and operated with funds provided by a poll tax "on All Negroes," but little else is known about it. Perhaps because of small enrollments or the difficulty of finding qualified faculty, the Free Schools of St. Mary's, Charles, and Prince George's counties in 1774 merged trustees, funds, and functions to form Charlotte Hall School at "Ye Coole Springs" in northern St. Mary's County, site of a public sanitarium and popular health spa since 1698.

Although six decades separated the founding of Charlotte Hall School for boys and the birth of St. Mary's Female Seminary at the other end of the county, the former established important precedents for the latter. First, Charlotte Hall's original board of trustees included prominent county leaders who affirmed monetary and moral support for local education. Second, these affluent trustees committed themselves to a boarding school plan that was unprecedentedly ambitious and expensive for Southern Maryland. (The original building, housing sixty boys, required 250,000 bricks.) Third, the steady growth and long life of Charlotte Hall School, which operated successfully from 1797 through 1976, indicated that even one of Maryland's most rural regions was capable of supporting a precollegiate education for boys—and would perhaps be inclined to do so for girls in the future.

St. Mary's Female Seminary was in many ways a sister institution to Charlotte Hall School, but the sixty-year delay in its founding reflected the enormous problems associated with public education in general and state-supported *women's education* in particular. Although "sumptuously endowed schools for the sons of fortune" and the "slavish ignorance of the [common] people" had both been condemned by the idealism of the American Revolution, most state legislatures in

Trinity Episcopal Church in a rare nineteenth-century photograph. Built in 1829, the church may have appeared very much like this when St. Mary's Female Seminary was constructed in 1844–45.

practice feared that the high academic standards of elitist colonial schools would be compromised by admitting an increasingly diverse population of all social classes and both sexes. In Maryland, the establishment of new nonsectarian institutions like Washington College in Chestertown (1782) and St. John's College in Annapolis (1784) had a much higher priority than the creation of a comprehensive system of statewide public education—which was proposed in 1826 but not implemented until 1865.

Women in the early nineteenth century found themselves largely ignored by male legislatures, much as Margaret Brent had been in her day. The lack of the vote and the belief that the "female mind" was incapable of benefiting from the liberal arts resulted in state support of collegiate education for men over any education for women, and even the rudimentary schooling of girls was often left to private entrepreneurs and re-

ligious groups. (The Commonwealth of Massachusetts, which had produced the most notable "patriot mothers" campaigning for women's rights, waited until 1839 to establish the nation's first female public normal school.) While private, nonsectarian girls' academies proliferated in the northern states—such as the influential Troy Female Seminary of Emma Hart Willard (1821) and Mount Holyoke Female Seminary of Mary Lyon (1837)—denominationally sponsored schools were predominant in the South. The Moravians, Methodists, Baptists, Presbyterians, and Catholics displayed a great enthusiasm for founding girls' schools by the dozen, which helps explain why only 18 out of the 182 American institutions established before 1860 and surviving to reach college rank by 1932 were created by state governments.

In this evolution of the educational prospects for young women, Maryland had an influential role to play—a role that reflected its unique amalgamation of

"Southern" and "Northern" traits and its dual legacies as the birthplace of both tolerant nonsectarianism and English Catholicism in the New World. After the American Revolution, Maryland regained its special place in the forefront of tolerant pluralism when the Protestant Episcopal Church, the Methodist Episcopal Church, and the Roman Catholic Church were all institutionalized as separate, independent American denominations within its borders. This reaffirmation of the liberal Calvert legacy particularly stimulated an important Catholic renaissance after nearly a century of official discrimination. Again enjoying freedom of conscience and political participation, Maryland's 16,000 Roman Catholics—representing two-thirds of all American adherents in 1790—responded enthusiastically, especially in the field of education. The Reverend John Carroll, S.J., a native son in "Maryland's own" Jesuit Order, served as the first Catholic bishop in the United States (1790–1815), and from his position in the dominant archdiocese of Baltimore, he was instrumental in founding several men's schools—Georgetown College (1789), St. Mary's Seminary (Baltimore, 1791), and Mount St. Mary's College (Emmitsburg, 1808)—as well as supporting Elizabeth Seton's creation of St. Joseph's Academy for women (Emmitsburg, 1809). Archbishop Carroll also built upon the traditional Catholic strengths in educating girls and in employing women teachers by dispatching Carmelites and Seton's new Sisters of Charity to establish girls' academies in Baltimore, Frederick, and Georgetown. Catholic lay teachers were more prevalent in St. Mary's County, where Polly Carberry and Jenny Digges conducted separate schools at Newtown and Mary Blades taught at both the Sotterley Plantation school and at the St. Mary's Academy for Young Ladies.

The Birth of St. Mary's Female Seminary

These general trends in women's education—both negative and positive, denominational and nonsectarian, national and local—all contributed to the founding of St. Mary's Female Seminary, but the specific, significant catalysts for its creation in 1840 came from Southern Maryland. Although the nation's first public woman's normal school had just been founded and the golden age of private female seminaries was in full flower across America, 1840 was a most inauspicious year in Maryland for the birth of this unique public institution.

The economies of the state and county had hit rock bottom and still suffered from the devastating impact of the Depression of 1837–1839. The State of Maryland, overzealous in its support of canal and railroad projects, was $15,000,000 in debt, owed annual interest payments of nearly $586,000 on its internal improvement bonds, and would soon be forced to institute a state property tax of 20 cents per $100 to raise revenues. The situation was even worse in St. Mary's County, one of the most distressed areas in the state. There, a population of 13,200 (6,000 whites, 1,400 free blacks, and 5,800 slaves) had declined by 2,300 people, or 15 percent, since the first federal census in 1790. St. Mary's County had the highest illiteracy rate among white adults in Maryland, and its single-crop tobacco economy made most residents commercially dependent upon Baltimore, unable to support a local newspaper, a bank, or a significant town within its borders. It was easy for Annapolis legislators to forget this depressed and isolated region, as was evident in 1834 when the State of Maryland totally ignored the site of St. Mary's City in celebrating the bicentennial of its founding.

If 1840 appeared to be the worst of times, it also held promise for becoming the best of times for a state

A Resident's View of Old St. Mary's City

Mention the city of {St.} Marie's, and the present generation will ask when and where it was. The headstone is buried under the moss of many years, and the child plays in ignorance over the grave of his mother. Like some wearied aspirant in ambition's race, that short-lived city stole unnoticed from the course and died unwept, while her sisters have reached the goal of empire and wealth.

. . .

It is strange, but it is true, that bosomed in these hills is the only spot in the western world where an Anglo-Saxon city once stood, not one foundation stone of which is now in its original place. After the removal of the capital to the present metropolis, the city pined and died, unnoticed and forgotten, like some heart-broken queen in the ruins of her palaces.

. . .

{The State House} . . . is a shattered pile of bricks and mortar, overrun with weeds and vines, like Caesar's robe, covering the ingratitude of his fall. . . . Our venerable state mother is gone and forgotten. We have inherited the fruit of her toil and her blood, and like heirs we have forgotten the giver in the fruition of the legacy. Few of her sons can point to her grave, fewer still have come to hang the pilgrim's cypress on her dismantled tomb.

—Source: Emily Regina Jones of Cross Manor, mid-nineteenth century, quoted in *The City of St. Maries, Maryland: A Story and Personal Recollections,* ed. Eugene and Jean G. Rea (St. Mary's City: The Press of William Nuthead, 1982), 1, 2, 6, 9–10.

and a county that had nowhere to go but up. The "sad remains" of ancient St. Mary's City consisted of "a few mouldering bricks," but the sacred site itself could be transformed into a vital resource of historical commemoration that no other county could claim. The local descendants of the first colonists, longing for the region's rediscovered fame and future growth, saw a glimmer of hope in the publication of John Pendleton Kennedy's historical novel, *Rob of the Bowl: A Legend of St. Inigoe's,* in 1838. This timely best-seller, the result of thorough research in rare seventeenth-century documents and containing "as much history as invention," generated public curiosity statewide about the origins of Maryland. By publicizing St. Mary's City as "the most wisely planned and honestly executed . . . society . . . found in the annals of mankind," Kennedy, a prominent United States Congressman and noted author, restored the forgotten Calvert capital to its rightful place in the minds of Marylanders. As a member of the new Philodemic Society of Georgetown College queried in 1842 after a group pilgrimage to the lost city: "Why are we so late in the proud ceremonial of this day? Why so far behind our brethren in Massachusetts in testifying veneration for the founders of this time-honored community?"

The citizens of St. Mary's County surely felt such neglect more often and more deeply than any tourist, and the three local representatives in the House of Delegates decided to exploit the widespread publicity that Kennedy's novel had stimulated. In 1839, Colonel William R. Coad, Colonel James T. Blackistone, and Dr. Joseph F. Shaw reportedly met at Coad's Cherry Fields plantation in Drayden, across the river from St. Mary's City, and formulated plans for the creation of a girls' academy that would be a living state memorial to the historic first capital. That was ironic, because the ancestors of Coad and Blackistone had been the rebel leaders most responsible for toppling the Calverts from power in 1689 and sending the old capital into a fast, fatal decline. Colonel Coad was a wealthy, 35-year-old Catholic planter (with total property valued at $63,000 in the 1850 census); Colonel Blackistone was an equally affluent, 25-year-old Episcopalian lawyer and future state senator from Leonardtown (whose in-laws owned Cremona plantation); and Doctor Shaw was a 38-year-old Episcopalian physician-farmer, graduate of the University of Pennsylvania Medical School and lifelong resident of Charlotte Hall. All were members of the Whig Party, but none seemed committed to politics as a career. It is not inconceivable that they gained election to the Maryland Assembly in 1839 for the sole purpose of founding a school that would help stimulate a regional renaissance, because all three men served only

briefly in the House of Delegates, only one before 1838 and none after 1840.

Delegates Coad, Blackistone, and Shaw journeyed to Annapolis in January 1840 to introduce their idea for a state monument school in the Legislative Session of 1839. (As was the custom in Maryland, a legislative session was designated for the year in which the assemblymen were elected, even though all of the business of the 1839 legislature actually occurred in 1840. Thus, the perennial confusion with the founding date of St. Mary's is owing to carelessness with prepositions; the school was created in 1840 by the legislature *of* 1839, not the legislature *in* 1839.) The three representatives from St. Mary's County received a good indication of

---

John Pendleton Kennedy on Old St. Mary's City

{T}he very spot where the old city stood is known only to a few—for the traces of the early residence of the Proprietary government have nearly faded away from the knowledge of this generation. An astute antiquarian eye, however, may define the site of the town by the few scattered bricks which the ploughshare has mingled with the ordinary tillage of the fields. It may be determined, still more visibly, by the mouldering and shapeless ruin of the ancient State House, whose venerable remains—I relate it with a blush—have been pillaged to furnish building materials for an unsightly church, which now obtrusively presents its mottled, mortar-stained and shabby front to the view of the visitor, immediately beside the wreck of this early monument to the founders of Maryland. Over these ruins a storm-shaken and magnificent mulberry, aboriginal, and cotemporary with the settlement of the province, yet rears its shattered and topless trunk, and daily distils upon the sacred relics at its foot, the dews of heaven—an august and brave old mourner to the departed companions of its prime.

. . .

{But} our pragmatical little city hath departed. Not all its infant glory, nor its manhood's bustle, its walls, gardens and bowers—its warm housekeeping, its gossiping burghers, its politics and its factions—not even its prolific dames and gamesome urchins could keep it in the upper air until this our day. Alas for the vaulting pride of the village, the vain glory of the city, and the metropolitan boast! St. Mary's hath sunk to the level of Tyre and Sidon, Balbec and Palmyra! She hath become trackless, tokenless.

—Source: John Pendleton Kennedy, *Rob of the Bowl: A Legend of St. Inigoe's* (Baltimore, 1838), ed. William S. Osborne (New Haven, 1965), 35–36, 39.

how their proposal would fare when the House of Delegates, with a huge Whig majority, appointed them to investigate the feasibility of their own idea. Coad, Blackistone, and Shaw knew that the legislature was inclined to provide some help to improve the dismal condition of education in St. Mary's County, because the state had recently appointed fifteen district school commissioners there and allocated $1,600 for the construction of elementary schoolhouses. The proposal for a secondary girls' academy, although ambitious, would succeed if legislation could be phrased in such a way as to appeal to the delegates' nostalgic patriotism while also addressing a practical, present need.

The bill "to Establish a Female Seminary in Saint Marys County on the Site of the Ancient City of Saint Marys" fulfilled all of the objectives in venerating the past, rectifying a present problem, and laying the groundwork for a brighter future. The County delegation introduced it into both houses of the Assembly in early February 1840. It passed the House of Delegates on 26 February, was approved by the Maryland Senate on 4 March, and was signed into law by Governor William Grason on 21 March 1840–"Enactment Day."

This bipartisan legislation, passed by a Whig Assembly and signed by a Democratic governor, reflected the sincere desire "to cherish the remembrance of great events and sacred places connected with the early history of our ancestors" at St. Mary's City–"where civilization and Christianity were first introduced into our State." The drafters of the act sought "to establish on that sacred spot a female seminary [so] that those who are destined to become the mothers of future generations may receive their education and early impressions at a place so well calculated to inspire affection and attachment for our native State." Thus expressed, there was little that was controversial in educating young women, destined to give birth to future citizens, at the birthplace of Maryland. Although the legislation specifically mandated a female seminary–which referred to a well-rounded precollegiate curriculum in the liberal arts and a seriousness of academic purpose not found in traditional finishing schools–the assemblymen definitely expected the new institution to produce cultured "Mothers of the Republic" and not spinster professionals or activists for women's rights in the mold of Margaret Brent. The female seminaries were the first schools in America to bridge the traditional male world of culture and the traditional woman's world of nature, but if the graduates of the better northern seminaries often became teachers or missionaries, few such vocational aspirations were intended or encouraged by southern schools.

St. Mary's Female Seminary was designed as a fitting, living, albeit belated, memorial to Maryland's bicentennial–the first and only American school founded as a monument to, and on the original site of, the colonial birthplace of any state. Consistent with its role as the Monument School that would forever honor Maryland's past achievements, the Seminary was required by the legislation of 1840 to collect and preserve meaningful archives and artifacts related to the early colony. This focus on history was an indispensable ingredient in creating the Seminary, because the State of Maryland would not have approved of a school in St. Mary's County anywhere but at the site of first settlement. Moreover, since the indebted state government could not and did not provide a penny for the school's con-

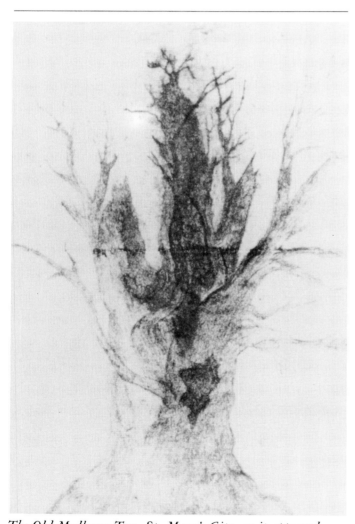

The Old Mulberry Tree, St. Mary's City, as it appeared when St. Mary's Female Seminary was constructed. This "treaty tree," the last of the capital's landmarks to survive from the seventeenth century, was drawn in 1852 by a Miss Piper, a student at the Seminary. Mrs. J. Spence Howard donated the drawing to Historic St. Mary's City, which granted permission to publish.

Trinity Episcopal Churchyard, St. Mary's City.

Creating the Seminary

An Act to Authorize the Drawing of a Lottery to Establish a Female Seminary in Saint Mary's County, on the Site of the Ancient City of Saint Mary's {as passed 4 March 1840}

Preamble

Whereas, *the disposition to cherish the remembrance of great events and sacred places as connected with the early history of our ancestors has ever been in all ages of the world considered praiseworthy and commendable, whether evinced by the institution of periodical celebrations or the erection of commemorative monuments;* and whereas, *a large and respectable portion of the people of Maryland have long entertained a desire to commemorate in some suitable manner the site on which stood the City of St. Mary's (in St. Mary's county), the ancient capital of the State, the sad remains of which cannot but recall to mind the transient nature of all* *things sublunary and the melancholy reflection, that nothing now remains but a few mouldering bricks to point out to the antiquarian the spot where civilization and christianity were first introduced into our State;* and whereas, ***the people of Maryland, and more especially the citizens of St. Mary's county, actuated by that delicate sensibility which prompts man to adorn and scatter flowers around the tombs of departed relatives and friends, desire to establish on that sacred spot a female seminary,*** *that those who are destined to become the mothers of future generations may receive their education and early impressions at a place so well calculated to inspire affection and attachment for our native State;* and whereas, *the object contemplated cannot be accomplished by private contribution and munificence and should for other good and sufficient reasons receive the countenance and support of this legislature. . .*

–Source: Laws of Maryland, Legislature of 1839, Chapter 190.

struction, having merely authorized a public lottery to obtain the necessary funding, the supporters of the Seminary counted on the popular, emotional appeal of nostalgia to fund this unique educational experiment. By authorizing a public lottery to raise up to $30,000 ($10,000 more than Colonel Coad had originally envisioned), however, the Maryland legislature provided official approval and thus encouraged thousands of individual contributors to make St. Mary's truly a Monument School of the People.

Although the legislature had used lotteries to fund other Maryland schools since 1809, one provision in the 1840 law made St. Mary's Female Seminary unprecedented and unique—it was to be *owned by the state* and operated as a *public boarding school for young women*. St. Mary's was the eighth female seminary in Maryland to be authorized and incorporated by the General Assembly, but it was the only one that was deeded to the state, that was subsequently supported by tax monies, and that survives today as a four-year college.

St. Mary's College, through its direct evolution from the Seminary, is thus the oldest state-owned institution of higher education in Maryland and the only one to have been continuously under state control for 150 years. St. John's College and Washington College had received state funds beginning in 1784, but they were never *owned* by the state; in 1805, the legislature withdrew its financial support, and both institutions struggled in the early nineteenth century before emerging as the independent colleges they have been ever since. In 1807, the legislature chartered Baltimore's College of Medicine, re-chartered it as the University of Maryland five years later, assumed control in 1826, and merged it with a small Baltimore academy and liberal arts college in 1830 to create a comprehensive state university. However, the medical professors rebelled against the state-appointed trustees and won a court battle to return both institutions to private ownership and operation, which the General Assembly agreed to in 1839. All of the other colleges in the state system were founded after the Civil War, and the present University of Maryland at College Park was not created until 1920.

In authorizing the lottery that would lead to the creation of the Female Seminary, the Maryland legislature appointed Colonel Cornelius Combs, Dr. Caleb M. Jones, and John White Bennett, all from St. Mary's County, as lottery commissioners and the first trustees of the prospective school. Although not as wealthy as Delegates Coad, Blackistone, and Shaw—the fathers of the Seminary—Combs, Jones, and Bennett were eminently qualified to be the first guardians of the new institution. All were trusted, middle-aged veterans of the War of 1812 who had demonstrated an interest in education through their service on the county commissions for primary schools. Colonel Combs (1783–1865), a prominent Catholic planter from Great Mills, had served on the St. Mary's County Levy Court and as judge of the Orphans Court. Doctor Jones (1788–1869), the Episcopalian owner of Cross Manor plantation at St. Inigoes, was a physician-planter with a medical degree from the University of Pennsylvania. Bennett (1796–1875), also an Episcopalian from the First District, had been postmaster of St. Inigoes and became a county commissioner in 1844. These trustees of both the lottery and of the eventual school assumed awesome responsibilities under the legislation of 1840. They were required to post personal bonds for good performance in administering the lottery and were legally liable "for the punctual payment of all prizes"—out of their own pockets, if necessary.

By the summer of 1844, Trustees Combs, Jones, and Bennett had raised $18,432.67, of which $1,124.42 was interest earned on bank deposits and another $3,438.56 interest on "City stock." Although this sum was far less than the ceiling authorized by the legisla-

The Charms of Women—1846

I would have her as pure as the snow on the mount
As true as the smile that to infamy's given
As pure as the wave of the crystalline fount,
Yet as warm in the heart as the sunlight of heaven.

With mind cultivated, not boastingly wise,
I could gaze on such beauty, with exquisite bliss;
With her heart on her lips and her soul in her eyes
What more could I wish in dear woman than this.

—Source: "Female Charms," *Godey's Magazine and Lady's Book*, XXXIII (1846), 52.

* * *

The Rights of Women—1848

The right to love whom others scorn,
The right to comfort and to mourn,
The right to shed new joy on earth,
The right to feel the soul's new worth.
Such are women's rights, and God will bless
And crown their champions with success.

—Source: Mrs. E. Little, "What are the Rights of Women?" in *Ladies Wreath*, II (1848–49), 113.

"The Seminary Building" (the original Calvert Hall), as it probably appeared soon after construction was completed in October 1845. A visitor in 1869 described it as "a large brick building that stands dreary and treeless, looking like a factory. . . . {The campus} would be an excellent place for a convent of Carthusians, but to banish lively girls to this lonely region, lovely though it is, . . . must have been the conception of some malicious and dyspeptic old bachelor."

ture, it allowed for the purchase of six acres of Trinity Church land from the Vestry of William and Mary Parish ($609.25) and the construction of the Seminary Building ($13,486.52), along with fixtures, furnishings, and fencing ($2,002). For an additional $100.00, the trustees also procured a right of way for "an avenue 20 feet wide," which by 1847 would connect the school to distant cities via the steamboat port at Brome's Wharf. (This road is still extant today, leading to the river alongside the Reconstructed State House.) On 3 August 1844, the trustees laid the cornerstone of the Seminary Building, with Randolph Jones, son of the trustee and heir to Cross Manor, delivering a stirring address. In dedicating the largest building to rise at the ancient capital in over a century-and-a-half, Jones reflected the local optimism for a brighter future: "May it be the morning star of moral light which brings in day, beautiful day, to Old St. Mary's." Three weeks later, Trustees Combs, Jones, and Bennett deeded the Seminary campus, including a portion "of the ancient city of St. Mary's," to the State of Maryland—probably the most significant single event that ensured the survival of the school to this day (21 August 1844, St. Mary's County Land Record JH No. 13, f. 381).

When contractor Thomas Evans completed the

two-story, double-porticoed "Plantation Greek" Seminary Building on 27 October 1845, the hopes and dreams of countless supporters seemed fulfilled. This original Calvert Hall*—although not officially named as such until 1955—was described by a Georgetown resident soon after construction as a "beautiful mansion." It was an imposing sight on a significant site and a fitting symbol of a community renaissance. The building's many chimneys and six white columns, thick and square, towered above nearby Trinity Churchyard, the tranquil resting place of colonial generations, and faced toward the Potomac River, alive with the traffic of commerce. Looking out upon the ruins of the old capital, this newest monument on those hallowed grounds contrasted sharply with the oldest—the massive but decaying mulberry tree that had greeted Leonard Calvert's arrival in 1634. The only other landmarks in St. Mary's City were Trinity Episcopal Church, which had been built with State House bricks in 1829, and the recently completed home of Dr. John M. Brome (1819–1887) at his St. Mary's Manor plantation in Governor's Field.

On 27 October 1845, the same day that Calvert

---

*Hereafter, "Calvert Hall" will be used instead of the "Seminary Building," since most people know this centerpiece of the campus by that name.

Hall (the Seminary Building) was completed, Trustees Combs, Jones, and Bennett began the process of making St. Mary's Female Seminary operational by convening the first official meeting of the Board of Trustees. In compliance with the legislation of 1840, they selected ten additional members to serve with them—Colonel Coad, Colonel Blackistone, and Doctor Shaw, who had conceived the school, and seven others: County Commissioner William Biscoe (1810–1876), Episcopalian owner of Pleasant Hills plantation, near St. Clements; Dr. William J. Edelen (ca. 1800–1873), a wealthy Catholic physician-planter and justice of the Levy Court; Colonel Benedict I. Heard (ca. 1793–1864), a Catholic from the Patuxent River with vast political experience on the state and county level; Judge Henry Greenfield Sothoron Key (1790–1872), an affluent Episcopalian lawyer who owned Tudor Hall in Leonardtown and the only known non-Whig on the Board; County Commissioner Henry Sewall (ca. 1805–1862) from the Second District; William L. Smith (ca. 1800–1853?), a school commissioner from the First District; and Richard Thomas, former speaker of the House of Delegates and president of the Maryland Senate, who declined to serve and was replaced at the December meeting by Thomas Loker (1798–1876), owner of Mulberry Fields plantation and former Levy Court justice.

This first Board of Trustees was an imposing group of prominent citizens from St. Mary's County, whose family dominance in public service and personal wealth was generally as great in the 1840s as it had been in colonial times. According to Whitman H. Ridgway's *Community Leadership in Maryland, 1790–1840,* "St. Mary's County was ruled by a dynamic oligarchy, whose power base was landed wealth, whose influence was enhanced by a persisting inequality in the distribution of property, and whose dynamic element was a social infrastructure of wide and expanding kinship associations." Service to the Seminary represented a civic duty to these community oligarchs and may have been the only personally unprofitable activity in which they participated. On 26 February 1846, the State of Maryland incorporated St. Mary's Female Seminary and officially made the Board of Trustees an independent "body politic and corporate," with the legal authority to acquire or dispose of all types of property, to use a common seal, and "generally to . . . promote the object and design of said corporation"—including the filling of trustee vacancies and the removal of members by a two-thirds majority. As one of the founding traditions of St. Mary's, its Board of Trustees has remained independent down to the present.

On Thursday, 13 November 1845, the Board of Trustees held the first business meeting since all thirteen members had been selected. The nine trustees present (Bennett, Blackistone, Coad, Combs, Edelen, Jones, Sewall, Shaw, and Smith) signed a pledge "to promote the interest and advance the prosperity of the institution"—which all subsequent Board members would sign for the next century. Colonel Combs was elected the first president of the Board and Bennett was chosen as register (secretary). Doctor Shaw introduced the only two motions of this first session: (1) that President Combs appoint a committee to draft rules and regulations for the governance of the Board (Shaw, Coad, and Jones were selected), and (2) that President Combs appoint a second committee to develop operational policies on teachers, salaries, and tuition (Shaw, Heard, Key, Jones, Coad, Edelen, and Sewall were chosen).

These subcommittees reported substantial progress at the next Board meeting on 14 January 1846. The one on operations, hoping that the Seminary could open by mid-March or early April, recommended the immediate furnishing of student living quarters "in a plain neat manner" and the hiring of three faculty members—a teaching principal at $400 per year, a teaching vice-principal at $350, and an assistant teacher at $300. The trustees decided to offer one-year contracts, reserving to themselves "the power and right of dismissing any teacher for incompetency, neglect of duty, or impropriety of conduct at any time within the year," but allowing the principal to suspend a teacher until the Board could take "final action on the subject." Committed to offering the curricula of the better female seminaries but at a much reduced cost, the trustees approved the following annual charges for students:

Tuition, Elementary Branch . . . . $ 20.00
(English Grammar, Spelling, Reading, Writing, Arithmetic, and Geography)

Tuition, Higher Branches of English 30.00

Instruction in French or Latin 12.00

Music Instruction, Piano (provided) 37.00

Music Instruction, Guitar (provided) 22.00

Drawing and Painting in Watercolors 16.00

Drawing and Painting in Oils 28.00

Stationery (optional) 2.00

Room, Board, Laundry, Fuel, and Oil for Lights 100.00
($10.00 applied to a fund for repairs)

The January 1846 meeting of the Board was among the most important and historic trustee gatherings in the 150 years of St. Mary's, for in addition to the measures already mentioned, the Board members determined the distinctive and critical core values of the institution that have endured until today. First of all, the trustees committed the Seminary to educational excellence in the liberal arts by pledging to "Secure . . . teachers talent to compete with the best established female Seminaries in the State, and offer as liberal and extensive [a] course of study as the highest standard of female education requires." One of the best institutions that the trustees investigated and emulated was the Patapsco Female Institute in Ellicott City, founded in 1834 by Mrs. Almira Hart Phelps, sister of Emma Hart Willard, known throughout America for the excellence of her Troy Female Seminary in New York.

Second, in recognizing that "the great object of this institution was not only to raise the standard of female education in our county, but to diffuse its blessings to as numerous a portion of the community as possible," the St. Mary's trustees consciously made tuition, board, and fees more affordable at the new Monument School of the People than at the "several female schools of established character in the State." St. Mary's charged a total of only $120 per year for a boarding student in the Elementary Branch and $130 per year for the advanced English curriculum. The total cost of taking every subject at the Seminary in an academic year (an impossible task) was a mere $267—substantially lower than the charges at sister seminaries across the state, which the Board had specifically researched: Frederick Female Seminary (1842), $365; Hamilton's Academy in Baltimore, $431; Baltimore Academy of the Visitation (1839), $445; and Patapsco Female Institute, $494. From the beginning, the trustees wanted St. Mary's Female Seminary to be self-supporting and actively sought "extensive patronage"—initially "Solicit[ed] Subscriptions" for a library fund—that would create a private endowment and continue to keep student costs low.

Finally, the trustees established the fundamental principles of strict nonsectarianism and liberal religious toleration in both the Seminary's internal operations and external relations, consistent with the school's historic ties to the Calvert legacy at St. Mary's City. While knowledge of Christianity would be encouraged among the students as a "great and important element of female education," the trustees were adamant that "no spirit of proselytism, no clashing of conflicting creeds, or controversial questions of churches shall be permitted within the walls of this institution, an institution founded on the consecrated spot where free toleration on the subject of religion was first promulgated." The Board "sincerely hoped that this spirit, like the good genius of the place, may hover over our institution and our children taught to respect each others religious creeds, and in the language of Saint John to 'love one another.'" All teachers and trustees of the Seminary were injoined "both by precept and example to carry out this principle, and thereby confer innumerable benefits and blessings upon the people of Saint Marys for ages to come." This principle was soon translated into policies that required an equal distribution of Catholics, Episcopalians, and Methodists—the dominant denominations in the population of St. Mary's County—among the teachers and the trustees.

"Placing A Daughter At School"

Dear madam, I've called for the purpose
Of placing my daughter at school;
She's only thirteen, I assure you,
And remarkably easy to rule.
I'd have her learn painting and music,
Gymnastics and dancing, pray do,
Philosophy, grammar and logic,
You'll teach her to read, of course, too.
I wish her to learn every study
Mathematics are down on my plan,
But of figures she scarce has an inkling
Pray instruct her in those, if you can.
I'd have her taught Spanish and Latin,
Including the language of France;
Never mind her very bad English,
Teach her that when you find a good chance.

. . .

Now to you I resign this young jewel,
And my words I would have you obey;
In six months return her, dear madam,
Shining bright as an unclouded day
She's no aptness, I grant you, for learning
And her memory oft seems to halt;
But, remember, if she's not accomplished
It will certainly be your fault.

—Source: Motte Hall, in *Godey's Lady Book*, XLVI (May 1853), 457.

	Mrs. Phelps Ellicotts Mills	Frederick Seminary	Visitation Academy. Balt.	St. Marys Female Seminary	Hamiltons Baltimore
Board per annum	$200.	160.	130	100	200
Tuition Common branches	40	25	40	20	40
" Higer branches of Eng	40	40	60	30	60
" Languages	30	20	20	12	32
Music on Piano	60	40	60	32	Professor charge
" Guitar	40 – 4	20	48	20	"
Use of Piano & Guitar	10 – 4	8	12	5 – 2	15
Drawing & Painting	30	20	20	16	Professor charge
Painting in Oil	40	30	50	25	"
Stationary	4	2	5	2	4

A chart of charges from the 14 January 1846 Minutes of the Board of Trustees, showing how St. Mary's was designed to be an inexpensive alternative to sister seminaries around the state.

A Rough Beginning

Blessed with conscientious trustees, a new campus, and laudable guiding principles, St. Mary's Female Seminary in the spring of 1846 lacked only two prerequisites for a successful school—teachers and students! In their enthusiasm for this unique educational experiment, the trustees were unprepared for the difficult task of recruiting accomplished faculty members to such a rural area—an endemic problem that would plague the institution for the next century. Mr. Edward J. Meany finally accepted the position of principal on Thursday, 2 April 1846, after thinking over the Board's offer for nearly a month, but the Seminary still desperately needed women teachers before it could open. Mrs. Meany, who had been hired to provide meals, oversee the dormitory, and chaperone the students, was pressed into service as a part-time teacher by the reluctant trustees, who promised to "appropriate such compensation [to her] as they can afford." The Board increased the annual salary of the vice-principal from $350 to $400 in an effort to stimulate applicants, but to no avail. Two well-known and highly regarded county teachers, Miss Agnes Magee and Miss Mary Blades, were offered teaching positions at $350 apiece (an increase of $50 from the Board's initial budget projections), but they both declined the appointments anyway.

After all the previous plans to open the Seminary in mid-March or early April or mid-May had been dashed by the failure to recruit instructors, a strange malaise beset the once-enthusiastic trustees. The scheduled Board meetings for 2 May, 16 June, 1 July, and 17 October 1846 all failed to attract a quorum, and on one occasion, three trustees waited several hours for others to arrive in the futile hopes of having a meeting. On 13 May, the Board ruled that, henceforth, five members—not the seven as stated in the state's 1846 act of incorporation—would "constitute a quorum for the transaction of ordinary business, subject to the approval by a quorum under the *charter* at their next meeting." The trustees, in evident desperation, passed the following motion at the Board meeting on 14 December 1846: "Resolved by the Trustees of St. Marys Female Seminary that when a Trustee of this institution fails to attend three quarterly meetings in succession, without a good and sufficient excuse, he will be considered as having vacated his seat, and that the trustees will, at their next

36

meeting, . . . elect someone to fill his place."

The Seminary was almost still-born, but to maintain momentum, the trustees encouraged a "very limited number of boarders"—mostly their own daughters and nieces—to take up residence at the school in the late spring of 1846. An additional teacher joined the Meanys that summer, and St. Mary's Female Seminary, after numerous delays, at last had its official opening on the first Monday in October 1846. No more than ten students began the first academic year, for the Board minutes of 11 November 1846 recorded only $92.95 collected in "Tuition fees." Mrs. Cecelia Coad Roberts, Trustee Coad's daughter and the last surviving member of that entering class, was only eight when she started at the Seminary. In reminiscences recorded in the mid-1920s, she recalled "less than twelve" initial matriculants, including Jane Bennett, daughter of Trustee Bennett; Sallee Biscoe, perhaps a niece of Trustee Biscoe; Mary Rebecca Loker, daughter of Trustee Loker; and Mary Milburn, daughter of Trustee James C. Milburn (who had joined the Board in March 1846).

These first Seminarians found the school a very congenial place to live. According to Colonel Coad's daughter, the girls' bedrooms shared part of the second floor in old Calvert Hall with large classrooms and a study hall. The dormitory rooms were quite spartan. Shelves and racks were not installed until October 1848, and the perennial lack of wardrobes and chests-of-drawers forced some two generations of students to store their clothing in the attic. The first floor of Calvert Hall was divided by a large central hallway facing toward Trinity Church and opening onto a huge, columned front porch. This may have been the only door to the building, since it was common practice in female seminaries of this era to monitor closely the movement of students. Pupils would have found it difficult to exit or enter the building unnoticed, because on one side of the central hallway were a teacher's bedroom, a parlor, the Trustees' Room (where the Board held its meetings), and a music room; the other side contained the principal's living quarters, another teacher's room, "the best music room," and the library. The legislature in 1840 specifically required a library "for the purpose of collecting and preserving all books and other relicks connected with and calculated to throw light upon the first settlement and early history" of Maryland. The basement of Calvert Hall contained the kitchen and dining area, in addition to a "lovely big room with fireplace" for the steward, the staff member in charge of student meals, accommodations, and the maintenance of the campus. To the rear of the building was a back porch (where students exercised in inclement weather) and behind it a bath house with hot and cold running water, several wooden storage sheds for food and fuel, a wash-house, an ice house, and a stable—reportedly constructed with bricks from the State House of 1676. Mrs. Roberts affectionately remembered Calvert Hall as "a wonderful place with all modern conveniences. I got my first shower bath there." Then, as now, the waterfront was the focus of student recreation; by 1852 if not earlier, the school provided "conveniences on a clean and bold shore for salt water bathing during the summer season."

Letters Home from an Early Seminarian

St. Mary's Seminary
January 22, 1849

Dear Parents

I received your kind and affectionate letter and it gave me much pleasure to hear from you all. . . . I hope you do not think hard of my not answering your letter before now, but . . . I thought it unnecessary to write again so soon. . . . I suppose you want to know how I spend my Sabbaths here. I go to Church every other Sunday and get Bible lessons every Sunday, so I spend my Sabbaths very pleasantly. . . . Tell Aunt Mary I think ink or paper must be very scarce with her else she would write oftener to me. . . . When you write to me again let me know whether little Brother can walk or not; and whether he can speak any words. Now I must conclude by sending my love. . . .

February 10, 1849

Dear Ma.

I cannot express my feelings on receiving your letter, for I was so much surprised to hear that little Brother had been so extremely ill . . . . The Trustees had a meeting last Wednesday and did not decide whether we would have any holiday at Easter or not but most of the girls expect to go home . . . . You said I must send you a memorandum of my studies. I am studying Chemistry, Philosophy, Arithmetic, and several others which I have not time to mention now, but these are the principal. Music I am very fond of and have taken two tunes and M. Sommervell has taken three and you know she knew some of her notes before she came here. . . . I remain, Your affectionate and loving daughter

Sarah J. F. Jones

—Source: Letters from Sarah Jane Frances Jones to Mr. and Mrs. Washington Jones of Mill Mount, Calvert County. Transcription kindly provided by Margaret P. Weems, Prince Frederick, Maryland, a descendant of the author.

The Dorchester *docking at Brome's Wharf, St. Mary's City. The Female Seminary was a steamboat school from 1847 to the mid–1930s, accessible to most of the Chesapeake region primarily through the twice-weekly docking of such vessels only 100 yards from the campus.*

Both beautiful and functional, the Seminary at long last reverberated with the energy of adolescent residents, and the ancient capital once again heard the sweet sounds of youthful excitement.

St. Mary's Female Seminary was always distinctive, because, as a boarding school, it sought to create a total educational environment of living and learning that would complement classroom activities. The academic year was divided into two five-month terms (October to March and March to July), with only a few days off at Christmas and only occasionally at Easter and a summer vacation of eight weeks. The trustees assured parents that the summer vacation was timed to avoid the "only season during which malarious sickness prevails even in the least favored parts of the county." Each July, as the academic year ended, the Seminarians had to pass an oral public examination in front of the trustees and other guests. The school day began at 8:00 a.m. and ended at 4 p.m., with a one-hour lunch break at noon. All classes lasted forty-five minutes and changed at the ringing of a bell. Two study periods were also scheduled in every class day; during the winter months, these were in the evening, as was an "exercise hour" year-round. When not studying or exercising, pupils were "encouraged to be industrious with their needles." An

early Seminarian also recalled how Mrs. Priscilla "Muddy" Greenwell, the school's third steward, promoted gardening as a recreational activity, allowing the girls to "plant what we pleased" in individual plots along the Trinity Churchyard fence.

In the 1847–48 academic year, all eighteen Seminarians were enrolled in geography, grammar, history, philosophy, arithmetic, and algebra; sixteen pupils had additional lessons in music and eleven in drawing. By 1852, St. Mary's advertised courses that seem surprisingly varied and sophisticated; in addition to the expected instruction in spelling, reading, penmanship, English grammar, composition, rhetoric, arithmetic, history, and geography, the school offered algebra, geometry, astronomy, botany, natural philosophy, chemistry, geology, physiology, natural history, "mental and moral philosophy," vocal and instrumental music, drawing, painting, French, Latin, and "the Evidences of Christianity." An advertisement in the *Port Tobacco Times* announced that the Seminary also had "all the instruments and apparatus necessary for the illustration of . . . [the] natural sciences."

That announcement revealed a dramatic improvement in the school's instructional facilities from just four years before. The principal's first report on instruction, dated 27 April 1848, had revealed "generally . . . good progress" in academic subjects but "moral health . . . [that] is not quite what is desirable." Students "in Geography might have advanced more rapidly had they had the use of Maps," and the drawing classes lacked suitable tables or desks. The school also suffered a severe shortage of books, especially for "read[ing] to the pupils at those hours when assembled with their Sewing, as well as on Sundays." Music students were "suffering great disadvantage by being compelled to practice on [an untuned piano that] . . . is forming them to bad habits." In addition, the Seminary still did not have the "grace hoops, battle doors, [and] jumping ropes" necessary for indoor exercise; the parlor was nearly devoid of furniture; and the principal desperately needed a stove in her quarters: "There being no fire in the wing I occupy, I was frequently compelled last winter to sit in the cold more than was conducive to comfort or health."

Aside from these early problems of an infant institution, the reasonably priced Seminary, "established for the public good" with some statewide fanfare, should have been overwhelmingly successful in recruiting students in its first decade. From the end of one depression in 1840 to the onset of another in 1857, the nation enjoyed widespread prosperity, producing almost a doubling of the population and an unprecedented building boom. However, the Seminary was not able to benefit from the growing numbers of families now interested in, and capable of affording, secondary education for their daughters, due to the endemic problem of finding and retaining qualified teachers in Southern Maryland.

Only three months into the Seminary's first academic year, a serious personnel crisis disrupted the school and exacerbated the teacher shortage. On 14 December 1846, the trustees fired Mr. Meany for "conduct . . . render[ing] him unfit for the office of Principal" and immediately relieved him of his duties as register and treasurer of the Board as well. Apparently the "unfit conduct" was public drunkenness, although there is also evidence to suggest a misuse of funds and Seminary property. Colonel Coad's young daughter remembered this scandal quite vividly. The members of the Board, including her father, met "most all day" in the Trustees' Room and finally summoned Principal Meany. "We [students] all hovered around, sort of subdued, expecting something. I wondered why there were so many carriages out in the yard and why our parents were there. Then the trustees came out and told our parents to take us home. The school was going to be closed. You see, Mr. Meany loved his toddy too much, so they had to get rid

of him, and they had warned the parents to be on hand." The "Meany Affair" aborted the 1846–47 school year after only ten weeks and gave the pupils an unexpected "Christmas vacation" that lasted ten months.

In the spring of 1847, during this hiatus in classes, the trustees secured the services of Miss Eliza M. Ohr as principal, at a salary of $250, and hired Miss Rebecca R. Hough and Miss Matilda Babb as teachers, at an annual salary of $250 each. Trustee Bennett took up Mr. Meany's duties as register and treasurer of the Board and agreed to serve as steward of the Seminary, in exchange for free tuition for his children. With a full staff and renewed spirits, St. Mary's opened to eighteen students the following October and finished 1847–48, *its first complete academic year of operation*, in fine fashion. The next year, however, enrollment dropped to thirteen stu-

Recruiting Faculty, 1852

St. Mary's Female Seminary
St. Mary's County, Maryland

TEACHER WANTED—*This institution offers to parents and guardians the best instruction in all the branches usually taught in female Seminaries, together with Music, Drawing, and the modern foreign languages on more moderate terms than is afforded by any similar academy in the State.*

It is now open for the reception of pupils under the care and instruction of MISS MARY BLADES Principal, MISS MARY P. THOMPSON, Vice Principal.

The Board of Trustees wish to engage the services of a more proficient instructress in vocal and instrumental Music, particularly on the Piano. This Assistant must be capable of giving some aid to the general course of study at the Seminary. To such a Teacher they will give three hundred dollars per scholastic year and board at the Steward's house. As they wish a fair representation of the different religious sects among the teachers, a preference will be given to a lady of the Methodist church, but invite proposals from all with testimonials of character and capacity, as they propose to secure the services of the best.

Applications may be made by letter, postage paid, to Col. C. COMBS, President of the Board of Trustees, Great Mills Post Office, . . . until the 4th Wednesday in November next, when the Trustees will meet to make the appointment.

By order WM. BISCOE, Register.

—Source: *Port Tobacco Times*, 14 October 1852.

dents (only three of them new), far below the eighty students that Calvert Hall was built to accommodate. Seeking better teachers who would hopefully boost enrollments, the trustees paid $50 to Mrs. Phelps of the Patapsco Female Institute in an unsuccessful effort to procure the services of one Madame Clarisse M. Plamondon, a French teacher from Canada.

Even though they were frustrated by the perennial problem of "secur[ing] the services of the best" teachers, the trustees were equally concerned about maintaining a balanced representation of Catholics, Episcopalians, and Methodists on the faculty. On 8 August 1849, the Board of Trustees passed a resolution—"that the Principal, Vice-Principal, and Steward be of different religions if they can possibly be"—which plunged the Seminary into its most severe and bitter crisis to date. This well-meaning attempt to preclude religious discrimination through the use of quotas backfired and, instead, unleashed destructive denominational tensions that were unexpected and explosive. The resolution had the effect of forcing Trustee Bennett, an Episcopalian, to resign as steward, because that denomination was overrepresented on the staff and it was unthinkable to drop one of the scarce women teachers. Bennett, the victim of this new policy, had voted against the August resolution, as did Trustees Blackistone, Loker, and Jones—signaling the emergence of an Episcopalian voting bloc that bitterly factionalized the Board. Soon it would be impossible for the trustees to agree on even trivial issues, such as the length of the students' Christmas vacation.

The religious crisis worsened by 1851, when Miss Marion Malone, a Catholic teacher of French and music, submitted her resignation because of ongoing confrontations with Principal Ohr, an Episcopalian. A contentious February meeting resulted in a series of 4 to 4 votes that prevented the trustees from formally accepting Miss Malone's resignation. The bad feelings carried over to 15 April, when the Protestant trustees convened the Board to consider the Malone affair—in the absence of Catholic members Coad and Combs, who had never before missed the same meeting. The specific charges against Miss Malone were that she had failed to perform her "police duties" at the school, denied music lessons to several students, refused to vacate the room needed for an infirmary, and, most damaging, had displayed "harsh treatment" and "violent authority" in her dealings with pupils. Colonel John H. Sothoron of The Plains plantation near Charlotte Hall, an influential citizen and future state senator, actually witnessed one such outburst while visiting the Seminary, and he immediately withdrew his daughters from the school.

Forced to rescue the fragile reputation of the new Seminary and to prevent Principal Ohr from suffering further insubordination, the Protestant trustees confronted Miss Malone. She "declined any meeting or interview with the board, on the grounds of absence of her friends . . . and the Catholic trustees." Nevertheless, at the 15 April meeting, Trustees Bennett, Blackistone, Key, Jones, Reeder, Milburn, and Shaw unanimously voted to dismiss the troublesome teacher.

The purge of the faculty would not end there, for within a month of Malone's firing, the full Board, led by Coad and Combs, investigated serious allegations against Principal Ohr herself. The principal admitted loaning and even selling two controversial books to Seminary students—*The School Girl in France* and *The English Governess*—which, according to several trustees, were scandalous, polemical works "calculated to excite unkind feelings among the pupils on the subject of religion, . . . reflecting & ridiculing . . . in the harshest and most insulting manner, on the Roman Catholic religion." Finding Miss Ohr guilty of violating the school's "liberal religious principles" and of ignoring specific Board policies on the selection of suitable reading material for students, the trustees voted 9-3-1 on 8 May 1851 to dismiss her. Apparently, however, at least four members did not believe, or little cared, that the incident made it "impossible . . . for Roman Catholic parents ever again to evince their confidence in the school while the present Principal is at its head," for Trustees Blackistone, Bennett, Jones, and Shaw continued to support Miss Ohr for her proven administrative abilities.

The divisiveness of the Board over the serious and fundamental issue of religious discrimination in the early 1850s rendered the trustees incapable of united action to stave off disaster by decade's end. Once the embittered Board members lost confidence in one another as neighbors with a shared heritage of toleration, the fortunes of the Seminary declined precipitously. Following the firing of Principal Ohr, the 1850–51 academic year ended on a sour note: the contentious trustees failed to achieve a quorum for the all-important, end-of-term public examination of pupils on 29 July 1851. The mistrustful trustees found it impossible to agree on prospective teachers throughout the decade, and in the face of continuing high faculty attrition, the Board itself was riddled by resignations, beset by poor attendance, and so thoroughly disillusioned as to allow the Seminary to fall into "a state of decay," both physical and spiritual. In a desperate effort to attract new students, the Board in 1852 *lowered* the room and board fee by $20 from that of 1846 and reduced the entire sched-

Late nineteenth-century students at St. Mary's.

ule of charges from $267 to $236. We can only guess at the devastating impact that this long administrative crisis must have had on enrollments, for the trustees did not leave any record of meetings after 1854. The school was apparently closed for the 1855–56, 1856–57, and 1857–58 academic years, and in late 1857, the situation was so bleak that the Board "petitioned the General Assembly for the sale of said Seminary and its property." The disheartened trustees suggested that the proceeds be distributed to the county primary school fund or to "another institution for purposes of female education upon some other site than . . . St. Mary's."

First Rising of the Phoenix

Fortunately, just as county leaders were preparing to deliver funeral orations over the corpse of their "living monument," concerned state officials quickly intervened to rescue the Seminary and to breathe new vitality into it. In its short and troubled history, St. Mary's Female Seminary had become too precious a symbol to the state for politicians in Annapolis to let it suffer so shameful a fate. Calling the trustees' decision to abandon the Seminary "a perversion of the monumental and educational object" of its 1840 legislation, the General Assembly reaffirmed its commitment to the people of Southern Maryland by passing "An Act to Preserve the Existence of the St. Mary's Female Seminary" on 24 February 1858. Governor Thomas Holliday Hicks (1798–1865), of the American, or "Know-Nothing," Party, signed the bill only six weeks into his administration, perhaps because of his "hatred of religious schools" and his dedication to preserve "the antient landmarks of the republic" against the threatening flood of foreign immigrants. The law of 1858 admonished the trustees for allowing the Seminary to deteriorate, and it replaced them with "a board of commissioners for . . . re-organizing" the school—including Dr. John M. Brome, George W. Morgan, and Benjamin Tippett.

These three commissioners met on 18 March 1858 and duly appointed eleven other trustees from St. Mary's County to constitute an entirely new Board. Four men so named declined to serve, perhaps an indication of bitter feelings still present, and were replaced by new appointees. On 27 July 1858, the following new trustees signed the oath "to promote the interest of the institution": John B. Abell (ca. 1818–1886), a Catholic farmer and later county commissioner; Colonel Chapman Billingsley (ca. 1804–1874)–elected president of the Board–a wealthy Episcopalian planter-politician from the Sotterley area who would later serve in the state senate and the Constitutional Convention of 1864; County Commissioner Brome, an Episcopalian physician-planter who owned most of the townlands of St. Mary's City; John E. Carpenter (1825–1892), a Methodist farmer from Chaptico, former school teacher and future county commissioner; James Kemp Jones (ca. 1827–1868), a Methodist from Drum Cliff who later served as a county school commissioner; Charles Medley (ca. 1807–ca. 1873), a Chaptico merchant-planter, one of the few countians who would serve in the Union Army during the Civil War; George Henry Morgan (1818–1870), wealthy Catholic co-editor of the *St. Mary's Beacon* and judge of the Orphans Court; George W. Morgan (ca. 1812–1884), a Catholic kinsman of George Henry Morgan who would later serve in the House of Delegates and as a member of the Constitutional Convention of 1864; Henry C. Neale (ca. 1817–1880), a shoe manufacturer from Leonardtown; James Shemwell (1788–1869), an affluent Methodist planter from Chaptico; Benjamin Tippett (1806–1876), county surveyor, school examiner, and promoter of the "Point Lookout Railroad"; Dr. James Waring (1812–1883), of Southampton plantation, a wealthy entrepreneur who invested in wharfs and warehouses with fellow Trustees Carpenter and George H. Morgan; William Watts (1836?–1903), a farmer and steamboat pilot from West St. Mary's

Manor; and James Thompson Yates (1808–1874), a Catholic farmer from Medley Neck who later served as county sheriff, county commissioner, and judge of the Orphans Court.

This second Board of Trustees approached the task of revitalizing St. Mary's Female Seminary with dedication and innovation, and they succeeded in putting religious controversies to rest. This Board assiduously maintained a balance of five Catholics, five Episcopalians, and four Methodists (five after 1904, when the Board was increased to fifteen members). All of the trustees lived in St. Mary's County and were loyal Democrats; they served for life and filled vacancies in their own ranks, usually from among valued friends and relatives. In this regard, the Seminary's Board of Trustees may have been one of the last vestiges of the old oligarchic system that had dominated affairs in Southern Maryland since the seventeenth century. The trustees' close connections to one another through blood and marriage helped them establish the mutual respect and much-needed stability and continuity that transformed the Seminary into the pride of Southern Maryland. The willingness of these influential community leaders to accept a complex challenge in the midst of controversy doubtless contributed to the state's growing confidence in, and financial support of, the struggling school.

Although a full record of these trustees' accomplishments is denied us, because Board Minutes for the 1860s were destroyed by a fire in 1872, the new trustees apparently tried an ingenious method of quickly reviving the Seminary soon after their appointment. According to the *St. Mary's Beacon*, the school was scheduled to reopen on 18 October 1858 with the largest enrollment in its brief history, because the trustees had arranged for Madame Despommier's French and English Academy of Baltimore to relocate to St. Mary's City and for the Seminary to absorb its faculty and students. In a handsome seven-page brochure, the trustees advertised the services of Madame Despommiers as co-principal and instructor in French and Mary Blades as the other co-principal and teacher of English. Listed also were the names and hometowns of ninety-four "Pupils in the Academy"–seventy-two from Baltimore City, sixteen from out of state, and one from St. Mary's County (Nannie Brome)–who would supposedly take up residence at the Seminary. This ambitious and somewhat comical attempt to buy and relocate an established school, with a respected faculty and cosmopolitan student body, to Southern Maryland proved to be an abysmal failure. Few if any city girls followed Madame Despommiers to the Seminary, and there is no evidence that the headmistress herself ever resided on campus. Although the Board reduced the annual charges for tuition, room, and board to $150—surely a bargain compared to any urban academy—the trustees quickly learned that no amount of well-intended zeal could reverse the fortunes of the Seminary overnight. The problems of recruiting a stable, competent faculty and of attracting sufficient enrollments for financial solvency would continue.

The new trustees were apparently undeterred by their initial failure in educational merchandising, and they continued to rely on hyperbolic advertising to recruit a student body. Between 1860 and 1862, newspaper advertisements in the *St. Mary's Beacon, Port Tobacco Times,* and *Baltimore Sun* attempted to attract pupils by claiming that the Seminary had "a corps of efficient and experienced Teachers," who offered coursework "as thorough as at any other institution in the country." In reality, St. Mary's at this time had only one *inexperienced* teacher besides the principal—who was a different person almost every year—and, under such conditions, the school could barely offer even the most basic courses.

There are frustratingly few sources about the Seminary during the critical years of the Civil War, for besides the missing Board Minutes, the publication of the *St. Mary's Beacon* was curtailed in the mid-1860s due to the imprisonment of its allegedly "treasonous" pro-Southern editor. Miss Lucy L. Gardiner was listed as the

---

Inventory of Seminary Property, October 1872

{Classroom Furnishings}

1 Dozen double cherry desks w/ seats	2 Settees large size
	2 Settees small size
22 old desks out of repair, in attic	1 Teachers desk and cane chair
4 black boards	1 Long form painted wood chair
2 clocks	

{Dormitory Furnishings}

12 Double bedsteads	1 double (painted) wardrobe
1 High post-double Bedstead	4 small square painted tables (old)
1 Single Bedstead	
1 Hair Mattress double	1 small table (painted white)
1 Hair Mattress single	
1 Feather bed double	7 racks-with-pegs for clothes
1 Feather bed single	
12 Mattresses (shuck) double	5 Large wash stands (painted brown)
9 Mattresses (shuck) single	
10 Bolsters (shuck)	4 small wash stands (old)
1 Bolsters feather	
5 Prs pillows—feather	12 Wash Baisins
2 Prs pillows Hair	4 Looking Glasses
4 single (painted) wardrobes	

{Parlor and Hall Furnishings}

1 Large book case	1 Hall Table
1 Mahogany Center Table	4 Hall Chairs
1 Rocking Chair	1 Hall Lamp
4 Pianos	oil cloth on floor (worn)

{Dining Room Furnishings}

2 Large (painted) Dining Tables	1 Gravy Boat
	1 vegetable dish & cover
3 small (painted) Dining Tables	2 Glass salt cellars
	5 Plated forks
5 Heavy Kitchen Tables	1 Large tea waiter
10 Dinner plates	2 stone jars
11 Desert plates	1 Biscuit Tray
12 Breakfast plates	1 Pastry Board & rolling pin
11 Cups & Saucers	
6 Tumblers	1 dripping pan
2 Large Meat Dishes	2 Washing Tubs
2 smaller Meat Dishes	2 Andirons
1 Tureen	

{Miscellaneous Furnishings}

1 Mahogany secretary	2 Rocking Chairs (old & broken)
1 Large Music stand	
1 Calico covered Lounge	1 Center Table (broken)
3 Dozen Chairs (old & broken)	3 Carpets (old & much worn)

—Source: Loose-sheet inventory by Principal Jeannette E. Thomas, inserted in Board Minutes.

Seminary principal in *Beacon* advertisements dated 1 September 1864 and 15 August 1867, and she probably remained in that post until her death in August 1869; however, newspapers were silent on the subject of the Seminary in 1863, 1865, and 1866. Textbooks from the school—*Elements of Mythology; or, Classical Fables of the Greeks and Romans* (21st ed., Philadelphia: Moss, Brother and Co., 1860) and Mary A. Swift's *First Lessons on Natural Philosophy for Children* (rev. ed., Hartford: William J. Hamersley, 1862)—reveal that one Lucy Dunbar, who signed and dated the inside covers, was attending classes at the Seminary in February 1864 and May 1865. Considering that teachers and students had been in short supply during the best of times; that several of the trustees were distracted by the war and even joined military units; and that few Southern-sympathizing county families would have wanted their young daughters away from home and so near to several Union Army encampments (Cross Manor, Point Lookout, and Leonardtown), it is incredible that the Seminary continued to hold classes for even part of the Civil War.

Second Rising of the Phoenix

After a troubled quarter-century of bare survival, the Seminary's perseverance in the face of scandal, indebtedness, and the turmoil of war was rewarded by the state. Less than a decade after it had first resuscitated the struggling school, the Maryland General Assembly thrice more rescued the Seminary from certain collapse between 1864 and 1868. The timely arrival of essential financial support from Annapolis finally put the Seminary on its feet and permitted the school to prosper for the next 120 years.

Immediately following the Civil War, the State of Maryland belatedly created a comprehensive system of free public education, but instead of closing the troublesome boarding school in St. Mary's City in the name of progress or conformity, public officials consistently regarded the Seminary as an essential part of Maryland's emerging educational future. Under the pro-Union, abolitionist Whig governor, Augustus W. Bradford, the state in 1864 appropriated $2,000 to help retire the debts of the Seminary. Bradford's successor, the "Know-Nothing" ex-mayor of Baltimore, Thomas Swann, signed "An Act for the Relief of the Saint Mary's Female Seminary," which had passed the General Assembly on 23 March 1867. This law appropriated $1,500 "or so much thereof as shall be necessary to repair and put in proper condition the said Seminary." A year later, on 28 March 1868, the General Assembly pledged a continuing annual allocation of $2,500, payable every 1 April, "for the preservation of the Institution"— especially Calvert Hall, which was described in the legislation as a "structure . . . of such magnitude and character that the incidental expenses necessary to keep up repairs has

Old Calvert Hall, with painted or white-washed walls, as it probably appeared from the mid-1870s until 1924. This rare view shows the two-story porch facing toward Trinity Rectory that would have served as a "fire escape" in this period.

A group of Seminarians, ca. 1898. The x marks the location of Miss Esther Schilling, Class of 1898.

devolved upon the State."

The significance of the state's commitment in 1868 for annual funding cannot be overemphasized, for it allowed the Seminary to realize its mission as the Monument School of the People down to the present. Trustee George Frederick Maddox, a member of Governor Swann's staff, doubtless promoted the idea of perpetual funding in exchange for the Board's sponsorship of full annual scholarships for "the advancement of young ladies of the State by a liberal education." By guaranteeing in advance both an operating budget and a sufficient core of students, state officials ensured the solvency of the Seminary, permitted it to broaden its influence beyond the borders of St. Mary's County, and gave girls of modest means a free education where Maryland's first pioneers had turned their dreams into reality.

Stability and Continuity At Last

Thanks to the state's continuing financial support, St. Mary's Female Seminary between 1870 and 1900 finally realized the institutional maturation that gave it a distinctive character and a long life. The economic collapse of the school was never again a possibility, as the annual state contribution of $2,500 continued and even increased to $3,000 after 1893. Beginning in 1899, funding was raised to $6,500, which allowed—indeed required—the Seminary to increase the annual number of full scholarships from ten to twenty-six, one for each of the counties of Maryland and each legislative district of Baltimore City. By September 1888, the Board of Trustees had retired the school's debts and had a surplus of more than $3,000—enough to allow the trustees to begin a modest endowment through investment in guaranteed mortgage bonds of the Cincinnati-Washington-Baltimore Railroad.

Another improvement over the Seminary's first quarter-century was the stability of the student body and the faculty. Already by 1871, St. Mary's had expanded the number of teachers (four) and pupils (thirty-three) beyond previous years, and by 1899, it had six instructors and fifty students—both records for the nineteenth century. The Board's promotion of three-year state scholarships had indeed created a diversified student body; of the thirty-seven pupils at the Seminary in 1895, twenty-one came from outside St. Mary's County—three from Anne Arundel, two each from Calvert, Charles, Dorchester, Prince George's, and Wicomico counties, two from Baltimore City, and one each from Harford, Kent, Montgomery, Queen Anne's, and Somerset counties, and the District of Columbia.

Institutional stability and progress were also evident in the policies and activities that were becoming part of the Seminary's traditions in the last quarter of the nineteenth century. The school granted its first printed diploma ("Certificate of Graduation") in June 1874 to Sallie Brome Morsell, who has the distinction of being the first official graduate. (Before this date, stu-

dents who had finished the prescribed course of study with outstanding grades had received a "first degree testimonial," perhaps a hand-written document or an entry in an official register. However, until opportunities for women's employment outside the home became more extensive in late nineteenth-century Maryland, there seemed to be little need for the bureaucratic formalities of transcripts and diplomas. It is definitely not true, as persistent school legends contend, that students "graduated" as early as the 1840s.) Four more students graduated by 1879, and in the decade of the 1880s, thirty-one diplomas were awarded, seven each in 1886 and 1889. Between 1890 and 1895, twenty-two pupils successfully completed the course of study at the Seminary. As the number of annual graduates increased, commencements became more formal and elaborate; special medals were awarded to top graduates, students read essays on current topics, and visiting dignitaries were commissioned to deliver orations to packed audiences.

Despite the growing reputation and formality of St. Mary's Female Seminary in this period, costs remained quite reasonable. The basic English curriculum cost $180 a year, including all living expenses, and the Sem-

A Seminary Commencement, 29 June 1885

It would be difficult to imagine a more delightful and appropriate spot for the location of an Institution of learning than that of St. Mary's Female Seminary . . . . From a glance at the beautiful beds of flowers around the yard and building, the fertile fields . . . of waving corn, and the lovely expanse of water presented a scene which few can exceed in beauty. A pleasant breeze came up from the water below and swept agreeably through the halls and spacious rooms. The stage and walls in the large parlor were beautifully and artistically decorated with flowers, ferns and wreaths, . . . and every available space seemed well filled with people.

On the stage sat the Principal, Miss A. E. Thomas, and Misses Long and Hortense Mallier, Teachers of the Institution, Dr. John M. Brome, the Secretary and Treasurer of the Board of Trustees, and Mr. B. Harris Camalier. Just before the stage were the pupils, looking charming in their white dresses, whilst directly in front of them sat the Trustees. The programme consisted of original essays, recitations, vocal and instrumental music, . . . and the execution of the pieces gave unmistakable evidence that the pupils had been well and carefully trained. . . .

Gold medals were conferred upon {the Valedictorian,}

Miss Emma Griffith (Montgomery County) for general excellence, . . . upon Miss Bettie Revell (Anne Arundel County) for the greatest improvement in Vocal Music, upon Misses Katie Polk (Baltimore), Edith Black (Frederick), and Marion Chamberlaine (Baltimore) in instrumental music. Premiums were awarded Misses Sallie Hinman (Calvert), Sadie Hollingsworth (Queen Anne's), Lulie Posey (Baltimore), Marion Chamberlaine (Baltimore), Lola Garner (St. Mary's), Sallie Cissell (Howard), Edith Black (Frederick), and Addie Hammond, Delia Ellis, Carrie Chamberlaine, Ethel Gray, and Mamie Smith (St. Mary's County).

After the distribution of premiums, Mr. Camalier . . . address{ed} the school in the absence of Col. Harris, President of the Board of Trustees. . . . After the exercises were over, the courteous and popular Capt. Geoghegan, of the steamer Sue, which was then lying at Brome's Wharf, invited all to take a little excursion down the classic St. Mary's and return, which was readily accepted by many and greatly enjoyed. Thus closed the day, long to be remembered among the brightest in the annals of the Institution.

—Source: Undated but contemporaneous clipping from an unnamed newspaper.

inary's full schedule of annual charges was a mere $287—only $20 more than in 1846. But many Seminarians paid nothing at all. On a consistent basis between the late 1860s and the late 1940s, at least half of the annual student body was attending the school on full scholarship. In 1875, the trustees' annual report to the General Assembly, required under the legislation of 1868, indicated that thirteen of twenty-three students had all of their expenses paid by scholarships, ten funded by the state allocations to the school and three provided by the Board from other sources.

The reasonable charges and generous scholarships at St. Mary's in no way implied an inferior education in the late nineteenth century. The *Report of the State Board of Education for 1878* revealed the academic breadth of the Seminary curriculum and refuted the implication that St. Mary's was merely a finishing school in the "parlor arts." In that year, sixteen students were enrolled in instrumental music, twelve in French, ten in rhetoric, eight in natural philosophy, four each in botany, chemistry, geometry, and algebra, and two each in logic, drawing, physiology, and English literature. The 1895 school catalog listed faculty positions in art and art history, English, French, Latin, German, home economics, natural sciences, "higher mathematics," and all types of music. Student accomplishments in such subjects were showcased annually in the end-of-year public oral examination, which apparently became a popular event in the local community. In 1879, a county newspaper reported that student performance on these examinations "reflected credit" on the Seminary and made the school in "merit at least equal to any within the limits of our state." The article concluded that "it is gratifying to note that proper interest is being manifested by friends of the female culture throughout the state towards this seminary."

Such praise and positive publicity were largely the result of the talents and dedication of the Seminary principals in the last quarter of the nineteenth century. As the trustees learned early in the history of the school, the top administrator could make or break the institution. Thanks in large measure to state funding in the 1860s, the Seminary gradually attracted, and increasingly retained, accomplished, committed teachers to the principalship. After eight principals had come and gone between 1846 and 1862, the local Gardiner family provided the first semblance of continuity in that office. Descended from seventeenth-century settlers, Miss Lucy L. Gardiner served as principal from August 1862 until her death in August 1869, whereupon her sister, Miss Mary Gardiner, succeeded her until August 1870. From that date until August 1872, the third sis-

A rare early report card from the Female Seminary, ca. 1870.

ter, Miss Lottie L. Gardiner, served as co-principal with Miss Henrietta K. Tilghman.

Another prominent county family dominated the office of principal for the next twenty-three years, bringing continuity in leadership during the golden age of the nineteenth-century Seminary. Mrs. James Richard (Jeannette) Thomas, daughter of Dr. Walter Hanson Stone Briscoe of Sotterley Plantation and wife of the St. Mary's City postmaster, was continuously elected to one-year terms as principal from September 1872 until her death in November 1881. Her daughter, Annie Elizabeth (Lizzie) Thomas '77 (after 1894, Mrs. John Gray Lilburn) stepped in to assume the duties of her mother in the middle of the school year, although she was barely older than many of the Seminary students. "Dear Miss Lizzie" remained in office until 30 June 1895, becoming the most popular and longest-serving principal of St. Mary's Female Seminary in the nineteenth century. This much-loved woman also served concurrently as the first female postmaster at St. Mary's

City (the post office was located in Calvert Hall), and she was fondly remembered by two generations of students as an inspiring teacher, administrator, and active member of the later Alumnae Association until her death in 1932.

When "Miss Lizzie" left office in 1895, seven candidates applied to be the next principal—a gratifying indication that the Seminary had finally attained respectability and stability. The Board elected as principal thirty-nine-year-old Miss Laurel Richardson Langley, daughter of the late James R. Langley (Seminary trustee, 1872–1886), and she remained in office for five years. Like the Gardiners and Thomases before them, the Langley family provided strong support to the Seminary; while Laurel was principal, her sister, Miss Leila Langley, taught English, and their mother, Mrs. Indiana Milburn Langley, taught home economics. (The family tradition continues with the current service of Trustee J. Frank Raley, Jr., a distant Langley descendant.)

In August 1900, Mrs. Lucy Virginia Maddox assumed the principalship of St. Mary's Female Seminary and achieved the longest tenure of any person in that position—twenty-three years, until her retirement on 30 June 1923. Standing for reelection each year, Mrs. Maddox was a patient and dedicated administrator who never had an office of her own and who often netted less than $200 in annual salary, after paying most expenses and all staff salaries out of a lump-sum allocated to her by the Board of Trustees. Her skillful and loving service to the Seminary harkened back to simpler times and in some ways kept the school in the nineteenth century until her retirement. After Mrs. Maddox, St. Mary's would have only two more principals/presidents until 1969.

The continuity and faithful service of the Seminary principals were matched by the long tenures and admirable harmony achieved by the Board of Trustees in the half century between 1870 and 1920. The trustees' collective and individual length of service reflected the success they brought to, and the satisfaction they derived from, the school. Of the fourteen trustees who were named to the new Board in 1858, Board President

Mrs. Annie Elizabeth Thomas Lilburn (1859–1932)—"Dear Miss Lizzie"—who had the longest tenure of any Seminary principal in the nineteenth century (November 1881 to June 1895). She was the only St. Mary's graduate (1877) ever to serve as the school's chief executive.

The Reward of Affection for a Teacher's Dedication

"Going Home"
In memory of Mrs. John Gray Lilburn, former Principal of St. Mary's Seminary, Maryland, and State Regent of Daughters of American Revolution, by her pupil, Lila Sadelia Gray '98.

We carried her home—not in her bloom of youth
And beauty—not in her crowded years—
But when her work was done. Uprightness and truth
She spread. Her energies and fears
Built sterling character, that could not fall
Beneath a fine ideal. Enthusiastic fire
Spread beneath rich consciousness—'til each and all
Possessed for life the pattern of her desire.
And now small Trinity receives her, and she sleeps
Beneath a cedar's shade she loved full well—
Nearby a rose bush blooms, and ivy silent creeps.
St. Mary's River will in music tell
Of sacred things—things beautiful—silent in her heart—
Associations splendor—grass, buttercups and clover,
The flirting butterflies and bees that sail and dart—
The sun, the moon, the stars that silently watch over.

—Source: Original typescript, undated, glued to a page in Betty Revell Wathen's journal of alumnae proceedings, St. Mary's College Alumni Archives.

The Seminary faculty in the late 1890s. Principal Laurel R. Langley is in the center.

Billingsley served sixteen years until his death in December 1874; Doctor Brome, twenty-nine years; John Abell, twenty-nine years; John Carpenter, twenty-eight years; George W. Morgan, twenty-six years; Charles Medley, twenty-five years; Doctor Waring, twenty-five years; Benjamin Tippett, eighteen years; and James Yates, sixteen years. Most of the other trustees from the mid-nineteenth century served at least a decade. The next generation of trustees included three men (Benjamin Harris Camalier, Stephen M. Jones, and C. Ethelbert Abell) who served on the Board more than forty years, three more who served between thirty-two and thirty-seven years (J. Marshall Dent, Joseph H. Key, and Noble L. Penn), and eight who remained in office at least twenty years (Louis C. Combs, Giles F. Dyer, John A. B. Shermantine, James Thomas Raley, J. Parran Crane, Robert T. Barber, Thomas F. Foxwell, and Richard H. Garner).

When vacancies occurred on the Board, the contin-uity of leadership was maintained by the appointment of close friends or family members. Edward S. Abell served from 1870 to 1889, concurrently with John B. Abell; James F. Abell assumed John's seat in April 1887 and served until his death in 1899, whereupon Charles Abell took over until his own death in August 1923. He was succeeded in that year by C. Ethelbert Abell, who remained on the Board until his retirement in 1964. When John E. Carpenter resigned in June 1886, his brother, J. Walter Carpenter, was elected to this "Methodist seat" and served until his death in 1898, the last ten years as Board treasurer. Leonardtown lawyer and former clerk of the Circuit Court John A. Camalier was elected to the Board in September 1874 and served until his death in June 1892, whereupon his son, Benjamin Harris Camalier, state's attorney and judge of the Circuit Court, assumed his seat and remained a valued trustee until 1936. George Frederick Maddox, aide to Governor Swann at a critical time for the Seminary and

Mrs. Lucy Virginia Maddox (d. 1949), the longest serving of any principal of St. Mary's Female Seminary (August 1900–June 1923).

later state senator, served on the Board in the late 1860s alongside his father-in-law, the Honorable Benjamin Gwinn Harris, United States Congressman (1863–1867) and president of the Board of Trustees, 1875 to 1895. Both men died at Ellenborough, the Harris estate south of Leonardtown, where a fire in 1872 destroyed the Board Minutes for 1854–1872.

Throughout the late nineteenth century, the close-knit native countians who comprised the Seminary's independent Board of Trustees developed enduring traditions and strong bonds of affection. The Board met every three months at a Leonardtown hotel (Moore's, Shank's, Down's, or Raley's) or at the Seminary itself, but it is clear that they kept in close touch between meetings. For eight decades, these prominent local leaders in politics, business, and the law nurtured a deep commitment to the Seminary and used the pride they felt for it to reinforce their common county heritage and old family ties. One can sense the affection that existed among the trustees, as the Board Minutes record the sorrow felt when vital records were destroyed by fire; the sensitivity toward colleagues all too obviously infirm; and the grateful acknowledgement of large cash advances to the school from the treasurer's own pocket. When death inevitably depleted the ranks

of long-serving "brother members," the trustees always composed moving eulogies, read them into the record, and had the tributes published in local newspapers. When two of the oldest and most faithful Board members, Captain Raley and President Harris, died within a month of each other in the spring of 1895, the trustees were "forced to the conclusion that the last links which bind us to the past and which so united and strengthened . . . this time-honored Institution are fast . . . breaking away."

A sense of nostalgia was ever present in the deliberations of the trustees, but so too was an enthusiasm for maintaining progress at the Seminary. With a growing administrative professionalism—demonstrated by the creation of standing committees of Finance (March 1870), Rules (May 1871), and Buildings and Grounds (April 1878)—the Board of Trustees established many important precedents in the last third of the nineteenth century that enriched the Seminary and continue to influence the College today. On 21 September 1870, the trustees awarded the first full merit scholarships at the Seminary, and twenty-three years later, they proposed competitive examinations for such tuition, room, and board awards. The Board authorized the school's first diplomas in June 1874, and in 1889, proposed the first seal or logo on those documents. In 1884, the trustees began granting honors and prizes to outstanding graduates, and in order to make commencement the most notable affair in the academic calendar, they recuited distinguished guest speakers (from 1887 on) and even paid for travel expenses ($9 in 1890). They also cultivated the strong historic values of the Monument School by authorizing the first school holiday for a commemorative event (the public dedication of the state's Leonard Calvert Memorial obelisk on 3 June 1891) and recommended the writing of the Seminary's first history in 1887. The Board helped stimulate the formation of student organizations by allocating $20 to the first one—the "Young Ladies of the Literary Society"—on 1 April 1885. Finally, as some of the most worldly-wise citizens in Southern Maryland, the Seminary trustees took care to prepare the school for the challenges of the future by authorizing, on 23 October 1888, the first investments toward creating an independent endowment.

The First Building Boom, 1890–1920

Only two decades after the state had stabilized the finances of the Seminary, growing enrollments necessitated an enlargement of the physical plant to better serve the students. Committed to the modernization, growth, and improvement of the campus, the trustees in the late 1880s fixed the roof and furnace of Calvert

A commencement program for 1901.

the Seminary opened in 1846, new campus construction was planned. Convincing officials in Annapolis that the "state scholars" needed "a Hall for gymnastic exercises . . . and public exhibitions," the trustees in 1891 obtained $1,000 in special funds from the General Assembly. They constructed a simple but commodious frame building with a large stage some twenty-nine feet from the river wall of Calvert Hall at a total cost of $1,551.87. Furnished with $105 worth of wooden chairs, this new building, soon to be known as "The Annex," was first used at the commencement exercises on 22 June 1892.

This initial success in lobbying Annapolis for supplemental funds and expanded facilities generated a momentum for still more improvements on campus. In 1900, with the "school full" and a new building considered "absolutely necessary," the trustees sought a special appropriation of $6,000—later raised to $10,000—from the legislature. The Board president, Circuit Court Judge J. Parran Crane, actually wrote the bill that he and two other trustees (a present and former state's attorney) lobbied for in the capital. The General Assembly in April 1902 voted the Seminary $8,000 for new construction. The trustees immediately engaged the services of George W. Corbitt, an architect from Washington, D.C., and hired Elias C. Milburn to construct a multipurpose brick building with a large assembly hall on the first floor and dormitory rooms on the second. However, the estimated costs proved too high, and the trustees were forced to retain (and relocate) the wooden Annex and to erect a smaller, less elaborate, brick build-

Hall and painted its exterior, terraced the riverbank, drilled a new artesian well, installed fire escapes and extinguishers, and repaired the outbuildings. However, the school still lacked space, and for the first time since

The "Alma Mater" of St. Mary's Female Seminary, written in 1895 by Henrietta ("Etta") Porter Coston Lockner—here pictured in her graduation portrait in June 1892.

Alma Mater - St. Mary's.
Words by Henrietta Coston Lockner, Class of 1892.
Dedicated to Mrs. A.E.J. Lilburn

1. On the banks of blue St. Mary's, near Potomac's strand
Stands our dear old alma Mater - best school in the land,
Built of bricks from the first state-house, near the mul-
berry's shade,
Where Lord Calvert, with the Indians, once a treaty made.

2. Like a beacon by the river stands she grandly bold,
Giving knowledge to her daughters - worth more
than pure gold.
Age and fire cannot destroy her, she has stood the test,
We will always love St. Mary's - she deserves our best.

3. We will ever love St. Mary's - love to praise her name,
Strive to make our lives add honor to her glorious fame,
Let your glad song wake the echoes, sing with voices
free:
Hail to Thee, Dear Alma Mater! Hail, all hail,
to Thee!

The above was written in 1895.
by Henrietta C. Lockner.

The fire alluded to was a small one confined to first
2 rooms in basement - on dining-room level. H.C.L.

ing flush against, but apparently not connected to, the riverside wall of Calvert Hall. This two-story "School Building," as it was called when completed in the spring of 1903, contained a study hall and three classrooms on the first floor and dormitory rooms on the second. During the construction, the contractor also apparently built the brick portals that still front on the wharf road, and in early 1905, a large iron gate was installed.

No sooner was the "School Building" occupied than the Board of Trustees, on 7 December 1903, outlined a strategy to "urge state aid to erect a new Hall & other improvements so much needed," especially the replacement of "the Frame Building [Annex] now so unsatisfactory." On 20 July 1906, the trustees met at the Leonardtown restaurant operated by Confederate Captain C. B. Wise to open sealed bids for the new building and even received one by "Phone." The Board accepted the bid of $7,825 from Elias Milburn, which was $2,000 to $5,000 lower than all the others. Although the work was often interrupted by controversies between the trustees and the contractor and in the end appeared "very rough" to architect Corbitt, the new "Music Hall" (the present St. Mary's Hall) was finished in time to hold commencement exercises there on 10 June 1908.

The "building boom" that had lasted seventeen years came to a sudden halt in 1908, and the state adamantly refused to pay for more improvements—even a desperately needed infirmary. It would be another seventeen years before the state would allocate additional funds for construction at the Seminary. Instead of lobbying legislators, consulting blueprints, and meeting with architects, school officials again concentrated on the "little things" that could improve the life of the Seminarians. They installed one hundred acetylene gas lights throughout the dormitories and classrooms by 1910 (replacing antiquated whale oil fixtures), repaired the furnace almost yearly, erected a new water tank behind Calvert Hall, and built the school's first tennis courts. In 1911, the trustees purchased a carriage and harness "for church going," and at times, they personally escorted students to the Sunday services of their choice. Four years later, the Board appointed the Seminary's first staff physician, despite the lack of an infirmary building.

In the era of World War I, Seminary officials had to make do with meager financial resources, and for the first time in the school's history, they found the state bureaucracy to be more of a hindrance than a help. In 1913, William H. Davenport, secretary of the Board of State Aid and Charities, through which the most recent

A rare view of the frame Annex (dedicated in June 1892)—the first academic building constructed on campus since 1845.

construction projects had been funded, visited the St. Mary's campus and made a thorough investigation of its operations. He criticized the unreliable water pumping system, the method of sewage disposal, deficient furnishings in classrooms and dormitories, the shortage of books in the library, the absence of science laboratories, and the byzantine accounting procedures that required the principal to cover virtually all expenses out of a single, annual Board appropriation of between $5,200 and $5,800. Much of Davenport's lengthy report smacked of an urban bias against an institution that he considered too rural and too small to justify state support in a new era of standardized, "efficient" public education. Davenport unfairly criticized the Board for not providing buildings, furnishings, and student services that only more money could have addressed; ironically, his investigation of the school immediately preceded a period (1915–1917) when the state treasurer failed to honor the financial commitments originally made to

the Seminary by the legislature in 1868. Forced to borrow thousands of dollars to meet routine operating expenses and to pay teachers' salaries, the trustees successfully weathered the crisis while continuing to support half the student body on full scholarships. Indeed, during this period, the bonds grew stronger between Board members and the Seminary's "efficient corps of teachers."

The students and staff of St. Mary's Female Seminary had learned long before that abundant financial resources and elegant campus facilities have little direct bearing on the educational excellence of a school. Even in its darkest, most destitute days, the Seminary had placed its emphasis on the close contacts between caring teachers and a small core of interested students. This boarding school aspired to create, and had largely achieved, a family of learning across the generations, in which a highly controlled academic environment nurtured the individual talents of varied students. In 1914,

A Seminary *outing on the steamboat,* Three Rivers, *in 1913. The students in the foreground are, from left to right, Josephine Saunders, Alice Minnick, and Mary Costin. With them is Captain Bill Geoghegan.*

A View of Student Life, 1911–1914

My trips to the school . . . were up the bay by Choptank River steamer, then down from Baltimore. We rode practically all night, from Pier 3 on Light Street, on the steamers Three Rivers *and* Northumberland, *of the Maryland, Delaware and Virginia Line. The steamers, leaving Baltimore at 4.45 PM, arrived at St. Mary's at 3 AM the following day, and Ernest, the school's handyman, met the students at the pier and hauled their luggage to the dormitory by wheelbarrow. . . .*

Our wardrobes were terribly plain. We wore middy blouses and navy blue skirts, with oxfords or tennis shoes. For evening wear we could dress in lighter colors, as long as the dress cloth was heavy. No slippers or low shoes allowed after November 1. No evening gowns, no cosmetics of any sort. With family permission, we could write and receive letters from a few friends, but only a few.

Our light was provided by gas jets. We had running water, but only when the wind blew. A windmill operated a pump which kept our reservoir filled in breezy weather. In calm weather we carried our own water and washed in basins. {In our dorm rooms} most of us created . . . what was the rage then—a "cozy corner" . . . {consisting} of a bed dressed as a couch, often with a colorful parasol suspended overhead, with pictures, photographs, fans and other souvenirs tacked on the walls nearby. . . .

We lived by a schedule which began at 6.15 in the morning with the rising bell and ended with the 9.30 PM lights-out bell. If we didn't get too many demerits through *the week for being late to meals or class, for running through the halls, for being untidy or unladylike in any other way, we were rewarded on our day off, Monday, with a trip by oxcart or wagon to Park Hall, 4 miles away. Park Hall's only attraction was a country store, where we bought candy, hair ribbons, black cotton hose, peanut butter, pickles, crackers, cookies and so on. We weren't supposed to eat in our rooms, but most of us had hidden hoards of food for after-hour snacks. We weren't supposed to play cards, either. . . .*

We had other activities. We put on plays and minstrel shows, recitals, dances (no male partners), Halloween parties. Our Colonial Ball was a tremendous affair, all in costume, . . . {with} imaginary guests—Mistress Brent, Lady Baltimore, George Washington, Thomas Jefferson. We danced the lanciers, the waltz and the Virginia reel and, . . . our behavior had to be ever so formal. We went swimming (seniors were allowed to go rowing) in the St. Mary's River. We tramped through the woods and gathered flowers and wild asparagus.

We were never bored. Once a year we made an all-day trip on the steamer Three Rivers *from the school over to Coan and Kinsale in Virginia. These two little towns didn't have much more to offer than . . . Park Hall, but the ride there and back was fun. We sang the then latest songs, "Too Much Mustard," "Red Wing," "Row, Row, Row," and the "Oceana Roll."*

–Source: Mildred Spedden McDorman '14, "Study and Fun at the 'Monument School,' " *Baltimore Sunday Sun Magazine,* 10 March 1963, 2.

Mrs. Maddox told the parents of prospective students "not to rush your daughters through school," for "the painstaking and serious task of acquiring an education" must be "very thorough." In that year, the Seminary required students to take thirty-six half-hour periods in a four-day week, not counting music lessons, which Secretary Davenport found to be "very heavy for Secondary school work." (St. Mary's traditionally held classes Tuesdays through Fridays into the mid-twentieth century.) Eight semesters of satisfactory coursework were now required for a diploma, and several students stayed an extra year to "pursue special studies" in a "Post-Graduate" program.

While Seminarians endured a rigid disciplinary code that governed their behavior and deportment both on and off campus, they enjoyed an extensive array of courses taught by highly qualified instructors. The 1914–15 faculty included Miss Madeline Bernays (Royal Conservatory, London), piano; Miss Alice Miller (Otterbein University), piano and voice; Miss Caroline Mullikin (A.B., Goucher College), mathematics, chemistry, and physics; Miss Alice Constance Moore (A.B., Synodical College), Latin and English; Miss Ethel Joy (Western Maryland College), American and English literature, ancient and modern history, mythology, grammar, rhetoric, composition, and French; and Miss Marjorie Hebb Maddox (St. Mary's Female Seminary '09), freshman spelling, elementary grammar, composition, reading, literature, United States history, political geography, arithmetic, and physiology. The academic reputation of St. Mary's had become so good in the late 1890s that the State of Maryland granted Seminary graduates "similar and equal privileges" with those of the State Normal School at Towson, which allowed them to "teach in the public schools of the . . . State without further examination." Between 1900 and 1910, 70 percent of the graduates of St. Mary's Female Seminary (fifty-seven out of eighty-one) adopted teaching as a profession. That trend was perhaps the most fitting expression of gratitude to the teachers who had encouraged the discovery and development of their students' abilities. A 1911 graduate, Lettie Marshall Dent, became the first female county superintendent of schools in the State of Maryland, serving her native county of St. Mary's and bringing credit to the Seminary in that post from 1928 to 1957.

The Seminary Legacy

St. Mary's Female Seminary had enjoyed such success in the late nineteenth century that it seemed to want to remain in that era long after the twentieth century had arrived. Although it kept pace with current educational trends, the school seemed "old-fashioned" in the appearance and ambience of its campus and in the Victorian values it cultivated into the 1920s. For those who knew the school best, these were special qualities to be cherished, and generations of women attended the Seminary precisely to experience the same things their ancestors had. Outside critics, however, increasingly found those characteristics objectionable after 1900. They accused the Seminary of being too isolated, too small, too

An Outsider's Appraisal of Life at the Seminary, 1913

The sewerage and waste water runs through the underground pipes to the bluff leading down to the River. The terra-cotta pipe conveying it has not been continued far enough but should by all means be run sufficient distance out into the River to avoid flies and the odors that arise.

The present method of disposing of garbage is to dump same in a chute which runs down into the River, where, in summer time . . . a flat boat is always kept anchored and . . . is pushed out into the . . . river and there dumped.

Most of the equipment in the class rooms is very inadequate. . . . The Recitation Rooms are also lacking in maps, pictures and other paraphernalia for properly teaching. . . . The teaching of chemistry and physics without laboratory work is everywhere now regarded as a farce and it is essential . . . that adequate laboratory facilities be furnished.

There are canoes and a boat supplied for rowing on the River and the girls also swim during the summer months. The croquet, basket-ball and tennis court also help to give sufficient exercise, in view of the fact that . . . the girls exercise at least one-half hour {each day} under the supervision of the teacher.

The Dormitory arrangements consist of sleeping rooms about 10 × 16, in which two and sometimes three girls room. . . . The furniture is fairly adequate but is exceedingly miscellaneous in character, there being hardly a complete set of furniture in any room. . . . The girls are obliged to hang their dresses and suits on racks or nails in the walls without any protection from dust or sunlight.

The students . . . are supposed to carry all thirty-six half hour periods per week in addition to music. This course strikes me as very heavy for Secondary school work, and I . . . suggest that . . . a system of election be installed which will permit even wider scope of studies.

—Source: Report of the Secretary (William H. Davenport) of the Board of State Aid and Charities, after a visit to the Seminary, 1–3 April 1913.

The School Building, completed in Spring 1903; shown here soon after construction and before it was painted to match the main building. Note the windmill to the left, which powered the pump for the artesian well.

An early view of Music Hall (now St. Mary's Hall), in the foreground. This building was dedicated in June 1908 and was the last construction on campus until 1925.

elitist, and too lavish in its spending on each student for a school in the twentieth century. Many called it an anachronism and an anomaly as a public boarding school for girls in an era of "progressive" education.

However, the legacy of the Seminary—an affectionate but defiant pride that graduates felt for the special place and the special people responsible for a uniquely-nurturing education—proved stronger than its critics. The resilience that kept the school alive was derived from the loyalty of its students to the traditional values of the Seminary. The formation of the Alumnae Association in 1917—a major institutional milestone that symbolized the ability and willingness of past students to assist those of the present and future—provided a tangible focus for pride in the Seminary and helped rally citizens to the school's defense on several key occasions.

The fierce loyalties of former students were instilled by the special environment of a four-year boarding school in an isolated place with a timeless heritage. Secretary Davenport was neither the first nor the last critic to denounce "the location of the Institution . . . [as] unfortunate." But the residents of the Seminary knew better. The rural isolation of St. Mary's City removed most of the distractions and diversions that interfered with academics, while encouraging a warm and congenial atmosphere to flourish among the girls of Calvert Hall. Moreover, the school's location amid ancient relics that recalled memorable principles of the past imparted a valuable perspective to youths thinking only of their individual futures. The place was, and is, the essence of the Monument School's enduring and endearing charm.

School pride was diffused across the generations and throughout the state because the Seminary's special people made people feel special. Attesting to this quality were hundreds of former students from several eras, who came from poor families and attended St. Mary's free of charge, proof positive that the school may have been isolated but never inaccessible. Among the most special people associated with the Seminary were "Dear Miss Lizzie" and "Madame Maddox," the past principals of affectionate memory who continued to serve the school years after they ceased drawing salaries. They instilled in their many students the genteel values of the nineteenth century long after it had ended and, in effect, demonstrated the *positive benefits* of institutional anachronism. In the trying, testing months that followed the complete destruction in 1924 of Calvert Hall, symbol and centerpiece of St. Mary's Female Seminary, nostalgia for the distinguished past of this old-fashioned school proved vital to its future.

The pride, the place, and the people who made the Seminary what it was are with us still, more relevant and meaningful than ever. The Monument School of the People lives on, because St. Mary's Female Seminary persisted with the innovations of the 1840s and retained them as the traditions of the 1900s—outlasting its many critics until the anachronism and impracticality of a small, rural, residential, public school of affordable academic excellence became valued once again.

An Estimate of Resources and Expenditures for the 1916–17 School Year

Resources

Continuing State Appropriation	$2,500.00
Current Appropriation	
(Omnibus Bill, 1914)	6,000.00
Fees from Boarding Pupils	
—15 pupils at $170.	2,550.00
7 pupils @ $150.	1,050.00
Fees for music pupils—	
15 pupils @ $ 40.	600.00
	$12,700.00

Expenses

Salaries—

Treasurer	$ 100.00
Principal (also allowed board & garden)	750.00
2 Music teachers @ $475 and board . .	950.00
4 Classical teachers @ $450 and board	1,800.00
Coal	700.00
Carbide for gas machine	150.00
Wood	50.00
Coal Oil	50.00
Ordinary repairs and furniture	800.00
School Supplies	300.00
Office Expenses, printing and postage	150.00
Commencement, Trustees' and visitors expenses	100.00
Insurance	150.00
Books (furnished free to scholarship students)	200.00
Board—60 persons @ $10/month × 8½ mos.	5,100.00
Losses and Sundries	900.00
	$12,250.00
Balance in hands of Trustees	$ 450.00

—Source: William H. Davenport, "Memorandum of Suggested Changes in Financial Methods of St. Mary's Female Seminary" (undated but ca. 1916–1917).

The Seminary "Prison" of 1898

St. Mary's Prison Cell No. 12
Sept. 24, 1898

Dear Mama,
Please let me come home, I could not stay here until Christmas if I was paid $10 per day. I cried myself to sleep last night & cried so much today that Miss Palmer (the nice

Miss Grace Linwood Gibson, *author of the accompanying "letter from prison," in her graduation portrait, June 1901. She not only survived those awful early days of homesickness to graduate from the Seminary, she became a teacher.*

teacher I told you about) had to make a baby out of me. . . . {O}h mama you know I can't bear such lonesome solitude as this, {if} you let me come . . . I will never say I dislike Centreville again.

. . .

I like most of my teachers very much, but they are so strict. We have 50 rules to keep.

. . .

When other things are sent, please send something to eat, I am starved. All you have to eat is fish and I don't love it much as you know, and the coffee is strong enough to walk out the door at 10 miles per minute. . . . We had warm rolls for supper, the first we have had. They were about the size of a walnut. . . . {On Sunday} we had chicken or rather a tough rooster and gravy that resembled slops and rice without either sugar or milk and one little sweet potato that nearly broke my heart, for mama, you know how I love them.

. . .

Mama please write a letter saying I can come home at any time and send me some money for boat fare and a dollar also for a berth for I will be on the boat from 6 p.m. until early the next morning.

. . .

Do all I tell you and oblige your poor home-sick daughter. Give my love to everybody in Centreville but don't tell them I am coming {home} for maybe when you say I can come I will want to stay. Kiss Helen, papa & May for me & give my love to Nellie if you see her.

Grace, poor hungry home-sick
Grace {L. Gibson}

Don't let Grace come home. She will be alright in a few days. She has the blues right now. I'll take care of her.
her schoolmate
Ella Hodgson

–Source: *Alumni Newsletter,* Vol. XVI No. 3 (Fall 1967).

Students of St. Mary's Female Seminary gather on the steps of Calvert Hall in 1915.

And when life's ray
Shall fade away
To evening's gentle warning
May we all look back
O'er its varied track
To this spot, where
All was morning.

—An alumnae tribute to Mrs. Maddox, at her last commencement as principal, June 1923

Calvert Hall, St. Mary's Female Seminary, as it looked before the fire of 1924.

The ruins of old Calvert Hall after the fire of 5 January 1924.

*This Maryland Bethlehem of kindness and
understanding . . . has been one of the great
educational . . . leaders of the country; its example
has contributed no little to enlarging religious and
educational freedom and in making bigotry . . .
abhorrent to all true descendants of the
Maryland-born at St. Mary's City.*
—An article on St. Mary's Female Seminary, *Baltimore
News-American,* 7 August 1924

TRIALS AND TRIUMPHS:
Miss France's Junior College, 1923–1948

Among the many transformations that brought St. Mary's College to this sesquicentennial anniversary, the Junior College years (1926–1968) represent a critical intermediate stage in the evolution of the mature, secure institution of today. If we envision the present four-year College as a blossoming flower, and the Female Seminary as the seed that imparted a timeless heritage, then the Junior College would be the stem of the plant—a sturdy stalk, resilient to the buffeting winds of change—that grew from the seed and permitted the flower to reach the sunlight.

St. Mary's Female Seminary-Junior College, the first junior college in Maryland, was a daring experiment that continued this school's reputation as an educational pioneer. This chapter will focus on the creation and operation of the Junior College in its first two decades, with particular emphasis on its founder, M. Adele France. Rightly regarded as the "School Mother," Miss France was an inspired and affectionate leader who served St. Mary's for twenty-five years—the longest tenure of any chief executive in the school's history.

The Dawn of a New Age
The 1923–24 academic year was one of the great turning points in the history of St. Mary's College, for events both destructive and creative brought the Female Seminary into the twentieth century almost overnight. The old Seminary, which perhaps had grown too secure in the stable and conservative administration of Lucy Virginia Maddox since 1900, was ripe for change

and ready for a challenge. When Mrs. Maddox announced that she would retire in June 1923, the Board of Trustees unanimously elected Miss M. Adele France, aged 43, as her successor. A native of Chestertown, Miss France graduated from Washington College in 1905 with a major in mathematics and earned Master's degrees from her alma mater and Teachers College of Columbia University. Miss France had been a "highly valued teacher" at St. Mary's from 1909 to 1913, leaving to become a supervisor of secondary schools in Nashville, Tennessee, and on Maryland's Eastern Shore. As one alumna wrote, Miss France was an ideal choice to make "St. Mary's a big little school . . . in the front rank of preparatory schools with all the rights and privileges of college certification." This Margaret Brent for the modern age was a native Marylander who knew the Seminary well, and yet she had traveled widely in gaining vital administrative experience. She appreciated the traditional heritage of the Seminary, and yet she was committed to progressive educational ideals and methods. And finally, Miss France seemed to bridge the gap between old-fashioned values of the nineteenth-century family and the professional aspirations of young women in twentieth-century society. Having obtained the right to vote in 1920, American women for the first time inhabited a world of expanded horizons. The graduates of St. Mary's, prepared and inspired by the first college-educated principal in the school's history, would grasp the new opportunities of that era.

Appointed at the unprecedentedly large salary of

The graduation portrait of Mary Adele France, one of the first women to receive a bachelor's degree from Washington College. She must have looked very much like this when she joined the Seminary faculty in 1909.

$2,000 per year and accorded the additional title of "Chief Administrative Officer," Principal France brought boundless energy and enthusiasm to this new job in a familiar, congenial setting. She corresponded with former faculty colleagues throughout the summer of 1923 in preparing copy for the new catalog. On 11 June, the last day of school under Mrs. Maddox's long tenure, a teacher wrote Miss France: "We are trying to 'round up' our year to-day. We want to leave things so that you may get a line on what has *gone before,* at least. We were distressed to learn that the whole Sophomore Algebra class cheated in their examination. The papers were thrown away and they took a second examination, with the exception of four or five, who either [will] repeat the work or do not expect to return. Yesterday was a beautiful day for our last Friday together. . . . Poor Mrs. Maddox was much in tears—a sort of final sorrow! My heart is in this dear old school and I am glad that someone who knows it and cares for it is going to continue the good work, but the 'mills of the gods grind exceedingly slow' in this part of Maryland, so don't be discouraged, you will come through all right in time!"

According to a Seminary brochure, "at the beginning of the scholastic year of 1923–24, the future of St. Mary's Seminary seemed especially bright, its prosperity well assured." But it was to be a new future, not always prosperous, and filled with more change than complacency. Miss France's leadership was already evident as the sixty Seminarians arrived for the fall semester and met "an entirely new faculty" that she had assembled in only three months' time: Ida de Loache (Columbia College), English and French; Mrs. Ethel Whitmore (George Washington University), history and Latin; Anne B. Horne (Converse College and Columbia University), science and household arts; Elsie V. Stanley (Posse Normal School of Gymnastics), elementary science and physical education; and Elizabeth O'Brien (University of Kansas), piano and chorus. Other new features at the old school included a reorganized curriculum that for the first time required sixteen units for graduation, the addition of two new departments (Household Arts and Physical Education), the first Spanish language classes, the opening of the school's first "real" library (with books systematically arranged on built-in shelves), the first specifically designed and well-equipped science laboratory, conversion of Music Hall into a gymnasium, and the first electric lighting throughout the campus. In addition, the first student newspaper, *The Seminary Signal,* began publication during the Fall 1923 semester; new clubs were organized ("each girl was compelled to belong to the Hiking Club, and also to join two others" from among Dramatic, Social, Music, and Current Events); and the activities calendar was vastly expanded, offering pupils more commemorative assemblies, historical pageants, lectures, debates, teas, dances, and intramural athletic events than ever before.

The Great Fire

St. Mary's Female Seminary was only four months into its "brighter future" under the new principal when a devastating fire destroyed eighty-year-old Calvert Hall and severely tested the spirit of the people who occupied that venerable structure. At dusk on Saturday, 5 January 1924, in the midst of a fierce winter storm, a fire broke out in the basement furnace room and quickly spread into the walls, fed by gale-force winds. The Reverend C. W. Whitmore, Rector of Trinity Church, was the first to notice the glowing flames in the descending darkness, but he and the school's two maintenance men were unable to control the blaze because the fire extinguishers had been recharged and locked away in an unknown location over the Christmas recess. By means of telephone party lines and the ringing of the Trinity

Church bell, the Whitmore family soon summoned a large force of eager volunteers to the blaze, and hundreds of local citizens worked in sub-zero temperatures for seven hours to save the Monument School of the People. The Leonardtown Fire Department never arrived, because its truck had a frozen engine, but county residents of all ages formed bucket brigades and courageously carried out school records, furniture from the first floor, pianos, library books, and bags of mail from the St. Mary's City Post Office (located in the rear of Calvert Hall). In the excitement, several well-meaning volunteers even salvaged logs from a fireplace and a withered Christmas tree! All of the students' personal possessions in the upper-story dormitory rooms were lost, but a huge and tragic toll in lives was averted due to the holiday recess. Rector Whitmore was the only casualty in the long night of fire-fighting. The strong winds blowing from the river spared Music Hall but endangered the rectory on the other side of Calvert. In trying to extinguish the many sparks that landed on his

Miss France's Rules and Regulations

Courtesy, punctuality, and neatness of attire and room are expected and required. Students make their own beds and care for their rooms and wardrobes.

Quiet after "room bell" and orderly behavior in the halls are required.

Students leave the grounds only when accompanied by a chaperon and visit only with the permission of parents.

Parents are earnestly requested, for the well-being of their daughters, not to send or bring them food other than fresh fruit and a limited amount of candy.

All packages are subject to examination and delivery at the discretion of the principal.

Pupils will not be called to the telephone during recitation or study hours and at other times only for parents.

Visits to oculists should be made before the school begins or during vacation. No dentistry or dressmaking should be done during school sessions except in case of emergency.

Pupils may receive occasional calls, by permission, from persons who are approved by their parents and the principal, on Saturday evenings and Sunday afternoons—provided the academic record and deportment warrant such privilege.

Parents should furnish the principal a list of young men of whom they approve as callers, or escorts for their daughters to occasional informal dances.

Pupils may receive visitors only with the knowledge and consent of the principal; all visitors must see the principal on arrival and departure.

Parents and friends of the pupils accompanying them to school or visiting them, if occasion demands, are charged at the rate of $1.50 per day.

The school is closed at Christmas. Board at the rate of $10.00 a week or $1.50 a day will be charged for those who remain at the school during the Easter vacation.

Borrowing clothing is strictly forbidden. Large amounts of money or expensive jewelry should not be brought to the school. We assume no responsibility for either.

Seminarians on a stroll in front of Trinity Rectory. They are looking at the entrance to campus; to their immediate left is Brome's Wharf Road.

Any article broken by a pupil must be replaced, and she must pay for any other damage, outside of ordinary wear and tear, for which she is responsible.

No chafing dishes, teakettles, alcohol, or electrical appliances are permitted in the pupils rooms. Special arrangements for pressing and for curling hair may be made through the principal.

Privileges are accorded only to those whose academic record and deportment are satisfactory.

We request that parents and patrons of the school assist us in the maintenance of order and obedience in the school family by not asking for exceptions to our rules.

Whenever the principal decides that a pupil's presence is detrimental to the school, on account of conduct, or for any other sufficient reason, she reserves the right to request her withdrawal.

—Source: Composite list from Seminary catalogs, 1920s–1940s.

The campus devastation that greeted Principal France on the morning of Sunday, 6 January 1924. The February 1924 issue of The Seminary Signal *(student newspaper, Vol. 1, No. 4) memorialized the old building: "It stood on the brow of a hill, Looking out where the blue water gleams; Stately and white and still—A castle of youthful dreams."*

home, Whitmore fell from his ice-coated roof and suffered injuries that incapacitated him for several weeks.

Returning from Christmas vacation on that Saturday evening, Miss France heard someone shout, "St. Mary's Seminary's burned to the ground!" as her bus pulled into Leonardtown. She arrived on campus in time to see the raging fire finish off the old building. As the new principal viewed the smoldering ruins, a pathetic memorial to eight decades of operation, Stephen M. Jones, a trustee since 1901 and now the Board treasurer, asked Miss France what was to be done. According to her recollection, she answered, very much in the spirit of Scarlett O'Hara: "We shall carry on!"

At dawn on Sunday, 6 January, all that remained of the Seminary's "beautiful mansion" were a few bleak and blackened walls and several charred chimneys. Pianos and furniture lay piled in Trinity Churchyard, while books, files, and paintings were stacked on the rectory porches. Community spirit was high, as the many local citizens who had fought the fire until 1 a.m. returned to the church ten hours later for a service of thanksgiving. Filing out of Trinity, they were greeted with tables of donated food, which would sustain them through long hours of moving salvaged possessions into Music Hall. Miss France rose early on Sunday morning and began the frantic task of calling the teachers and

students to tell them that the school would not reopen on the following day as scheduled. For the rest of Sunday, the principal held an unending series of meetings with school trustees, local officials, and the county's legislative delegation to discuss the future of St. Mary's Female Seminary.

Not everyone believed that the old school with only sixty students would or should survive, and even the most optimistic supporters had difficulty predicting where and when it could reopen. The trustees considered holding classes at Porto Bello, the well-known eighteenth-century manor house in Drayden, owned and offered by Trustee J. Allan Coad, but a newspaper article on Monday, 7 January, announced that the school would resume operations within two weeks at the Scotland Beach Hotel near Point Lookout. After two tense days of doubts, fully expecting state officials to close the school permanently, Miss France finally received the welcome news on Monday evening that Governor Albert C. Ritchie and the State Board of Public Works had given preliminary approval to construct temporary housing *on campus*—a vital commitment that would allow the Seminary to reopen and ultimately to remain at the historic first capital. As it had done so many times before, the persevering St. Mary's "phoenix" would rise again from the ashes, this time literally. But on this occasion, the school enjoyed phenomenal good luck, since Ritchie, a strong supporter of public education, was the first Maryland governor ever to be re-elected to a successive term. Since the inauguration was to be held on Wednesday, 9 January, no other governor, lame duck or new, would have been able to make such a commitment to the Seminary in those critical first days after the fire.

As soon as they received Ritchie's promise to continue operations on the historic campus, the Seminary trustees immediately allocated $2,500 for the construction of a two-story, T-shaped, frame dormitory down the hill from the ruins of Calvert Hall. Sleeping thirty students on borrowed Army cots in one huge room on the second floor, and providing bathrooms, kitchen facilities, and a dining hall on the first floor, the crude but functional "Barracks" was finished in three weeks, allowing the school to reopen on 2 February, only one month late. Still, because all sixty pupils returned for the spring semester, local citizens were asked to house students in their homes. Throughout that term, Miss France and two dozen Seminarians stayed with the Whitmore family at the Trinity Rectory. It must have been a trying experience for thirty-one adults to share a house with no electricity and one bathroom. Fifteen-year-old John Whitmore (who did not mind the

Medallion portrait of Albert Cabell Ritchie, Governor of Maryland (1920–1935), whose unwavering support preserved the Seminary. This Tercentenary Medal was created by Hans Schuler.

attention from so many new "sisters") recalled that the girls devised a detailed schedule that allowed everyone a turn in the bathroom—except Rector Whitmore. Other students and teachers moved in with Mrs. Lilburn

The "Barracks," temporary housing for most of the student body from 2 February 1924 to 9 June 1925. Note the board sidewalk that helped students avoid the muddy construction site of Calvert Hall.

("Dear Miss Lizzie"), the former principal who lived where the College Advancement Office now stands. Makeshift classrooms were created in spacious Music Hall, music classes were held around the Trinity Church organ, and students carried bowls of milk and flour in all weather to home economics classes conducted in the kitchen of Mr. and Mrs. Charles M. Robinson, who lived where the Admissions Office is now.

While the local community pulled together and shared an exciting rebirth of school spirit, influential politicians were also rallying behind the Seminary. Before the end of January, Southern Maryland legislators led by State Senator George C. Peverley of Mechanicsville (whose daughter, Corinne, was attending the Seminary) obtained an appropriation of $100,000 from the General Assembly to rebuild Calvert Hall on its original foundations. Although that amount was only half of what would eventually be needed and was not payable until 1 August 1925, the Seminary was fortunate to obtain any state assistance in 1924. The University of Maryland at College Park, recognized as the state university only four years before, had its budget request cut 67 percent at almost the same time, in what some reporters described as the "most desperate struggle in the legislative history of the present century." With $100,000 from the state and another $20,000 from an insurance settlement, the Board of Trustees quickly secured the services of Baltimore architect Stanislaus Russell and accepted the low bid for construction from the Salisbury contracting firm of Hastings and Parsons. Work on the new Calvert Hall began on 2 June 1924, with much of the first summer devoted to clearing the site and cleaning the charred bricks of 1844–45 for re-use in the new building.

Once again, the close physical and historical connection between the Monument School and old St. Mary's City had proven to be an indispensable asset for the Seminary. While some people wanted to replace the living educational memorial with less expensive marble monuments to the state's "Plymouth Rock," eighty years of public identification with the endearing, if troublesome, old school encouraged what A. S. Goldsborough called a "promptness that ever characterizes the truly patriotic act . . . to the task of rebuilding Maryland's tribute to her founders." Goldsborough was the executive secretary of the Baltimore Association of Commerce, and only two days after the Calvert fire, this tough-minded businessman and political insider had emphatically informed the press that "the State would aid in the rebuilding program . . . [because] the seminary was considered a State memorial, commemorating

the landing of the first Maryland colonists."

Patriotic nostalgia went only so far, however, and there were many practical reasons that compelled state officials to rebuild the Seminary. Governor Ritchie probably saw his commitment to the school as a means of rewarding the staunch Democratic majority in Southern Maryland for supporting his re-election, but as the "education governor," he was also sincerely concerned that each county receive an equal share of state funding for public schools. St. Mary's County was certainly most deserving of his support. According to the 1920 census, the county ranked near the bottom of all Maryland jurisdictions in educational opportunities, public school attendance, size of population, per capita income, and value of farm property. Forty-three of its fifty-three public elementary schools had only one room and one teacher, and it would not have a conventional public high school until Great Mills opened in 1927. Governor Ritchie could not afford to exacerbate this already bleak educational picture by closing the county's one successful secondary school that gave local residents their "only opportunity for graduation from a 1st class, 1st group public high school." What is a little-known fact today perhaps proved decisive in Governor Ritchie's decision in 1924–that St. Mary's Female Seminary had long accepted local boys as day students and was prepared to provide them with even more educational opportunities in the near future. Captain Alexander Kennedy's son had attended the Seminary as early as 1902, and at least three other boys (Alfred Saunders, Cleveland Potter, and Robert Stevens) took classes as day students in the 1920s. (The first recorded male graduates from the Seminary's high school curriculum were Edwin Birch, Class of 1929, and Benjamin Weiner, Class of 1930, both of St. Inigoes.)

In the final analysis, St. Mary's Female Seminary was saved in 1924 because so many citizens dedicated themselves to reviving the old school, so dearly loved in the past and so clearly needed for the future–and the politicians knew it. The Monument School of the People, though physically destroyed, truly proved that its greatest worth was not in brick and mortar, but in the love and loyalty that it both imparted to and received from the people of Maryland, rich and poor, near and far, across the several generations.

Those feelings of affection were translated into tangible financial support for the Seminary when the Rebuilding Campaign of 1924–25 solicited contributions to match the state's appropriation of $100,000. That fund-raising effort–directed by Baltimoreans A. S. Goldsborough, J. Spence Howard, Mrs. J. Dawson Reeder (president of the Alumnae Association), and

Edward M. Thomas of the Century Trust Company—published the following financial statement at the beginning of the statewide campaign for private donations in September 1924:

Cost of new building, under construction, minus one wing	$123,700
Cost of adding the wing now being omitted from plans	25,000
Cost of water tower, engine, electric lights, sewerage	11,000
Cost of equipment and furnishings (estimated)	35,000
School expenses since the fire, including Barracks	5,000
Accumulated indebtedness and contingent expenses	15,300

THIS SIDE OF CARD IS FOR ADDRESS

Hon. Geo. C. Peverley,

St. Mary's Female Seminary Office

Leonardtown, Md.

You are cordially invited to a

Dinner Meeting

at the St. Mary's Hotel, Leonardtown, Md.
on Monday Evening, Sept. 29, at 6:30

The Re-Building Program of St. Mary's Female Seminary, will be presented by prominent St. Mary's County speakers

Dinner Complimentary.
No Solicitation of Funds

Kindly reply promptly.

Hon. Geo. C. Peverley
Chr. County Com.

Hon. J. Allan Coad
Chr. Business Com.

Advertisement for a local fund-raising dinner, September 1924.

An Honor Roll of Fund-Raisers, 1924–1925

Joseph Addison	*R. Bennett Darnell*	*Dr. N. E. B. Iglehart*	*Clayton Purnell*
Matthew Page Andrews	*Walter I. Dawkins*	*Stephen M. Jones*	*Daniel R. Randall*
Mrs. C. W. Bassett	*Henry C. Dent*	*Willis R. Jones*	*Mrs. J. Dawson Reeder*
James M. Bennett	*J. Marshall Dent*	*Mrs. Frank Killian*	*Gov. Albert C. Ritchie*
Rev. Dr. Hugh Birckhead	*T. Raymond Dixon*	*Charles H. Knapp*	*Thomas Robinson*
Duke Bond	*T. Howard Duckett*	*Rabbi Morris S. Lazaron*	*Alfred G. Sanner*
James A. C. Bond	*Robert M. Duvall*	*E. Brook Lee*	*William S. Stanley*
Mrs. K. M. Brevitt	*Dr. J. M. T. Finney*	*Mrs. J. G. H. Lilburn*	*J. Noble Stockett*
John P. Briscoe	*Stephen T. Foxwell*	*Charles J. Linthicum*	*J. C. Taliaferro*
William Cabell Bruce	*Bishop James Freeman*	*Mrs. Robert Loker*	*Armstrong Thomas*
Howard Bryant	*George A. Frick*	*William M. Loker*	*Edward M. Thomas*
George L. Buckler	*Henry G. Garner*	*John N. Mackall*	*Henry B. Thomas, Jr.*
B. Harris Camalier	*A. S. Goldsborough*	*Rev. Dr. James Magruder*	*James W. Thomas*
J. Allan Coad	*Charles S. Grason*	*William L. Marbury*	*Mrs. T. Rowland Thomas*
Arthur C. Combs	*C. Benedict Greenwell*	*Ridgeley P. Melvin*	*Mrs. Felix E. Wathen*
Key Compton	*Samuel Hayden*	*Theodore K. Miller*	*George Weems Williams*
R. Keith Compton	*Mrs. George W. Hodges*	*Mrs. Frederick Mosher*	*Lawrence P. Williams*
Albert S. Cook	*W. Meade Holladay*	*Bishop John G. Murray*	*J. Dallam Wise*
Robert Crain	*Allen B. Howard*	*Mrs. Frank J. Parran*	*Dr. Walter D. Wise*
Randolph N. Dame	*J. Spence Howard*	*George C. Peverley*	

Interest payments due until 1 August 1925	5,000
Total deficits	$220,000
Amount covered by legislative appropriation, payable 8/1/25	100,000
Fire insurance settlement	20,000
Amount to be procured from private contributions	$100,000

This call for contributions produced a groundswell of citizen support from across Maryland. The people of St. Mary's County, as they had done so often, responded magnificently and pledged $10,000 in one month's time. The local effort was spearheaded by the Seminary's many influential trustees, including former State Senator Charles S. Grason of Cross Manor, Circuit Court Judge B. Harris Camalier, Delegates J. Allan Coad and Lawrence P. Williams, and past or present County Commissioners George L. Buckler, Arthur C. Combs, J. Marshall Dent, Samuel Hayden, Stephen M. Jones, and Alfred G. Sanner. In addition to citizen donations, the Leonardtown Branch of the Eastern Shore Trust Company (where Trustee Jones was cashier) provided several timely loans that saved the school in its darkest days of indebtedness. Statewide fund-raising was substantially assisted by the support from an impressive fifty-member "Honorary Committee," which included Governor Ritchie himself, former Governor Phillips Lee Goldsborough, Maryland Attorney General Thomas H. Robinson, Secretary of State E. Brooke Lee, United States Senator William Cabell Bruce, Congressman J. Charles Linthicum, historian Matthew Page Andrews, numerous judges, clergymen of all faiths, and dozens of devoted alumnae.

The fund-raisers quickly discovered that the memorable past of the Monument School held the key to its future. Contributions poured in so that "this shrine" on the site of Maryland's founding could "be put in first class order . . . [in time] for the Tercentennial pilgrimage to St. Mary's . . . in 1934." Although no citizen offered to build a new auditorium (for $10,000), Mr. and Mrs. James M. Bennett of Philadelphia (she the daughter of Doctor Brome, the former trustee) donated a completely equipped infirmary, while Miss Bessie Kibbie of Washington, D.C. gave a fully furnished library. Most of the funds for refurnishing Calvert Hall, however, came from hundreds of small contributors, in much the same way that the original structure was financed in the 1840s. The public responded most enthusiastically to the idea of furnishing dormitory rooms in the new Calvert Hall at $200 apiece, so that "some mother's girl away from home will be your perpetual guest." The overwhelming success of this campaign was due largely to the school's policy of placing inscribed brass plates on the doors of dormitory rooms, which identified the donors and the loved ones they were memorializing by their gift. By 1926, thirty-one such "memorial rooms" had been furnished in this way, and there was intense competition to endow specific sites in the new building that corresponded to where ancestors had lived in the old one. Several contributors, for instance, wanted to furnish Room 7 on the second floor, and one donor agreed to buy dormitory furniture only for "a bright room with windows to the front of the building."

Nostalgia also became a prominent theme for the Seminary students, as school officials emphasized the special relationship that had always existed between the past, the present, and the future at St. Mary's. In March 1924, after only a month back on campus, students and staff celebrated "Enactment Day" for the first time, delivering patriotic speeches and dressing in nineteenth-century costumes to commemorate the 1840 legislation that created the Seminary. On 31 May, St. Mary's students began a long tradition by staging an elaborate historical pageant for the general public, depicting key events in the school's past and highlighting "the part that woman has played in the history of Maryland." Commencement Day, 1 July 1924, was extra special, as ten girls received diplomas and Judge Camalier delivered an optimistic address, now assured that there would be future generations of graduates. On Independence Day later that week, the new Alumnae Lodge was dedicated. The original Seminary stable, which had contained bricks from the 1676 State House, was rebuilt using bricks from the 1844 Calvert Hall. As the most historic building on campus, the renovated Lodge truly symbolized the living spirit of a noble past that would continue into the future. The trustees had given a rundown structure to the Alumnae Association, and the contributions of former students had paid for its renovation; but instead of enjoying their new facility, the alumnae gave the building back to their alma mater because current and future students were in such desperate need of classroom space following the fire.

There was still one event to come in this summer of celebrations and that was the cornerstone laying of the new Calvert Hall. On Sunday, 3 August 1924, eighty years to the day from the cornerstone laying of the original building, some 1,500 persons gathered to dedicate themselves anew to the principles and purposes of the Seminary. The guest of honor, silver trowel in hand, was eighty-five-year-old Cecelia Coad Roberts—the oldest living alumna and a member of the entering class

A typical dormitory room in rebuilt Calvert Hall, furnished by donors as memorials to loved ones.

The Memorial Rooms of Calvert Hall, 1925–1926

In Memory of Fendall Marbury of "Wyoming," Prince George's County. Donor: William L. Marbury

In Memory of George W. and Susanna Rankin Watson of Anne Arundel County. Donor: Mrs. Joseph C. Dalton

Dedicated to the Memory of Mary Eliza Howard by Her Sons and Daughters

In Memory of Henry Briscoe Thomas, M.D.

In Memory of Georgeanna Weems Williams By Her Children: George Weems Williams, Elizabeth Chew Williams, Matilda Williams

Richard H. Garner, Trustee from 1888 to 1904
    Donor: Mrs. Richard H. Garner

In Memory of Alexander Magruder, Dr. John Briscoe, Rev. William Wilkinson, Edmund Howard, Capt. Thomas Dent, and Capt. Henry Hawkins—Early Settlers
    Donor: The Rev. James M. Magruder, D.D., and Margaret M. Magruder

Washington-Custis Room. Presented by the Washington-Custis Chapter, Daughters of the American Revolution

In Memory of Mrs. Elisabeth Briscoe Cashner (nee Bessie Briscoe). Donor: J. Douglas Cashner

In Memory of Cecilia Dent Harrison, 1792–1853, by Her Descendants. Donor: J. E. Harrison

Presented by the Society of The Ark and The Dove In Memory of Those Who Planted the Province of Maryland.

Theodora M. Anderson, St. Marys F. Seminary, 1850—A Memorial by Her Children: Alice Norris Parran, Bennet Biscoe Norris, Sophie Biscoe Norris, Bessie Biscoe Woodley, Arthur F. Norris, Jennie Biscoe Brooks, Ellen Dabney Miller

Emily Bishop Room. Donor: Beatrice Fenton, Marjorie D. Martinet, Anne W. Strawbridge

In Memory of T. Rowland Thomas by Several of His Friends. Donor: R. J. Brome

In Memory of Father and Mother—Thomas Dashiell France and Emma Price France. Donor: M. Adele France

Presented to St. Mary's Seminary by the Maryland State Society of Washington

In Memory of George Frederick Maddox and Susan Harris Maddox. Presented by their Daughter, Martha Maddox Key

In Memory of St. George Barber

Furnished by Mr. and Mrs. Franklin V. Killian

Furnished by The Thomas Johnson Chapter, Daughters of the American Revolution, Mrs. David M. Robinson, Regent

Endowed by "The Maryland Line" Chapter, Daughters of the American Revolution

*Furnished by Chapter I, The Colonial Dames of America

*Furnished by Dr. and Mrs. Alexander Hodgdon as a Tribute to Mr. and Mrs. George W. Hodges

*Lucy Virginia Maddox, A Tribute from Mr. and Mrs. H. S. Wherrett

*Dedicated to Our Principal, Miss France, by Delta Phi Sigma Sorority

Furnished by Judge Walter I. Dawkins, Baltimore

In Memory of Thomas F. Foxwell, Trustee, 1898–1919. Donor: Stephen M. Jones

In Memory of Jeannette Yates Clagett Wilson, Wife of Joseph Sollers Wilson. Donor: E. Brooke Lee

In Youth We Mold the Coming Nation. Margaret A. Albright

*Furnished by Delta Phi Epsilon Sorority

In Memory of Mrs. Lilburn, Principal

*Indicates plates on "Special Rooms" (not dormitory rooms)

    —Source: File A262-Markers-26: Memorial Rooms of Calvert Hall, College Archives.

in 1846. Joining her for the festivities were school officials, local politicians, other descendants of the first trustees, and representatives from the Society of the Ark and the Dove, the Daughters of the American Revolution, and the Maryland Historical Society. The keynote speaker, A. S. Goldsborough of the Rebuilding Campaign, reminded the audience that the bigotry of "religious fanatics" (like the revived Ku Klux Klan) was again threatening the ideal of toleration. "The lesson of the Ark and the Dove, the foundation stone of St. Mary's Seminary," he said, "is a badly needed plank to our almost shipwrecked society of today. . . . [S]o long as we uphold and cultivate such institutions in our midst, no one can say of us that we do not try to deserve that noble reputation bequeathed by the Calvert Lords . . . only a few feet away."

Getting Back to "Normal"

Following a year of such unparalleled trials and triumphs, crises and celebrations, it was natural that the staff and students of the Seminary would find it difficult to adjust to a more normal existence. The 1924–25 academic year was indeed "Hell on Earth," according to Miss France. The beginning of the fall semester was delayed until 1 October in the false expectation that Cal-

vert Hall would be ready for residents, and when the disappointed students did arrive, they faced a critical shortage of housing. The "Barracks" had to be enlarged to accommodate more boarders, since the patient hospitality of the local community was running thin. Forced to live in cramped quarters and to relinquish most of their holidays for the year, the students were inclined toward "much dissension." Among the teachers, "there seemed to be constant illness, which made it necessary that they go home or to a hospital." To make matters worse for Principal France, an epidemic of scarlet fever hit the Seminary in January 1925, soon after the students returned from Christmas vacation, and the school had to be closed (the second in Maryland to do so). However, the academic year ended on a happy, hopeful note when Calvert Hall was finished while school was still in session. According to Miss France: "We were promised the new building would be completed by Christmas, then February, then Easter. Finally, two weeks before Commencement I was told the building was completed, BUT there were no screens for the windows, yet—and the flies and mosquitoes were terrible! I told the girls the situation and they were unanimous in their decision to move in. So after classes that day [9 June 1925], we moved in and were all established in

The cornerstone–laying ceremony for the new Calvert Hall, Sunday, 3 August 1924—eighty years to the day that the original cornerstone was laid. The speakers' platform shown here was situated near the foundations of the old building, looking toward Music Hall and the St. Mary's River. The woman facing the camera, near the center, is thought to be Cecelia Coad Roberts, the oldest alumna and guest of honor.

The Alumnae Lodge, reconstructed from the Seminary stable with some $2,000 in alumnae donations and dedicated on 4 July 1924. In June 1922, the Association's 200 members endowed the Alumnae Scholarship (still given), and the organization received a state charter of incorporation on 22 March 1927.

two hours! And the miserable year ended happily after all!" At Commencement on 26 June 1925, eleven students graduated, having been denied a typically serene Seminary experience their last two years. Probably only one of those graduates, Elizabeth M. Dixon, had any reason to welcome the Seminary fire, for she met and soon married Baltimore architect Bernard Evander, who had come to St. Mary's to work on the reconstruction of Calvert Hall.

The 1925–26 academic year was much calmer. A growing percentage of the current student body had not even known old Calvert Hall, and they looked forward to spending the first full year in the new building, now three stories tall and equipped with all the modern conveniences. Although the riverside wing shown on the architect's plans would not be added until 1929, the white-columned building closely resembled the original structure and perpetuated the ambience of a traditional academy of the antebellum South. Moreover, Calvert Hall was furnished by benefactors who were conscious of the school's unique ties to regional heritage, so that "practically everything was of historic value." Such donated items included a painting of the first settlers, from the State House in Annapolis; a circa-1816 mantle from the Throughton/Traughton-Brome House of St. Mary's City, donated by Mr. and

Mrs. J. Spence Howard (she the daughter of Doctor Brome); a mounted composing table, alleged to have come from "the First Printing Press in the American Colonies"; a conceptualized "portrait" of Governor Leonard Calvert; a large painting for the entrance hall, donated by Mrs. T. Rowland Thomas of historic "Clocker's Fancy"; two eighteenth-century Chippendale chairs; and books contributed by Governor Ritchie, the Maryland State Library, and Enoch Pratt Free Library.

Appearances were deceptive, however, for the emphasis on the Seminary's plantation past masked progressive educational goals that would soon transform the old-fashioned boarding school into a modern, innovative junior college. Although St. Mary's Female Seminary had developed into an excellent academic institution of its type, traditionalism and provincialism had limited its horizons before 1924. The very destructiveness of the fire that year proved to be an important catalyst for a new beginning. Because that tragedy had brought unprecedented attention and assistance to the Seminary, school officials were encouraged to reevaluate and redefine its future. When Governor Ritchie and members of the 1924 General Assembly came to campus on 22 May 1926 for the dedication of a memorial plaque thanking them for their support, they could little imagine that this old, traditional school would

The central entrance foyer of the new Calvert Hall, 1925, showing several of the historic furnishings donated to the school. The open door to the right now leads to the President's Office.

The new Reception Room in rebuilt Calvert Hall, furnished as a tribute to Mrs. Lucy Virginia Maddox, past principal (1900–1923). Note the "portrait" of Leonard Calvert above the early nineteenth-century mantle from the Throughton/ Traughton House in St. Mary's City. Today the mantle is in the Provost's Office, Calvert 104.

soon "enter upon an enlarged field of honor and usefulness"—and change the future of Maryland education.

Launching the Junior College

The Seminary trustees in the 1920s proved to be as farsighted and courageous as their nineteenth-century predecessors in not permitting short-term problems to disrupt their long-term dreams. On 19 February 1926, the trustees' executive committee voted to borrow another $5,000 to meet current expenses and discussed "eliminating at least two teachers [one-third of the faculty] and curtailing the course of study" to stem the school's mounting indebtedness. However, at a meeting held *only three weeks later,* the full Board promptly dismissed such pessimism. At this historic 10 March meeting, the trustees approved a resolution by Judge Camalier and Delegate Williams that directed the principal and the executive committee to confer with the State Superintendent of Education at the earliest opportunity

"with a view to raising the standard of the school to that of a Junior College." On 21 April, Miss France reported on the committee's encouraging meeting with Superintendent Albert S. Cook, and two days later, the Board of Trustees formally agreed to offer a first-year junior college curriculum in 1926–27, with second-year coursework to follow soon after.

This was a remarkably daring step for a school that had been on death's door just two years before, but it followed the typical, traditional pattern at St. Mary's, for, since its founding, the Seminary had always rebounded from a crisis stronger than before. Now, St. Mary's would surprise everyone who thought of it only as a nostalgic reminder of the nineteenth century and would reward the state's confidence with a sudden, creative shift to collegiate instruction.

The Fall 1926 catalog announced the new venture for the school. St. Mary's was described as a "boarding school for girls, on the high school and junior college

Seminarians waiting for a steamboat at Brome's Wharf, St. Mary's City. When the Junior College was created in 1926– 1928, steamboats were still an important means of transportation in Southern Maryland. Vessels of the Baltimore and Virginia Steamboat Company left from Baltimore at 4:30 p.m. every Monday, Wednesday, and Saturday and arrived at Brome's Wharf about 4:00 a.m. on Tuesdays, Thursdays, and Sundays. Students were met by the Seminary custodian, who transported their trunks to Calvert Hall by cart or wheelbarrow. The steamboat age came to a sad and sudden end by 1935, due to company bankruptcies, increased competition from automobiles and improved state roads, and a fierce storm on 23 August 1933 that destroyed many of the region's wharves.

The cast-iron arch donated by the high school seniors in 1927.

level, . . . conducted for service, not profit." The Seminary, according to Miss France, was committed, "first of all [to being] an excellent school, organized on modern lines [and] flexible enough to meet different needs." Explaining that "the time is past when we educated our daughters for ornaments only," the principal pledged the Seminary to "greater service" in preparing its graduates for "an economic place in the world." The new Junior College Division promised to be innovative because it offered a personal, caring approach to postsecondary education—which was a tradition at the "small home-like" Seminary but was almost nonexistent at the huge university campuses then emerging. As Miss France announced to parents and prospective students, she and the school were committed to giving freshmen college women, who were often intimidated or overlooked at large, impersonal universities, a "square deal," by providing an education "under careful guidance, in close association with Principal and teachers, near home, at small cost."

The addition of the Junior College Division placed St. Mary's in the forefront of the national junior college movement and was the key to the future prominence of the institution. The first junior colleges in the United States were founded around 1910 in response to mush-

rooming high school enrollments, and between 1920 and 1930, these more accessible, less expensive "people's colleges" grew at a phenomenal rate, from 52 schools enrolling some 8,000 students to 277 institutions serving more than 55,000 students. St. Mary's, which had already outlived most of its contemporaneous sister seminaries, was one of a few exceptional secondary schools with the vision and the tenacity to respond in a timely fashion to the national trends in junior college education. When it did so, St. Mary's occupied a special—perhaps a unique—niche among all two-year collegiate institutions in the United States. It was a public junior college when most were private; it served women only when most others were male or coeducational in nature; it was rural when virtually all others were located near large urban population centers; it stressed the traditional liberal arts when many others focused on vocational training; and it was on the East Coast when the vast majority of early junior colleges were established west of the Mississippi River. In 1926, St. Mary's may well have been the only public junior college in the country to have a chief executive, a faculty, and a student body exclusively comprised of women. Within Maryland, this oldest state-owned school and only public boarding school for women added to its distinction as an educational pioneer by becoming the first junior college in the state. Baltimore's Mount Saint Agnes became the second one in 1933, but no others, public or private, were founded in Maryland until after World War II.

St. Mary's Female Seminary was able to add junior college courses to its curriculum in the fall of 1926 because it indeed had concerned, "well qualified teachers"—and obviously versatile ones as well. The eight faculty members in 1926–27 (an increase of only two since 1924–25) had vastly expanded responsibilities at the new multi-functional and multi-dimensional school. They staffed two separate four-year high school programs (a general curriculum and a college preparatory curriculum), offered a one-year program in secretarial and business subjects for high school graduates, and taught seven, year-long Junior College courses of six credits each. These included English Composition, Advanced Algebra and Trigonometry, British History (Roman Britain to the Present), Biology A–Botany, Elementary French (elective), Latin A–Cicero and Virgil (elective), and two electives in Household Arts (Food and Nutrition; Textiles and Clothing)—consistent with national trends at the time. When the Junior College curriculum was expanded two years later, the St. Mary's faculty would have to be more versatile still, serving students (both Seminary graduates and new enrollees) who wanted either a terminal associate degree or who wished to complete the B.A. elsewhere.

The creation of the Junior College Division immediately became the catalyst for the recruitment and retention of a superior faculty. St. Mary's again had a high attrition rate among teachers, but unlike the situation in the mid-nineteenth century, school officials promoted the turnover in the search for the best qualified faculty. Miss France regularly and vigorously "pruned" her staff according to a March 1928 directive of the Board of Trustees, which "authorized [the principal] to engage all of the most important Teachers as early as possible [while] leaving the most unimportant ones to be selected later." In that year, four of the eight Seminary teachers had master's degrees— three from prestigious universities—but Principal France was the sole instructor remaining from the faculty of 1924–25, and Mrs. Sallie T. Davis (A.M., Lebanon Female College) and Elizabeth Lindsay (graduate, Bowling Green Business University) were the only other teachers who had been on the staff for three consecutive years. Ethel R.

The members of Delta Phi Epsilon Sorority, 1929.

Cohodas (M.A., University of Michigan) had recently replaced a diplomate of the Sorbonne, while Majorie Smith (M.A., University of Pennsylvania) was hired in preference to a predecessor with only a bachelor's degree. A decade later, in 1938–39, eight of the twelve instructors at St. Mary's had master's degrees and all had some graduate training:

M. Adele France (A.M., Washington College; M.A., Columbia University)

Mrs. Mildred K. Chenoweth (graduate, School of Speech, Northwestern University; English and speech)

Ellen M. Doherty (graduate study, University of Iowa; business)

Mrs. Mary D. Faison (M.S., Woman's College, University of North Carolina; home economics)

Margaret E. Hight (M.A., University of North Carolina and additional graduate study at University of Virginia and Columbia; social studies)

Lura Frances Johnson (M.A., Emory University; mathematics and psychology)

Ghissell E. Klein (A.M., University of Michigan and additional graduate study at the Pasteur Institute, Paris; science)

Mrs. Helen L. Manson (Library School, George Peabody College and library apprenticeship at the U. S. Naval Academy; librarian)

Evelyn Mitchell (M.M., American Conservatory of Music and additional graduate study at Northwestern University; piano, voice, violin)

Mary B. Renshaw (graduate study at Johns Hopkins; physical education)

Claire V. Stickney (M.A., Catholic University and additional graduate study at Middlebury College; French, Latin, Spanish)

Mrs. Minnie J. Swindler (M.A., Columbia University and additional graduate study at the University of Chicago; English)

It was doubly ironic that the excellent teachers who were recruited to St. Mary's largely due to the demands of collegiate instruction earned the high school branch of the Seminary its first national accreditation just when the institution was most committed to the Junior College. On 29 December 1930, after eighty-four years of operation, St. Mary's was finally accredited by the Commission on Secondary Schools of the Association of Colleges and Secondary Schools of the Middle States and Maryland. The Seminary's official ranking as a "First Class, First Group High School" by the Maryland State Department of Education in 1931 was also belated recognition for an institution that now saw its future in collegiate, rather than secondary, instruction. St. Mary's prospered over the next twenty-five years because of its dual focus; the high school curriculum gave it stability as a traditional program known to many Marylanders, while the Junior College Division provided the educational innovativeness that attracted a new student constituency and enhanced the school's reputation beyond the borders of the state.

The St. Mary's Female Seminary-Junior College (as it would eventually be called) was in full operation by the beginning of the 1928–29 academic year. Because only one student took college courses in 1926–27, the initiation of a second-year Junior College curriculum was delayed one year. In 1928–29, however, the school added a two-semester, two-credit course in Speech to the first year requirements (which remained English Composition, Advanced Algebra and Trigonometry, British History, Botany, and Physical Education), and began to offer an extensive array of second-year courses. Collegiate sophomores would now take year-long, six-credit courses in English Literature and Science B: Physiology and Hygiene and choose electives from General Psychology, Economics, Sociology, French Literature, Intermediate Latin (Horace, Tacitus, Livy), and Home Economics (Advanced Clothing; Home Designing and Interior Decoration).

From these tentative beginnings, school officials conscientiously improved and expanded the curricular offerings of the Junior College Division. Only a decade later, the 1938–39 catalog listed ninety-five courses, enough to permit students to group them according to specific concentrations: Liberal Arts, Home Economics, or Music for those wanting to transfer to senior colleges; General Culture, Homemaking, Creative and Applied Arts, Secretarial, General Business, or Recreational Leadership for students who regarded the two-years as "terminal." The Liberal Arts concentration in 1938–39 was as follows:

Year One	Credits
English Composition	3, 3
Biology, Chemistry, or Math	3, 3
History of Europe	3, 3
Speech	1, 1
Art Appreciation	1
Study Technique	1
Physical Education	.5, .5
Electives:	
Math (Algebra/Trigonometry)	3, 3

French Literature	3, 3
Biology	3, 3
General Chemistry	3, 3
U.S. History Since 1865	3
Introduction to Sociology	3
Year Two	*Credits*
Survey of English Literature	3, 3
Personal and Community Health	1, 1
Music Appreciation	1
Bible Appreciation	1
Physical Education	.5, .5
Electives:	
Masterpieces of World Literature	3
Contemporary Literature	3
Latin: Virgil's Aeneid	3, 3
French, Latin, or Spanish	3, 3
Spanish Literature	3, 3
General Chemistry	3, 3
U.S. History Since 1865	3
Introduction to Sociology	3
Human Physiology	3
Introduction to Psychology	3
Introduction to Economics	3
Federal Government	3

Having a well-designed curriculum and a qualified faculty before it had students, the Junior College Division grew slowly but steadily from the single enrollee in 1926–27. The Board of Trustees had already designed the collegiate diploma by 1928, and school officials must have been greatly relieved when the first Junior College class of four students finally graduated in June 1930 (along with twenty pupils from the high school program). The first collegians to finish–Katherine M. Bowdle of Denton, Dorothy Connor of Eckhart, Irma K. Mumford of Ocean City, and Virginia Dare Sollers of Lusby (the only alumna of the Seminary high school)–had completed a minimum of sixty-two credits, with at least forty-six graded C or better. The number of Junior College graduates remained a consistent four to six per year until June 1934, when twelve received diplomas, compared to seventeen high school graduates. In June 1935, the Junior College Division graduated nine, including the first male–Charles D. Birch of Stewartstown, Pennsylvania, who would return to teach at Great Mills High School after receiving his B.A. from Western Maryland College. The Junior College Class of 1935 was 82 percent as large as that year's high school class–the highest proportion ever–and throughout the

rest of the 1930s, that percentage was matched or bettered all but once. Clearly, the new collegiate curriculum was catching on, and the growing popularity of this educational experiment would lead to further innovations at the Seminary.

Another Threshold: The Four-Year Junior College

St. Mary's Female Seminary-Junior College reached a crossroads in Spring 1935, and school officials did not hesitate to gamble everything on the new future of collegiate instruction. With the advice and support of the State Superintendent of Education and the Junior College alumni, the trustees reorganized St. Mary's into a *four-year Junior College* between 1935 and 1937. They discontinued the freshman year of high school beginning in September 1935 and eliminated the sophomore year beginning in September 1937, so that by the 1937–38 academic year, St. Mary's offered a four-year junior college curriculum that incorporated the junior and senior years of high school ("Lower Division") and the freshman and sophomore years of college ("Upper Division"). This unusual reorganization was significant to the enhanced reputation of St. Mary's, for it was the

The St. Mary's basketball team, 1932. Team captain in front center is Martha Morris Blackistone, Seminary high school '30 and Junior College '32.

"MONKEY"

"CONNOR"

"SCREECH"

"KAY"

Most of the College Group
In the corners, our first Junior College Graduates

The first graduates of Maryland's first junior college. Clockwise from top left, they are: Irma K. Mumford, Dorothy Connor, Katherine M. Bowdle, and Virginia Dare Sollers.

only junior college in Maryland to offer a four-year curriculum and was one of only twenty-five institutions in the nation to do so. The Seminary was reoriented at this time for several compelling reasons. Great Mills High School had been in operation for a decade and had diminished the pool of ninth- and tenth-graders who in years past would have attended the Seminary. More importantly, the restructuring of the St. Mary's curriculum permitted an increasingly talented faculty to focus on higher level coursework and allowed an expansion of the collegiate population by freeing dormitory space previously occupied by high school freshmen and sophomores. Higher enrollments had become a priority, since the school was required to have a minimum of fifty Junior College students to be considered for national accreditation. Statistics from the first decade of the Junior College Division revealed that only 17.7 percent of its ninety-six graduates had attended the Seminary high school and that the collegiate curriculum was most popular among out-of-county and out-of-state students. Thus, the new four-year Junior College was designed to attract mature students who wanted more than two, but less than six, years at St. Mary's and who preferred an institution with a collegiate, rather than a high school, identity.

An additional, and perhaps the most compelling,

reason for the creation of the four-year Junior College at this time was the well-publicized campaign that the League of Women Voters in Maryland launched against St. Mary's in 1932. In October of that year, the League's annual convention in Baltimore issued a critical report by Mrs. O. H. Williamson, claiming that the Seminary had "no apparent place in the present public school system." Committed to reforming and economizing Maryland government in the midst of the Great Depression, the League charged that the state-owned Seminary cost the taxpayers "nearly four times as much" as a conventional public high school did to educate a student, because it "operated as a private boarding school managed by its own Board of Trustees and [was] not under the jurisdiction of the State Department of Education." A resolution at the League's convention recommended that the state should either close the Seminary or have its "purpose redefined and the institution reorganized to serve . . . some specialized group."

St. Mary's responded to that recommendation by creating the four-year Junior College and indeed found a "specialized group" to serve in a growing population that desired an affordable alternative in collegiate education. The reorganized curriculum and redefined mission helped quiet the critics, while truly fulfilling Miss France's dream of "serv[ing] the people." That innovation also appreciably enhanced the reputation of the Seminary in Annapolis and across the state. The elimination of the freshman and sophomore years of high school elevated the status of St. Mary's—reflected in the substitution of "president" for "principal" as the title for the chief executive officer (May 1937)—and gave the institution a higher priority for state support. In February 1937, the Seminary for the first time was included in the regular state budget on an equal basis with the other public educational institutions of Maryland. Although the school fell under the Maryland Department of Education, its previous funding had always come from special legislative appropriations for scholarships and construction projects, which the Board of State Aid and Charities administered. Beginning with a $14,000 appropriation for the 1938–39 fiscal year, the State of Maryland elevated St. Mary's to a new budgetary status that it has enjoyed ever since. (It is most curious to realize how little-known the Seminary was in government circles before its inclusion in the regular budget, despite the extensive state funding after the fire of 1924. In describing the budgetary deliberations in 1937, a re-

Miss France poses with graduates on Commencement Day.

What Did You Do After Graduation?

In January 1940, President France put together "a perfectly stupendous questionnaire" that asked recent Junior College graduates about their lives since leaving St. Mary's. Some of the responses:

After graduation from the Seminary I entered Washington College the following fall. I had no trouble in having all my credits accepted and this past June graduated from there with an A.B. degree. I had planned to take up teaching as a profession but was not so fortunate as to obtain a position in any of the counties. In August I went with the Department of Public Welfare as a social worker. . . . I will be only too willing to do anything I can for the Seminary. They were the most marvelous days of my school life. —Mary B. Fraser

After graduating from St. Mary's I enrolled at the University of Maryland. During the first semester, I belonged to no class, but I was allowed to take third year work. At the end of the term, I was on the honor roll and my past credits were accepted. In May of my senior year I was elected to Phi Kappa Phi, the national honorary scholastic fraternity. As a consequence, I graduated from the University on June 4, 1938 with first honors. In early September, I was called to a teaching position at Catonsville High School. It will be a real pleasure to see St. Mary's an accredited Junior College. —Mary Jane Hoffman

I entered the nursing profession at the Union Memorial Hospital, Baltimore, on September 3rd, 1935, for which hospital I have been working since graduation—as a member of the nurses staff in the operating room and dispensary. I am glad to hear of the apparent progress the school is making. I often think of you and wish I could relive the two happiest years of my life. I will also add—two very profitable years. —Leanna Riedy

{F}ollowing graduation from Hood . . . {I moved to Baltimore, where} I met a rich elderly lady who lives in a fourteen-room antiquely furnished suite in the Belvedere. She is paying all my expenses at the Peabody and also for my apartment furnished with a baby grand piano and a Hammond electric organ. I am studying piano under Couradi & pipe organ under Virgil Fox. —Jeannette Roelke

I entered the University of Maryland after leaving the Seminary. . . . In February 1939, I entered the Graduate School of the University . . . {majoring} in Plant Pathology, with research in tobacco. —Betty Wise

In September following my graduation from S.M.S. I entered Washington College as a junior. There I found that my two years' work at the Seminary had given me preparation superior in most cases to that received by my class-mates at Washington. . . . In October 1938, I became assistant Postmaster in Sudlersville and have continued there. I do wish you the greatest success in your endeavor. S.M.S. will always be a place I'll recall fondly. —Kathleen Powell

—Source: Accreditation Files, 1940–41.

porter wrote: "A stranger popped up tonight before the Legislature. There's nothing new about [the Seminary] . . . but this is the first time the State had recognized that it owned it and put it in the budget as a Maryland institution, . . . [causing] a lot of wondering among the legislators as to when the State had taken it over"!)

The decision to transform St. Mary's into Maryland's only four-year junior college was clearly the right one at the right time. President France's "high hopes of service to the State and to Youth" were certainly realized through this innovative institution. In 1939–40, only the second year of the reorganized curriculum, St. Mary's admitted a record twenty-nine Junior College freshmen (high school juniors), eighteen of whom had not attended the Seminary previously and only four of whom lived within a fifty-mile radius of the campus. More importantly, the Junior College was living up to its promise of providing an excellent education that focused on the development of the individual student. Over 40 percent of the sixty-three Junior College graduates between 1935 and 1939 went on to receive bachelor's degrees from senior colleges, several with honors. The institutions most frequently attended by St. Mary's graduates in this period were: Western Maryland College (five students), University of Maryland-College Park (three), Johns Hopkins University (two), George Washington University (two), Goucher College (two), Hood College (two), Washington College (two), Peabody Conservatory of Music, Corcoran School of Art, University of North Carolina, Pennsylvania State University, and Mary Washington College (all one each). The success that former students experienced brought credit to the school that nurtured them and helped earn "St. Mary's Female Seminary Junior College" much-deserved accreditation. On 17 April 1941, after a thorough survey of the Seminary's alumnae and an extensive investigation of its operations, the Maryland State Department of Education accredited the four-year Junior College. Dr. Albert S. Cook, the State Superintendent of Schools who had approved the first experimental Junior College classes at St. Mary's fifteen years before, signed the authorization of accreditation.

Accreditation was a triumph for President France and the trustees, because they had reinvigorated the old school with innovations while preserving the best of its traditions—and had done so in the midst of the Depression. Curricular change, faculty and student recruitment, and the expanded scope of operations came at a high price, but to their credit, school officials did not abandon the original principles of the Monument School of the People. As Miss France explained in 1937,

"against the urging of individuals and agencies to raise the charges, . . . rates have been kept low to permit those in moderate circumstances . . . to secure the outstanding advantages, educational and otherwise, offered by St. Mary's Female Seminary." Throughout the 1930s, annual tuition remained $100, room and board $300, for *all* resident students in either the high school or Junior College divisions, and commuting day students from St. Mary's County could still take a year of courses for only $50. Moreover, the school continued to provide twenty-nine full scholarships to about half of the student body and increasingly supplemented those funds with privately endowed awards (e.g., the multiple scholarships contributed by the Daughters of the American Revolution and the Margaret Roberts Hodges Memorial). Seminary officials were, in fact, so committed to the principle of affordability that they allowed students to enroll, take classes, and even graduate despite owing money to the institution. Over the course of fifteen years, from 1932 to 1947, a total of $4,311.34 in overdue student bills went uncollected.

Refusing to charge more or to expel delinquent students, despite a five-year operating deficit in the mid-1930s, school administrators relied on creative frugality to get them through the tough Depression years. In 1933–34, the Seminary fed each of seventy-eight boarders (including faculty) for less than twenty cents per day. Despite the state's budget-line support in 1938–39, St. Mary's remained the epitome of a non-profit institution, spending an average of $434.95 to educate each student and receiving an average income per pupil of $435.00! At a nickel per pupil, the Seminary could not afford lavish salaries for its faculty. In the late 1930s, teachers earned $900 and those with administrative duties an additional $100, plus free room, board, and laundry for all. They received $50 raises their second year and "subsequent increases in proportion to the value of the incumbent." President France, who refused to accept a $1,000 raise in 1931 due to the "existing business depression," reported that St. Mary's retained good teachers despite low salaries, because at least the school met every payroll when other institutions did not. Throughout the Depression, the Seminary truly functioned as a caring college for the people, and everyone associated with it met the challenge of hard times as most families did—by pulling together. Although the ongoing and increasing financial support from the state was vital to the school's survival, the bureaucrats in Annapolis could not understand why the St. Mary's trustees sought out poor farm children to educate free or why they once paid a speeding ticket for a manual laborer at the Seminary.

Two Seasons of Celebrations

In the dark days of the Great Depression, the State of Maryland and St. Mary's Female Seminary offered the public two special celebrations that relieved the tension of troubled times. The first, in 1934, was the 300th anniversary of Maryland's founding at St. Mary's City; the second, in 1939–40, was the 100th anniversary of the Seminary's founding as the Monument School. Both events were hopeful reminders of the benefits of perseverence, recalling that the residents of this site in the distant past had survived crises and surmounted challenges to create a notable collective legacy of persistent struggle for all the present and future citizens of Maryland.

The Maryland tercentennial presented quite a contrast to the state's bicentennial in 1834, for finally, one hundred years later, St. Mary's City and its Monument School were to be the main focus of activity and attention. Since the founding of the Seminary, school officials had dreamed of such an occasion to increase the public's awareness of the ancient capital and its antebellum academy. Maryland's 300th birthday party loomed large in the minds of Seminary administrators and state officials, and every campus improvement for five years before the anniversary was justified on the basis of the huge crowds and extensive press corps that would visit St. Mary's City in 1934.

In May 1927, the high school senior class donated the large, ornamental cast-iron arch that graced the Seminary entrance gate until the late 1960s. In April 1929, Trustees J. Allan Coad, George C. Peverley, and Lawrence P. Williams finally convinced their colleagues in the state legislature to pay for the construction of the riverside wing of Calvert Hall, which would complete the building as the architect had originally conceived it. With the General Assembly's appropriation of $30,000 and Governor Ritchie's personal assurances of an additional $10,000 to come later, the Board of Trustees borrowed the money that allowed construction to begin immediately. On 11 September 1929, after nine feverish months of work by contruction crews, arriving students moved into the newly expanded Calvert Hall, complete with a fresh coat of whitewash on its square columns and a huge painted-iron replica of the state seal perched high on the front portico. As luck would have it, the Seminary finished the campus centerpiece and symbol just in time—only six weeks before the stock market crash on "Black Tuesday," 24 October 1929.

With optimistic preparations for Maryland's 300th anniversary taking precedence over the gloomy projections of an expanding national economic crisis, the Seminary undertook several other projects that improved its appearance or efficiency. For the first time since the campus was purchased in 1844, the school acquired additional land for expansion, buying Mrs. Lilburn's small lot across Brome's Wharf Road following her death in 1932. The trustees granted a 99-year lease on part of the property to the State Tercentenary Commission as the site of Hans Schuler's "Freedom of Conscience Monument"; on the other portion of the Lilburn lot, they relocated the "Caretaker's Cottage," or "White House," which had been built from the "Barracks" of 1924 and which today houses the Advancement and Alumni offices. Storage sheds and the school garage were constructed on that site as well, housing a growing fleet of Seminary vehicles that included a 1928 bus (called "Our Pride and Joy") and a 1933 pick-up truck. In 1931, the school was connected to county electricity for the first time and converted the small brick building that had housed its Delco generator into a science laboratory. About the same time, another well was drilled and a new pump, water tank, and chlorinator were installed.

The final campus project, and one of the most memorable, was completed just before the official tercentennial activities commenced in June 1934. Two years earlier, the Board of Trustees had given permission

A later view of Calvert Hall, clearly showing the wing (in the foreground) that the architect designed in 1924 but was added only in September 1929.

for the Alumnae Association to convert the Calvert Hall vegetable plot into a "Garden of Remembrance." Beautifully landscaped and furnished with donated benches and a fountain, this memorial garden was dedicated as a tercentenary gift to the Seminary on Sunday, 10 June 1934. Ever since, it has served as a reminder of the grateful affection that St. Mary's alumni have felt for and from their alma mater.

The dedication of the "Garden of Remembrance" was the first event in a week-long series of special activities that would culminate in the Tercentenary Celebration on Friday and Saturday, 15–16 June. There had never been, and will probably never be again, such intense excitement on this campus in any seven-day period. Seminary officials were only partially prepared for the demands that state officials and the general public would make on campus facilities. In March 1934, the school had lent Music Hall to the U.S. Postal Department for the sale of first-day issue Maryland Commemorative stamps, but now the state wanted to convert Calvert Hall—the "only 'business building' in the area"—into a tourist hotel within hours of the last

A student outing at the Seminary in the early 1930s. The 1928 school bus, "Our Pride and Joy," was purchased for $1,866.50 and remained in service for two decades.

Capital Outlay, 1 October 1933 to 28 February 1937

Land $3,336.99
   (*Lilburn lot $1,800.00, filling in land, new tennis court, retaining walls, grading and seeding lawn*)

Water & Sewerage System $4,107.24

Main Building   486.70
   (*New partition in Home Economics Room, remodeling library, new outlet for light*)

Commencement Hall   110.66
   (*Partitioning off music practice room, new light outlet, changing radiator*)

Chemistry Laboratory   789.93
   (*Expense of changing Delco House to Chemistry Lab*)

Pump House, Tank & Well   841.53

Alumnae Lodge   2,432.05
   (*Expense of remodeling lodge, building furnace room, installing heat, etc.*)

Caretaker's Cottage (Moving & Remodeling)   1,096.13

Garage (Moving & Remodeling)   297.46

Tool House (New)   175.00

Office Equipment (Desk, file cabinet, bookcase, typewriter)   88.75

Household Equipment (Library table & chairs, vacuum cleaner, desks)   285.06

Motor Vehicles (New bus)   1,866.50

Educational & Recreational Equipment   701.82
   (*Chairs for Home Economics Lodge & Study Hall, 2 typewriters, 3 second-hand pianos, Frigidaire for Lodge, Grand Piano, New machine, stove and furniture for lodge*)

Laboratory Equipment (for Chemistry Lab; microscopes for Biology Lab)   985.12

Other Equipment (Wheelbarrows for W.P.A., new street light)   108.45

   —Source: Adele France's notations, loose papers, College Archives.

The Garden of Remembrance, dedicated on Sunday, 10 June 1934. In her remarks on that occasion, Alumnae Association President Betty Revell Wathen thanked the Seminary for "happy memories of friendships, associations, studies, and some good old fashioned discipline. The best her children can do at this time . . . is to present a gift expressive of beauty and charm, a Garden of Remembrance which finds fulfillment in love and life—a memorial to our beloved ones, roots reaching out, extending far into the past."

final examinations in the academic year. This prospect created a special air of expectation and a sense of urgency about finishing the spring term and clearing out the dormitory. Students tried to concentrate on studying for finals amid countless banquets, an endless stream of vehicles, and the deafening noise from invading brigades of construction workers. At commencement exercises on Monday, 11 June, the Seminarians presented "The Vestal Flame," an elaborate pageant about the school's history, and then promptly packed up and vacated Calvert Hall. The keepers of the vestal flame were safely away before the arrival of one British and two American warships in the St. Mary's River later that week, and they missed the local newspaper notice that read: "Please send out an S.O.S. for some girls to make the sailors happy. Tell them the boys need dancing partners."

With the students on their way home, the Seminary maintenance staff readied the "Calvert Hall Hotel" for 150 overnight guests (only some in rooms) on each of the two festival days. The school administration building also served as the base of operations for the Tercentenary Celebration, the nerve-center of the State of Maryland in those last hectic days before the 15–16 June birthday party. Calvert Hall was described as "a beehive of activity [and] the headquarters of scores of newspapermen, newsreel cameramen and radio announcers"—all of whom communicated with the outside world by means of the Seminary's single telephone line. The normal serenity of the campus vanished during that special week in June, as an army of carpenters hastily constructed a 10,000-seat "stadium" on the State House grounds; county farmers brought sickles, scythes, and ox-drawn carts to clear fields for parking; endless convoys of trucks and boats delivered ice, beverages, and ice cream from Baltimore; some 500 countians donned seventeenth-century costumes to rehearse the gigantic outdoor pageant, "St. Maries, the Mother of Maryland"; and highway crews were completing the new road (present Route 5) specifically to serve the throng of motorists who would soon descend on the old capital. When the two days of festivities finally got under way, St. Mary's Female Seminary contributed the most critical single element to the success of the tercentennial celebration—fresh drinking water, which was piped from the campus artesian well to over 700 National Guardsmen, mounted state police, and U.S. Army medical corpsmen camped near the Brome House. In a final tribute to the school's key role in this gigantic birthday party, Governor Ritchie returned to "his" Calvert Hall and hosted a mint julep luncheon for visiting dignataries on "State Day," 16 June.

The front page headline of the Washington Times, *Saturday, 16 June 1934.*

When the long-awaited Tercentenary Celebration Weekend finally arrived, St. Mary's City was immediately transformed into the state's third largest urban area. The front-page headline in the *Washington Times* for Saturday, 16 June, trumpeted the news: "100,000 AT ST. MARYS CELEBRATION SEE HISTORY ROLL BACK 300 YEARS: Parades and Pageantry Mark Tercentenary in Two-Day Fete." The *Baltimore Evening Sun* for Friday, 15 June, proclaimed: "THOUSANDS SEE ARK AND DOVE ARRIVE: Old St. Mary's Host to Crowds for Pageantry." Hundreds of power boats, schooners, bugeyes, excursion steamers, Chesapeake crab boats, and yachts of every description jostled for position in a clogged harbor to catch a glimpse of Governor Ritchie's flagship, *Dupont,* the British cruiser *H.M.S. Dundee,* two American destroyers, *U.S.S. Manley* and *Overton,* Sea Scouts in a miniature replica of "Old Ironsides," an oyster-patrol schooner refitted as the "*Ark,*" and a naval motor-launch similarly disguised as the "*Dove.*" Special channels in the St. Mary's River were kept clear of boats for the landing of the several sea-planes that circled the festival site. On the ground, the thousands who mingled, and the dozens who fainted, in the stifling 100-degree heat, included Brit-

ish sailors futilely trying to buy American hot dogs with shillings and pence (a Baltimore bank set up a currency exchange at the last minute); pageant "Indians in full headdress [who] elbowed their way to . . . the temporary bars . . . [and] tossed off their steins of real beer"; concessionaires in a tent-city of food stands, dispensing some 14,000 gallons of lemonade, 40 half-barrels of beer, and 2,500 pounds of hot dogs; and police officers from six states patrolling the grounds for known pickpockets (Baltimore City detectives nabbed a couple). One of the most noticed revelers was 102-year-old Mary Ellen Jones ("Aunt Pigeon"), a former Langley family slave who was the cook for the Seminary in the late nineteenth century, as she sat under a shade tree surrounded by dozens of her descendants.

After two exhausting days of speeches, unveilings, dedications, tributes, gun salutes, band music, historical pageants, and evening light shows from the harbor, the revelers departed and allowed the ancient capital city to return to its tranquil repose.

Nothing could match the magnitude of Maryland's tercentenary party, but six years later, the 100th anniversary of St. Mary's Female Seminary-Junior College had an equivalent emotional intensity for those closest to the institution. The year-long commemoration of the school's founding began on Commencement Day, 12 June 1939, with Governor Herbert R. O'Conor delivering the address to nineteen collegiate and twenty-three high school graduates. The theme of graduation weekend, "The Birth of the State's Living Monument," was carried through the next academic year. The centennial of "Enactment Day" was celebrated in grand style on Thursday, 21 March 1940. Press reports estimated that some 500 visitors attended the ceremonies, including the oldest living alumna (Mrs. Cornelia D. Jones, 86, an 1869 graduate); Mrs. Maddox, the former principal; representatives from Hood College and Charlotte Hall Academy; and the Leonardtown Fire Department, "in full regalia with its new equipment." The Seminary Glee Club appeared in period costumes on the stairway of Calvert Hall and presented songs from the 1830s–1840s, and at "high tea," all of the faculty members and several distinguished alumnae dressed in hoop skirts to serve as hostesses. Katherine Scarborough, a reporter

for the *Baltimore Sun,* wrote of the occasion: "Nobody gave a speech. None was necessary. The school spoke for itself, and in the exhibition room there were relics in plenty to tell the story of what had gone before." These included Board of Trustee Minutes from the 1840s, one of the Seminary's original desks from the 1850s, and "a silver fork used by two generations of girls at a time when students furnished their own cutlery." Trustee Grason, 84-year-old grandson of the governor who signed the Seminary legislation in 1840, even loaned a newel post from the seventeenth-century State House.

Less than three months after the "Enactment Day" festivities, Commencement Week of 1940 brought a second, and even grander, centennial observance. An event-filled weekend began with public recitals by the music and speech departments on Friday, 7 June. Saturday was devoted to "our earliest and latest alumnae," and at an evening banquet, the oldest graduates inducted the Class of 1940 into the Alumnae Association. Congressman Lansdale G. Sasscer of Prince George's

The Tercentenary Celebration adjoining the Seminary campus, from the Baltimore American, *Sunday, 17 June 1934. Notice the new replica of the State House of 1676 and the bleachers (center left) for the pageant, "St. Maries, Mother of Maryland." The large tents (center) occupied part of the old townlands where Anne Arundel Hall would be built twenty years later. To the right, is the new road (present Route 5) that was cut specifically to direct the heavy traffic away from campus and toward the parking areas. Many thousands of revelers slept in their cars for two days due to the shortage of overnight accommodations.*

Seminarians in 19th-century gowns serenade visitors on the 100th anniversary of "Enactment Day," 21 March 1940.

County addressed the alumnae, and Mary E. W. Risteau, former state senator from Harford County, was the guest of honor. The following day, Sunday, 9 June, the Reverend John LaFarge, S.J., assistant editor of *America Press* and former pastor at nearby St. James and St. Peter Claver churches, delivered the baccalaureate sermon

A Centennial Poem

Daughters of St. Mary's
We salute you on this day;
One hundred years behind you,
Still forward press your way.

Never there springs a harvest
Where seed has not been sown;
Today, Oh fair St. Mary's,
You come into your own.

Fruit of long days of labor,
Of tender tear-wet dreams;
Of glorious hopes and splendid,
For you the future gleams.

Hold fast the Vision Splendid,
Still set the noblest free;
Put ever first the Kingdom
Which seeks Eternity.

St. Mary's, dear St. Mary's,
Breaker of Living Bread,
Go thou with God, the Giver,
Into the years ahead.

—Source: Written by Eleanor
B. North, June 1944.

and hosted a student supper in the Garden of Remembrance. The "Centenary Commencement" was held on Monday, 10 June, with fifteen students graduating from high school and ten receiving Junior College diplomas. The highlight of the ceremonies was the performance of "The Pageant of the Hundred Years," written and directed by faculty member Muriel Stemple. Every student and teacher had a role in this elaborate production, which used an outdoor stage to dramatize key events in the Seminary's history and portrayed the "ideals of St. Mary's"–"Motherhood, Tolerance, Proper Conduct, Liberal Education, Thoroughness, Accreditation, Community Service, Adjustment, Social Relationships, Homemaking, Perseverance, Alumna Activities, Junior College, [and] Self-Government." Students performed the "Garden of Remembrance Dance," while the Glee Club sang the "Centenary Song," as well as selections from Handel, Haydn, Wagner, and Tchaikovsky.

Because of special circumstances, the Seminary's centennial celebration extended beyond the 1939–40 academic year. Spring 1941 brought two notable events that were considered part of the anniversary festivities. The State of Maryland's birthday gift to St. Mary's–the $85,000 Gymnasium and Recreation Building (today's

Kent Hall)—was finally completed after several delays and dedicated on Enactment Day, 21 March 1941. Designed by Baltimore architect Bernard Evander, the new Gymnasium was a multi-purpose building that provided the Seminary with much-needed indoor recreational and assembly facilities. Only three weeks after this dedication, the state presented its second gift to St. Mary's—accreditation of the Junior College on 17 April. Now the century-old Seminary had academic respectability as well as a major new addition to its physical plant. Considering the significant achievements of its centennial "year," 1939–41, St. Mary's had every reason to expect a bright and confident future as it entered a new decade. But it was not to be.

Trials and Tribulations: War on the Homefront

St. Mary's Female Seminary-Junior College endured one of its most trying decades in the 1940s, as global war and local problems nearly depleted its reservoir of confident optimism. On the eve of World War II, the Seminary was in many ways still a fledgling institution, despite its 100-year history. In its haste to grow and

change since 1923, the school had never paused long enough to attain stability and security, and with the massive, unsettling transformations that World War II introduced throughout Southern Maryland, the once congenial and serene environment of the Seminary would be lost forever. The old reliable ways of doing things—such as traveling by steamboat, depending on county residents for labor and food, and expecting a Board of local trustees to be available for emergency decisions—became mere memories after 1941. Four years of crises and challenges changed the character of the Seminary forever, and the symbol of that change, of the realization that a very different institution had crossed the threshold into a modern postwar world, was the retirement in 1948 of President France, weakened and exhausted after years of struggle.

Even before Pearl Harbor, 1941 brought a significant change to the traditional organization and operation of St. Mary's Female Seminary. Coinciding with the good news of the new Gymnasium and Junior College accreditation, school officials were dismayed to learn that Governor O'Conor was determined to dismantle

School Events Calendar for 1939–40

September
Get-acquainted Party
Athletic Association Picnic
Boat Ride Picnic
Visit to Old County Homes

October
Series of President's Teas
Artists and Lecture Program
D. A. R. Luncheon
College Club Initiation
Dramatic Club Tea

November
Athletic Association Fall Prom
Junior Play
Tea House
Thanksgiving Banquet

December
Senior Bazaar
Artists and Lecture Program
Basketball Game
Christmas Banquet

January
Tea House
College Club Informal Dance
Athletic Association Banquet
Artists and Lecture Program
Basketball Games

February
Freshman-Sophomore Dance
School Play or Operetta
President's Birthday Party
Basketball Games

March
Artists and Lecture Program
Tea House
Junior-Senior luncheon
St. Patrick's Party

April
Dramatics Club reception
Apple Blossom Festival
Visit to local homes and gardens
(during Garden Club week)
Artists and Lecture Program

May
Junior-Senior Formal Dance
Home Economics Club Tea
Freshman party for Sophomores
Sports Day with outside school
Boat Ride for Seniors
Artists and Lecture program
Charlotte Hall Tennis Matches
Strawberry Festival
Graduates Day

June
Cookery Class Luncheon for Trustees
Field Day and Athletic Banquet
Alumnae Banquet
Garden Party
Commencement

Informal dances, here and at Charlotte Hall, held on free week-ends.
Birthday dinner each month for those having a birthday.

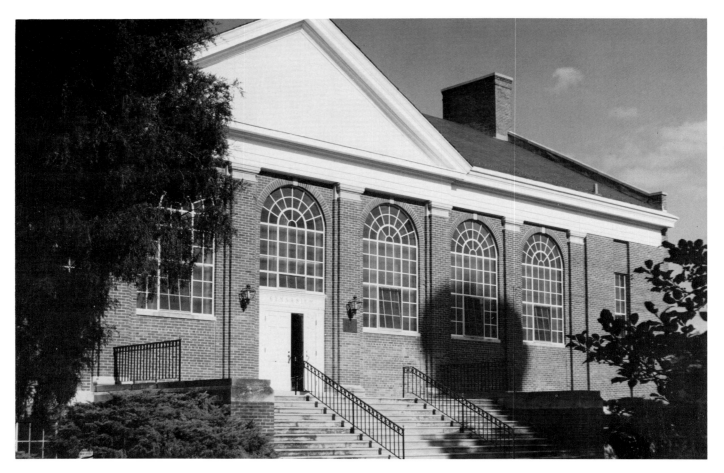

Exterior and interior views of The Gymnasium, dedicated on 21 March 1941. This is now Kent Hall, where the Division of Natural Science and Mathematics is located.

the Board of Trustees as it had existed since 1858. Although the trustees had had more clashes with state officials over building the Gymnasium than over any issue in recent memory, the decision to change the governance of the Seminary was never linked to any impropriety, incompetence, or ideological position of the Board. Rather, the legislative initiative in Annapolis seemed to be focused on modernizing the Board of Trustees, by requiring representation by women as well as men, from every area of Maryland, for fixed terms of six years. Governor O'Conor was personally committed to having women on the Board of the Female Seminary, for as he explained at the St. Mary's Commencement in June 1939: "women are expected to contribute their share toward the proper functioning of everything that concerns the public good." The timing for this change may be explained by the recent deaths of several of the oldest and most politically powerful trustees—including Circuit Court Judge B. Harris Camalier (deceased in 1936 after forty-four years on the Board), Henry C. Dent (d. 1937, twenty-five years of service), George L. Buckler (d. 1941, twenty-six years), and former State Senator Charles S. Grason (d. 1941, thirty-one years as a trustee).

The prospect of changing such a time-honored tradition was anathema to most St. Mary's alumni, and they lobbied hard to retain the old Board of Trustees. Not only did school supporters resent the involuntary retirement of fifteen eminent trustees from St. Mary's County—five Catholics, five Episcopalians, and five Methodists with a total of 260 years of collective service to the Seminary— but they feared that the new Board of twelve trustees, without the guarantee of lifetime tenure, would doubtless be more dependent upon the whims of state officials. Throughout the spring of 1941, Seminary traditionalists sent a "swarm" of angry letters to the governor and the General Assembly, which reporters described as unprecedented for a legislative issue of this type. State Senator J. Allan Coad, a trustee since 1923 with a century of family ties to the school, declined appointment to the reorganized Board as a matter of principle. He attacked Governor O'Conor's plan as "nothing short of vandalism"—a way "to reduce appointments to the Board of this venerable and venerated institution to the status of mere ordinary political patronage." From the alumni side, Mrs. Betty Revell Wathen, '85, co-founder and past president of the Alumnae Association, persuaded the United States senators from Maryland, Millard E. Tydings and George L. Radcliffe, to oppose the measure, and she enlisted support from Circuit Court Judge Ridgely P. Melvin, State Comptroller J. Millard Tawes, and several prominent at-

The President's Address to the New Trustees

{U}nder the previous Board of Trustees, I have served St. Mary's Female Seminary to the best of my ability for eighteen years, putting into the administration of the school my love, my entire interest, my utmost effort for its betterment and advancement, so I pledge to this new Board of Trustees my utmost effort and most loyal cooperation in continuation of the work begun.

I have sincerely and earnestly tried to keep alive in the school the ideals of the first settlers: of tolerance, respect for God and God's laws, respect for the integrity of the individual, consideration of others, independence of thought and freedom of speech, {and} democratic government . . .; and, also, to keep alive, and pass on to succeeding generations through our future mothers, the traditions of helpfulness, kindliness, courtesy, gracious living, hospitality, politeness, et cetera, which our first Maryland settlers established.

In this work I have had the full support of the Board of Trustees, the Alumnae, and the true friends of the Seminary; and while we all naturally take pride in the material development and progress of the school, I feel . . . that those intangible qualities subtly built into the hearts and souls of our students, through precept, example, association, are the most valuable assets. . . .

I believe in St. Mary's Seminary; I believe the unique idea of its founding—to keep alive the glorious history of Maryland and to pass it on through the mothers of men—is a sacred trust given into the keeping of each administrator and trustee of the school. {As} the only school in the United States that stands as a monument to mark the settlement of a State, St. Mary's Seminary deserves to be more widely and better known because of its unique and interesting establishment and history; and I believe it has something to give its students—over and above the thorough and excellent all-round education they receive—which makes their attendance here tremendously worthwhile.

With all my heart I hope this Board of Trustees will understand the sort of educational institution with which they are connected, that they will use their best endeavors to make it more widely known and appreciated—especially in its own State—and that they will see to it that it does not lose those peculiar and 'different' characteristics and features that give it its own individuality. Knowing you and knowing of you, as I do, I feel sure you will accept the sacred trust—and carry on.

Respectfully submitted,
M. Adele France, President

—Source: President's Report, 24 September 1941.

torneys, bankers, and physicians from Baltimore.

In the end, the governor and the legislature succeeded in reconstituting the Seminary's Board of Trustees, effective on 1 June 1941. The old Board was allowed one final meeting, on 3 June, to say their good-byes and to savor their first and last triumphant moment as trustees of the recently-accredited Junior College. The intense lobbying of school supporters had resulted in the provision that six of the current trustees would be appointed to the new Board of twelve. The reorganized Board of Trustees met for the first time on 24 September 1941, and included: Stephen M. Jones of Leonardtown (first appointed in 1901), who was re-elected president; Lawrence P. Williams of Ridge (who had served since 1923); T. Raymond Dixon of Mechanicsville (1923); C. Ethelbert Abell of Leonardtown (1929); Dr. Robert V. Palmer of Palmers (1929); and Dr. L. J. Sothoron of Charlotte Hall (1933). The new trustees included three former Seminarians—Mrs. Felix E. Wathen (Elizabeth Revell '85) of Baltimore, Mrs. George L. Ewalt (Anne Weeks '25) of Baltimore, and Mrs. Lansdale G. Sasscer (Agnes Coffren '12) of Upper Marlboro—in addition to the Reverend Dr. James M. Magruder of Annapolis (chaplain of the Alumnae Association), R. Ames Hendrickson of Frederick, and Mrs. J. Kemp Stevens of Denton. Contrary to the worst fears of the critics, the new trustees demonstrated their steadfast devotion to the Seminary and retained virtually all of the endearing traditions of the old Board, with one exception: the Minutes would finally be typed after ninety-six years of handwritten records.

Before the reconstituted Board of Trustees could hold its second meeting, the United States was plunged into World War II. The rural isolation of Southern Maryland could not protect its citizens from the impact of this global conflict, and the needs of the nation soon transformed the lifeways of St. Mary's County and the Seminary. In September 1941, the U. S. government selected 6,400 acres of prime farmland and rich oyster beds at Cedar Point along the Patuxent River, some eight miles from the campus, as the site of a major military installation. Little changed in the three centuries since the Jesuits established the mission post of Mattapany, Cedar Point was thrust into the complex modern world within a matter of months. Construction began on the Naval Air Station–Patuxent River in April 1942, and by year's end, the new facility was employing some 7,000 people in a county that had a total population of only 14,600 in 1940. The Navy built a railroad just for base use, paved new roads from Waldorf, threw up trailer cities that resembled the raucous mining camps of the Alaskan gold rush, initiated county-wide bus service for the first time, and created the town of Lexington Park, naming it after the famous aircraft carrier. At the same time, the federal government also constructed the 770-acre auxiliary base at Webster Field in St. Inigoes, the Jesuit headquarters in the seventeenth century and only four miles from the Seminary.

While the local population welcomed the shops and services that emerged to tap the huge federal payroll, St. Mary's Female Seminary faced immediate problems in trying to keep its staff and students on campus and military personnel off. An abundance of high-paying, war-related jobs here and throughout the state made it difficult to find qualified teachers and even maintenance workers for the school. Miss France spent every summer of the war replacing one-third to one-half of her twelve-member faculty and was often forced to pay exorbitant salaries for even young and inexperienced teachers, especially in the fields of home economics and physical education. It became commonplace for teachers to break their contracts in late summer and for school to begin each fall with faculty vacancies. Once on campus, many teachers were openly disgruntled and defiant, and in 1943, Miss France feared for her life until a particularly unruly instructor was committed to an insane asylum. Moreover, the several custodians, groundsmen, cooks, and waiters who had long served the Seminary now left for the "easy jobs" and "big money" at the Naval Air Station, and students, teachers, and even the president herself took turns preparing meals. The Seminary nearly exhausted its meager supply of rationed gasoline in transporting a few loyal employees to and from the campus, but when the cook did not report for work one morning in late 1941, Miss France "got a woman out of a corn field to help out." The following year, she reported that food rationing was made "even more difficult when one has to watch the mood and temper of the cook! Often some item on the menu has to be changed to placate the cook and keep her satisfied to stay." The shortage of support personnel was partially alleviated in 1943 when the school began employing parolees from the Woman's Prison in Jessup—without whom "it would have been impossible to keep the Seminary open."

Worse still were the problems with the students. Addressing the "Quality and Character of Students" in the President's Report for 1944–45, Miss France noted the "change in girls . . . . The graciousness, courtesy, thoughtfulness, kindly interest, pleasant manner—all these attributes to which we have been accustomed and which we have tried to uphold as standards are gone!" Although the four academic years of wartime saw near-capacity enrollments of between eighty-two and ninety-

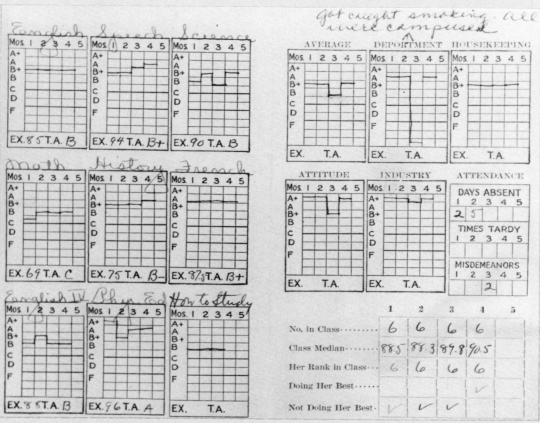

A report card of a first-year Junior College student, June 1932, in Miss France's handwriting.

Miss France's Method of Evaluating Students

May I, at this point, give you a brief explanation of our report system, one which we have worked out over a period of years. Its distinctive characteristics:

(1) in form, a personal letter from me to the parents, to which I invite a reply—the letter takes up one or more general school problems;

(2) an individual rating for each student, arrived at from the previous school attended, various tests given here at entrance, and the letter grades of all the faculty members over a three week period, without their knowing her previous record or the test results. The result is a grade based on the ability of the student, which she can raise or lower according to the work she does; it eliminates discouraging competition with people of higher mentality and compels each student to compete against herself alone;

(3) constructive comments from the various faculty members on work and conduct;

(4) the discussion of the report by the President and student, alone, before the report goes to the parent.

It took a few years before this type of report became appreciated, but last year and so far this year I have received a number of most understanding letters from parents. I should like to give you a few exact quotations:

"Your personal interest and that of the staff members in each student is gratifying, and your comments, because of your interest, are enlightening, since they show us parents our child an an individual, a fact that we sometimes lose sight of."

"Your comments convince me that you too have recognized many of the faults which H must learn to overcome. With the many advantages of your splendid school and the inspiration of your guidance and interest, . . . H will be able to correct them."

"Except for the profanity angle, D's report contained no surprise for Mrs. D and me. . . . So far as I can tell from her letters and what she had to tell us when she was home over last weekend, D is really in love with the school. Her English teacher may be horrified to know that everything is 'swell'—the teachers are 'swell,' the food is 'swell,' the girls are 'swell.' However, we feel it is 'swell' that she feels that way."

"I would like to take this opportunity to tell you how much better we think M is doing this year. The school has done wonders with her in all ways."

–Source: President's Report, inserted in Trustees minutes following the meeting of 3 December 1941.

one students, with sixty graduating from the Junior College, the school had record numbers of withdrawals, scholastic failures, and expulsions. With the distractions caused by battlefield news, parental fears, frequent turnover in teaching staff, air raid drills and blackouts, boyfriends back home, and the proximity of a large male population, the academic performance of the Seminarians declined and disciplinary problems increased. A student with previous mental disorders suffered a nervous breakdown in 1941, claiming that God had turned her into a boy and made her a prophet; a group of girls ran away to Washington; and several others were caught frequenting bars in nearby Park Hall and smoking in their dorm rooms. Two students were expelled for "improper relations" with men (one became pregnant), and in March 1945, five more students were kicked out—four for breaking into a local residence and stealing whiskey and another for making poison in the chemistry lab at night. In June 1946, six members of the Junior College graduating class were found off campus in the company of Pax River sailors on the Saturday night before commencement; they received their diplomas but were forbidden to attend the ceremonies. So many items were stolen in 1946 that President France had everyone on campus finger-printed—instructors as well as students—because she believed that "two or three of the young teachers . . . did not uphold our standards, . . . set bad examples to the students, and condoned their breaking of regulations."

Miss France dealt with many of these crises singlehandedly, because the full Board of Trustees, with members now scattered throughout the state and dependent upon rationed gasoline, met infrequently during the war years. With the support of Trustee R. Bascom Broun, Jr., and the school attorney, John H. T. Briscoe, both of Leonardtown, the president made key decisions that kept the Seminary operating, despite rampant inflation, a shortage of provisions, and unpaid student bills. Miss France convinced the trustees not to raise tuition (although the 50-percent discount for local residents had to be discontinued in 1943–44); she calmed students and their parents in the fall of 1941 when a case of polio was discovered at the school; she supervised the airplane observation post on campus, maintained by students twelve hours a day, seven days a week, for three years; she escorted Seminarians to dances at Charlotte Hall Academy and the Naval Air Station to alleviate their isolation; she personally drove the school cook to a Baltimore hospital to have an operation; and she steadfastly tried to uphold high academic and disciplinary standards against enormous odds. Having earned the praise and confidence of the trustees

for two decades as both Seminary president and Board treasurer, Miss France left an important legacy to all subsequent chief executives at St. Mary's. When wartime crises necessitated the transfer of many responsibilities from the trustees to her, this woman with Victorian values, like countless other women who were liberated during the 1940s, clearly demonstrated how effective and decisive a leader she could be.

The Final Crisis

St. Mary's Female Seminary-Junior College survived World War II, but it very nearly did not survive the peace. In 1947, twenty-three years after the Great Fire, Miss France had to save the school one last time in her long tenure as president. The skill with which she did so ensured that this would be the final threat to the Seminary's existence and the final triumph of her distinguished career.

On 1 February 1947, the Maryland Commission on Higher Education, appointed by Governor O'Conor and chaired by Baltimore attorney William L. Marbury, issued a controversial report to then-Governor William Preston Lane, Jr. In its comprehensive summary, entitled *Higher Education in Maryland,* the Marbury Commission expressed dismay that Maryland ranked forty-fourth among the forty-eight states in the percentage of eighteen- to twenty-year-olds in school. To serve a growing, veteran-swelled population, Maryland desperately needed to create a "State-wide system of locally controlled junior colleges" and to "abandon" several public institutions of higher education that did not meet the Marbury Commission's specifications—including St. Mary's Female Seminary. Rehashing the same old prejudices that had always plagued the Seminary, the Commission advised the legislature to close the school because it was too costly, inaccessible, small, and academically deficient. "Apart from sentiment, there can be no sound reason for continuing the existence of this institution. . . . To bring St. Mary's Female Seminary up to standard would increase the cost per student, already abnormally high, and would be an unjustifiable expenditure of public money."

In reaching that conclusion, totally oblivious to how perfectly St. Mary's fit into the new system of higher education it was proposing, the Marbury Commission overlooked or ignored several key facts: that the Seminary had pioneered the junior college movement in Maryland, that it granted degrees to men as well as women, that it was fully accredited by the state, and that it was the only collegiate institution in the three counties of Southern Maryland. School officials and supporters, angered by the Commission's seemingly

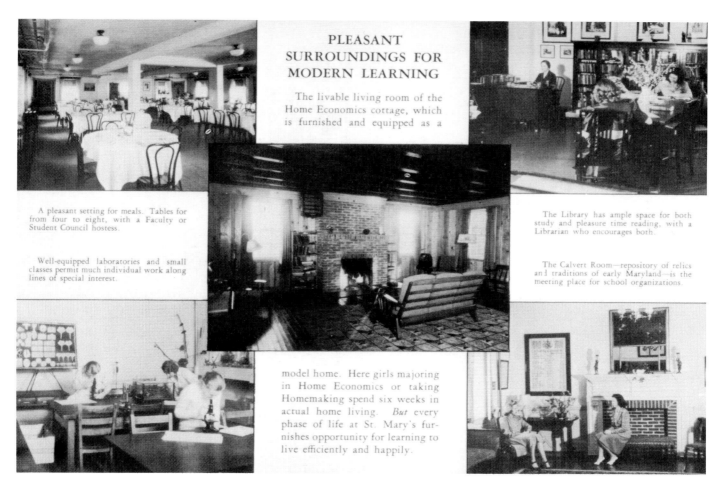

A page from the Seminary viewbook of the 1940s. Note at upper left the Dining Room, located in the basement of Calvert Hall between 1845 and 1969.

careless reliance on erroneous information, rose up with righteous wrath to save the Seminary from extinction yet another time. The Alumnae Association organized an extensive and effective letter-writing campaign within each legislative district, while the Board of Trustees printed and circulated a resolution of protest against the Marbury Commission report. Dated 14 February 1947, the trustees' resolution "deplore[d] the fact that the said Report appears to be based upon the findings of a single investigator, whose survey failed to include consultation with those duly appointed to administer the Seminary's affairs." The trustees who signed this challenge—Hendrickson, Magruder, Ewalt, Broun, Sasscer, Williams, Sothoron, and Palmer—not only demanded that St. Mary's be spared but urged state officials to "give further study to the important part which St. Mary's Female Seminary can assume in meeting Maryland's avowed urgent need for educating immature youth beyond high school graduation, to the end that this School shall fulfill its destiny by its worth as a Junior College—in which capacity it has served the State since 1926."

In the tough bureaucratic battles that lay ahead, Miss France played a critical role by assembling the evidence and arguing the case for the Seminary's survival in both the trustees' resolution and in a printed pamphlet she authored and circulated with the Board's approval. At a special meeting of the trustees on 14 February 1947, President France reported on the visit of a two-member survey team from the Marbury Commission in the fall of 1946, noting that their "repeated comment had been, 'It's too small! You don't have enough land! You need to have more students, et cetera.'" She then read her rebuttal to the Commission's recommendations, which the trustees unanimously agreed "was just what we needed to get before the public." In that rebuttal, subsequently sent to all legislators in Annapolis, Miss France argued that "sentiment" should indeed count a great deal when the object of that sentiment was the 107-year-old Monument School, erected by the state to honor the founding principles of Maryland. She stated that a small school was preferable to a large one in achieving educational excellence; that St. Mary's had consistently been Maryland's leader in the

The Seminary faculty of 1947–48 and Acting President Louise K. Rotha (February–June 1948), A.B., Woman's College of the University of North Carolina, M.S., University of Chicago. Miss Rotha was registrar and advisor of the Student-Faculty Government both before and after her service as the only acting president in St. Mary's history. She encouraged the students to call her "Ma." These photos come from the inaugural issue of The Castellan, 1948, *the first student yearbook.*

junior college movement; and that in return for its budgeted appropriation from the state ($19,000 in 1946), the school gave the public twenty-nine full scholarships. Moreover, the president noted, the Seminary was less isolated than it had ever been, with a total of thirteen buses a day running between Lexington Park and Baltimore or Washington, while the Naval Air Station constituted a large local population center that provided new conveniences as well as many potential students for the school.

On 2 July 1947, President France was present in Annapolis when Mr. Marbury formally reported the recommendations of the Commission on Higher Education to the Legislative Council of the General Assembly. Responding to the false allegation that St. Mary's was unaccredited, she and Trustee Ewalt "cornered [Marbury] outside [the] Assembly Room [and] reminded him that the Seminary's accreditation by the State Department of Education and the University of Maryland is printed in a Book gotten out by [his own] Commission." Before the next public hearing, Miss France compiled a two-page information sheet, entitled "Some Pertinent Facts about St. Mary's Female Seminary Which All Marylanders Should Know," and read it at the 16 July meeting of the Legislative Council. Encouraged by Dr. Thomas G. Pullen, Jr., State Superintendent of Schools ("who seemed interested in keeping the school alive"), she also compiled supplemental information on "The Feasibility of Using St. Mary's Seminary-Junior College As One of the State Junior Colleges Suggested and Urged by the Marbury Commission." Addressing the Legislative Council on that memorandum, Miss France argued that the state should not only preserve the school but *increase* support to it, since the Seminary had successfully served the only two western shore counties (St. Mary's and Calvert) that were considered too underpopulated to warrant a junior college.

By late 1947, the Legislative Council recommended to the General Assembly that St. Mary's Female Seminary-Junior College be continued as a vital state institution of higher education. The final decision on St. Mary's was rendered a year later, on 1 December 1948, by the Educational Committee of the General Assembly, which completely rejected the Marbury Commission's view of the school. The legislators criticized the Commission's obsession with student per capita costs and demonstrated less concern "with numbers in the student body [than] . . . with the quality and thoroughness of the courses." Once again, the past of the Seminary helped assure its future, as the legislators' final report stated: "This school . . . was erected at the site of the first landing in Maryland and was intended as a monument . . . permanent in nature. Through the years it has been a real cultural center and has sent out many young women equipped with a culture and refinement which is all too rare in modern education. The cost to the State is relatively small. The school should continue."

Unfortunately, by the time the Educational Committee issued its favorable recommendation on the Seminary, Miss France was no longer at the school. Suffering a coronary occlusion in December 1947, just when legislative opinion turned in favor of St. Mary's, the veteran president was unable to resume her duties throughout the spring term of 1948 and tendered her resignation, effective 30 June 1948. From February through June 1948, St. Mary's had its first and only "acting president," when Miss Louise K. Rotha, beloved science teacher and school registrar, carried out the responsibilities of chief executive until Miss A. May Russell assumed the presidency. Miss Rotha had abandoned a promising career as a scientific researcher at New York University and Cornell University Medical School because of arthritis, and she served as acting president of the Seminary while almost completely deaf.

Miss France lived six more years at the Shady Nook Nursing Home in Catonsville until her death on 17 September 1954, at age seventy-four. After funeral services at Emmanuel Episcopal Church in Chestertown, she was laid to rest in the town of her birth.

The Legacy of Adele France

The strain of a quarter-century at the helm of the much-buffeted old Seminary, with trials and triumphs in equal measure, exacted a heavy toll on the woman whom all revered as the "School Mother." Miss France had transformed a small and often-ignored female seminary into an innovative junior college that was belatedly praised by state officials. Along the way, she earned distinctions for herself and the school. She was elected to the Executive Committee of the Junior College Council of the Middle Atlantic States, and in 1942, Miss France stood alongside Eleanor Roosevelt to receive an honor-

Mary Adele France (17 February 1880–17 September 1954), the "School Mother," A.B., A.M., Litt.D., Washington College; M.A., Teachers College, Columbia University. Principal of St. Mary's Female Seminary, 1923–1937; founder of the Junior College, 1926– 1928; president of the Seminary and Junior College, 1937–1948. Portrait by Colonel James M. Wharton of Baltimore, 1947.

ary doctorate from Washington College. The student evaluation procedures that President France instituted at St. Mary's earned the Seminary recognition from the American Association of Junior Colleges, the Junior College Workshop, and Johns Hopkins University. At times, outsiders appreciated the school more than state officials did. In February 1942, Mrs. Marian W. Pease, a psychologist and guidance counselor from New York City, wrote of her recent visit to the campus: "I was prepared to find the most unique college in the United States, and I was certainly not disappointed; as a matter of fact, I have been talking about St. Mary's ever since."

Miss France was responsible for the unique qualities at St. Mary's Female Seminary-Junior College. Her special blend of old values and new pedagogy perhaps had most to do with saving the school from oblivion in 1947. The Legislative Council twice visited the Seminary and observed, among other quaint customs, the "daily evening family prayer" led by the president herself. Of course, such old-fashioned traditionalism appealed to the legislators, who commended the school for "the excellent manner in which it is conducted." But the point is, the students also seem to have appreci-

President France in her beloved flower garden, seeking serenity during the turmoil of World War II. She was fond of advertising the Seminary as "A Home School in a Garden Setting."

ated the nostalgic, affectionate, and homey environment at the Seminary, despite—or because of—the fast-changing values of modern American life.

Miss France was committed to the cultivation of the timeless social graces and of a warm family atmosphere at St. Mary's. She cared for her students and demonstrated that caring like few other college presidents ever had or would again. Creating a home-like Victorian environment on campus, she found the time in a hectic schedule to write verses to the students during exam week, to plant and pick flowers for the dining tables, to hug all of the girls as they departed and returned at holiday time, and to lead the evening candle-light procession to Trinity Church every Christmas season. Miss France was old-fashioned and only grudgingly admitted that the gentility and grace of the nineteenth century had faded forever, and yet she welcomed the creation of the Naval Air Station for the new social outlets it would provide her isolated students. She was rigid about discipline and academic standards, but that inflexibility in the search for excellence would serve the school well as it evolved, increasingly prepared and respected, into senior college status.

This special, tireless woman departed the Seminary she loved in the only appropriate manner for someone with her energy and devotion—carried out, seriously ill and incapacitated. As she lay, confined and inactive, in a distant nursing home, she was always gladdened by news of "her girls."

The mission and the vision of Miss France continue to influence St. Mary's today. She left future presidents with a model of devoted leadership and energetic perseverance that had saved St. Mary's from extinction in her first, and again in her last, year in office. But Adele France's greatest legacy will always be her pioneering Junior College. By experimenting with the school curriculum in 1926–27, she consciously united tradition and innovation to create a hybrid institution that reaffirmed the old Seminary's caring virtues on a collegiate level and introduced modern standards of academic excellence that were hard for the public to ignore and virtually impossible for the state to abandon. Through the expert nurturing of a patient gardener, Miss France's little seedling survived for forty years until it blossomed into St. Mary's College of Maryland—a most special flower indeed.

The Seminary candle-light service that was traditionally held in Trinity Episcopal Church every Christmas season while Miss France was president.

Stately she stands on the shore of her bay
Watching the tides that sweep over the land,
Sounding the depths of the waters that play
In the night watches, when moments are grand.

· · ·

Monument through which the warm blood of life
Pulses in heart throbs its vision again,
Moulding as beacon through calm and in strife
Daughters of women, mothers of men.

· · ·

Challenge of centuries, mark us today!
Yesterday's needs with its moments are gone,
Out through the present we measure the way
Spirit with spirit is carrying on.

—Attributed to Miss France, written on the occasion of the school's centenary.

FOREVER YOUNG:

The Old School and the New College, 1948–1990

CHAPTER IV

Rescued from oblivion for one final time in 1947–48, St. Mary's Female Seminary-Junior College looked forward to a bright future of greater service to the citizens of Maryland. It has never looked back since. Under three talented and dynamic presidents in the postwar era—Dr. A. May Russell (1948–1969), Dr. J. Renwick Jackson, Jr. (1969–1982), and Dr. Edward T. Lewis (1983–present)—St. Mary's has matured and modernized rapidly, enjoying increased state support for an unprecedented building boom. But St. Mary's also became better as it grew bigger, retaining the traditional intimacy and timeless values of the old school even as it was transformed into a new senior college of the liberal arts. What we celebrate in this sesquicentennial anniversary year is that successful blending of old and new at St. Mary's—the continuity with meaningful principles first expressed in the 1840s and the many changes that have prepared this institution for the complex challenges of the twenty-first century.

Enter May Russell

Since 1900, each chief executive of St. Mary's has left her or his successor a much-improved institution on the threshold of a new era. Lucy Virginia Maddox turned

Calvert Hall—centerpiece and symbol of the old school and the new College—as it was rebuilt in 1924–25 on the foundations of 1844.

over a reputable, old-fashioned female seminary to M. Adele France, who directed its critical transformations into a modern, accredited high school and then into an exceptional, pioneering junior college. When she retired in June 1948, after a quarter century of service, the school had emerged from crisis stronger than ever, but it was at another critical crossroads. What did the future hold for the institution, and how would it adjust to the new challenges and opportunities of the postwar period? Would St. Mary's remain a four-year junior college for women, or become a more conventional two-year junior college for both women and men? Or did St. Mary's possess the potential to seek the most ambitious and difficult goal of all—transformation into a coeducational baccalaureate college?

Since Adele France had greatly expanded the powers and responsibilities of the Seminary president, making that office the source of present missions and future visions, the trustees knew that their selection of her successor was probably the most crucial one in the school's history. In a momentous meeting held on 21 May 1948, the Board of Trustees convened in Congressman Lansdale G. Sasscer's office in Washington, D.C., to interview and vote on three candidates for president (two women and a man). Vice-Chairman R. Bascom Broun, Jr., of Leonardtown, nominated thirty-three-year-old Anna May Russell, who received "a large majority of the votes" and was declared unanimously elected. She had obviously impressed the trustees with her person-

The young, determined May Russell, as she appeared in the 1949 yearbook at the beginning of her long presidency.

ality and leadership abilities, because she was the only one of the three candidates who did not hold a doctorate. Miss Russell immediately accepted the presidency, effective 1 July, at an annual salary of $5,500 plus "full maintenance."

Born in Maddox, a St. Mary's County community some thirty miles from the Seminary, President Russell had earned her B.S. at Western Maryland College and, like Miss France, had taught high school mathematics before receiving a master's degree from Teachers College, Columbia University. She had done additional graduate work at the University of Michigan, Johns Hopkins, and Harvard (and would receive an honorary LL.D. from Western Maryland College in May 1950). Before coming to St. Mary's, a school she knew well because her sister Mary Eliza had graduated from the Seminary in 1926, President Russell had taught at Margaret Brent High School in her home county, at Annapolis High School, at the Horace Mann-Lincoln School of Experimentation at Columbia University, and at Salisbury State Teachers College. While at Columbia, she had taken several aviation courses, which led her to teach aeronautics to future Navy pilots during World War II. Miss Russell received her pilot's license in 1947, and perhaps the eighty-one flight hours in her "little red

monoplane" helped prepare the young president to navigate the old school into a daring and uncharted new future.

As impressive as Miss Russell's academic credentials were, her greatest strengths were her intangible qualities—the dynamism of youthful energy, a lifelong commitment to the educational needs of her native county, and a fierce, personal determination to master every challenge. These qualities were much in evidence from the beginning of her long tenure, as she made an immediate impact on old St. Mary's. President Russell had been in office only five months when, in November 1948, the Board of Trustees unanimously commended "her great understanding of the problems confronting the school and the masterly manner in . . . solving them." By that date, she had already proposed the elimination of the eleventh and twelfth grades and suggested the name change to St. Mary's Seminary Junior College—dropping "Female" in the hopes of making the institution fully coeducational. (The latter provision was approved by the General Assembly, signed into law by Governor William Preston Lane, Jr., on 6 May, and became effective 1 July 1949.) In her first year in office, President Russell aggressively recruited collegiate students, sending a Seminary slide-show to some fifty high schools statewide; proposed the remodeling of Calvert Hall for more dormitory space and the erection of a large modern classroom building; made provisions for black students to take the school's competitive state

The logo of St. Mary's Seminary, from a letter-sweater of the early 1950s. "Female" was officially dropped from the school name beginning in the 1949–50 academic year.

scholarship examinations; raised annual tuition and boarding charges to $700 ($200 and $500, respectively); and instituted the first student honor code at St. Mary's. These efforts paid off by the president's second year in office, as full-time enrollment jumped from 73 to 107, with a doubling of Junior College students.

The dynamism of the new president was also evident in her outreach to the surrounding community. The Artist and Lecture Series was improved and expanded to bring cultural enrichment to local citizens; the College choir regularly performed at area schools and churches; Seminarians more actively participated in joint programs with Charlotte Hall Military Academy, the U.S.O. at the Naval Air Station, and the United States Naval Academy; and the Gymnasium was made available to county groups for a variety of activities. The school's colorful May Queen Festival drew much press attention every year, and President Russell surpassed even Adele France's love of pageantry by producing a new outdoor historical drama, "The Birth of Tolerance," from 1950 through 1959. Written by a young Georgetown University playwright, David V. Turnburke (who was engaged to a teacher at the Seminary), this elaborate "pageant-play" involved the entire student body and used various sites within the old capital to explain the colonial legacies that influenced the Monument School. Many alumnae fondly recall the 1950s—the golden age of the four-year Junior College and its last decade of existence—because of the exciting and glamorous extracurricular activities that May Russell encouraged.

President Russell's early initiatives for increased enrollments, expanded facilities, and greater public visibility were designed to transform St. Mary's into a modernized, coeducational two-year junior college as quickly as possible. But her ultimate goal, indeed her personal dream, *from the beginning* extended far beyond that. When the *Southern Maryland Times* reported in May 1951 that Dr. Russell's "long-range aim . . . is to convert the school into a four year college," few trustees and virtually no state officials shared her confident optimism. One virtue of the president's plan was that regional and national trends favored the rapid expansion of collegiate facilities in the 1950s and 1960s; another was that every state-funded improvement to St. Mary's Seminary Junior College could be and would be used to justify the creation of St. Mary's College of Maryland. In making her personal dream a public reality, President Russell had to balance her visions of a future senior college with the pragmatic, day-to-day administration of the Junior College, which held the key to that future. One of her strengths as a leader was her ability to main-

May Russell's Honor Code

Since 1949 the Honor System has provided an excellent background against which students have learned to understand and accept personal ethics. The Honor System at St. Mary's is based on the belief that students can successfully accept the responsibility of establishing and maintaining standards in social and academic life.

. . .

Each entering student must feel . . . that he can give his active support to the Honor System. The entering freshman student should realize that its success, which is of great importance to him personally and to the whole student body, and indeed to the college itself, depends upon the willingness of each individual to contribute to an atmosphere of integrity and mutual confidence that is, in the final analysis, the total purpose of the Honor System on the St. Mary's campus.

. . .

During orientation, and before registration, each new student is required to sign a pledge card and to place his signature in the Honor Pledge Book. This, in effect, states that he understands what is expected of him under the Honor System and that infractions of the Honor Code at any time during his student days may be punishable by dismissal from the college.

The Pledge

As a student of St. Mary's, I pledge to uphold the Honor System in that I will not lie, cheat, or steal. I further pledge to report any infraction of which I have firsthand information.

I realize that the success of our Honor System depends upon every student's awareness of his own responsibility in helping not only himself but also others to maintain the ideals of our Honor System.

—Source: *The Honor System Handbook,* St. Mary's College of Maryland, 1965.

tain a congenial and enriching campus environment for the traditional Seminarians even as she implemented ambitious policies that would eventually transform St. Mary's into a very different institution.

In May 1950, President Russell initiated a significant program of campus expansion and capital improvements that have led to forty years of growth and modernization. At that time, the school added the first significant land to its campus since 1844 with the purchase of four acres of seventeenth-century Governor's Field from Trustee J. Spence Howard and his wife, Jean-

Visiting Artists and Lecturers

Throughout the 1950s, St. Mary's sponsored a wide variety of extracurricular programs that alleviated the isolation on this rural campus. In addition to the annual field-trip to Colonial Williamsburg and the frequent commutes to concerts in Washington, D.C., St. Mary's students were treated to campus visits by distinguished artists and lecturers. Among the most notable were:

1949—Stephen Hero, violinist
1950—Evelyn MacGregor, vocalist
1951—Peter Melnikoff, concert pianist
    Bennington College Dance Group
    Irene Hawthorne and members of the Metro-
      politan Opera Ballet Company
1952—William L. Shirer, journalist and historian
    Two plays by the Barter Theatre of Virginia
1953—Jean Carlton, vocalist
1955—Cornelia Otis Skinner, actress
1956—Lilian Kallir, pianist
1957—Charlie Ruggles, actor
    Dr. I. M. Levitt, astronomer
1958—Sir Cedric Hardwicke, actor
    Susann McDonald, harpist
1959—Remo Bolognini and the Baltimore
    Symphony Orchestra
    Barter Theatre's production of "The Mouse-
    trap"
    Baron Flary von Blomberg, diplomat

    —Source: Scrapbook of newspaper clippings, Alumni Archives.

Dr. Russell had "bowed smilingly" before him. Not forgetting how the past could influence the future, she told the *Washington Sunday Star* that "charm is as important now as it was in the days of the hoop-skirt and curtsy."

President Russell's elation with the growth and change on campus was to be short-lived, however. Patience and perseverance would be the watchwords for the next several years, as declining enrollments threatened both the immediate and long-range plans for the school's development. The 1949—50 enrollment of eighty-eight boarding students had been so large that the school had required advanced room deposits for the first time in St. Mary's history, but the student population declined precipitously soon after. The enrollment of full-time boarders dropped to 69 in 1950—51 and to 57 in 1951—52, before beginning a gradual resurgence: 72 in 1952—53, 78 in 1953—54, 88 in 1954—55, 97 in 1955—56, and 102 in 1956—57. President Russell explained to the trustees that the sharp decline in students for the 1950—51 academic year was "due to the fact that sixteen of the counties of Maryland were without graduating classes in June, 1950, because of instituting another grade in the elementary schools."

That fluke cost the Seminary dearly. The Junior

A scene from the 1957 "Birth of Tolerance Pageant," depicting Mistress Margaret Brent demanding the right to vote from the Assembly. This popular pageant-play was the brainchild of President Russell and was performed each spring from 1950 through 1959.

nette, principal heir to the extensive Brome family estate at St. Mary's City. Combining surplus funds with a new $500,000 state appropriation, the Seminary erected two buildings on this key parcel—Margaret Brent Hall in 1951 (providing much-needed faculty housing) and Anne Arundel Hall in 1954 (the first structure in the school's history designed exclusively for classroom use). The state's unprecedentedly large financial commitment resulted from the legislative sponsorship of State Senators Paul J. Bailey (St. Mary's County), Louis L. Goldstein (Calvert), and James B. Monroe (Charles) and the strong support of local citizens, most notably the nationally known radio commentator Fulton Lewis, Jr., of Hollywood, Maryland. The press also hinted that Governor Theodore R. McKeldin had signed the appropriations bill on 30 April 1951 because

The ground-breaking ceremony for Anne Arundel Hall, 8 June 1953. Governor Theodore R. McKeldin mans the shovel, while President Russell appears in one of her trademark stylish hats.

College was denied accreditation by the Middle States Association of Colleges and Secondary Schools on 3 May 1951–the same day the press reported the state funding for Anne Arundel Hall–because it was unable to attract "sufficient numbers of students to insure stability." Although the Middle States visitation committee recognized that "the College is in a state of transition," it could not excuse the fact that the forty-two resident collegians fell far short of the minimum of seventy-five full-time students needed for junior college accreditation, or that nineteen of the sixty-nine catalog courses had no enrollees that year. Despite St. Mary's fine reputation among peer institutions–symbolized by its hosting of 171 delegates to the Maryland Association of Junior Colleges annual convention in April 1951–the serious enrollment deficiencies created an "urgent need for a re-examination of the purposes and objectives of the college," according to the Middle States report.

The Years of Uncertainty

St. Mary's Seminary Junior College would have to endure the next eight years without nationally recognized

accreditation, and only the continuity and creativity of the president and trustees brought it through those dark, uncertain days. The events of May 1951 sent mixed signals to school administrators, and they faced perplexing dilemmas in trying to build new facilities for declining numbers of students and to enlarge enrollments at a junior college lacking an academic seal-of-approval. One proposed solution was to drop the eleventh and twelfth grades and to create a conventional two-year junior college; however, the trustees were reluctant to do so because the High School Division had been reaccredited by the Middle States Association (despite having its lowest enrollments for the twentieth century). The accreditation decisions of 1951 apparently had an enormous impact on the public perceptions of St. Mary's, and school officials were forced to react accordingly. The positive recommendation on the high school curriculum resulted in an influx of new students to that division, while the negative report on Junior College accreditation dropped collegiate enrollments to their lowest level since the 1930s. President Russell and the trustees were now obliged to retain the anachronistic four-year Junior College in order to keep St. Mary's solvent, and they faced the enormous challenge of doubling collegiate enrollments at a time when there were growing numbers of newer and more conveniently located community colleges in many parts of Maryland.

President Russell knew that St. Mary's was at a critical crossroads in the early 1950s, and she applied herself to the daunting task of recruiting more students to a distant, rural, and unaccredited school that lacked adequate facilities (Anne Arundel Hall would not open until 1954) and charged the highest fees in Seminary history (tuition, room, and board of $800 in 1952). Rising to the challenge, she hired the Seminary's first professional admissions officer, who visited 108 high schools in the 1951–52 academic year alone. Russell also produced expensive recruitment materials beginning in 1952–53 and appointed a "Publicity person" for 1953–54 to handle both admissions activities and media relations. This new director of public relations was Harrison E. Tawney (M. Ed., Kent State University), the first male member of the administrative staff at St. Mary's since Mr. Meany in 1846. In his first year, Tawney visited every public high school in Maryland, several more in Pennsylvania, Virginia, and Delaware, and many private secondary schools in Baltimore.

Despite these impressive efforts at statewide recruiting, the immediate solution to the Seminary's enrollment problems was found in St. Mary's County itself—in the form of local, non-boarding "extension students" who needed no introduction to the school. The population of the county in 1950 was double that of 1940, and a higher percentage of the surrounding community sought collegiate instruction than ever before. In becoming more of a "people's college" than even Adele France had envisioned, St. Mary's admitted twenty-six full-time commuting students in 1951–52, who ac-

Scenes from campus life at the still-traditional St. Mary's Seminary Junior College of the early 1950s.

counted for 54 percent of the collegiate enrollment that academic year. The numbers declined slightly in the next two years, but in 1954–55, St. Mary's Seminary Junior College enrolled seventy-seven commuters as full-time students (sixty-three in the four-year-old Evening Division), which represented almost twice the number of resident collegians. By the following academic year, commuters accounted for a majority of *all* students at the school. The sudden growth of the Evening Division alone—from no students in 1949–50 to 228 in 1956–57—solved the enrollment dilemma but created other problems for an institution in transition.

The successful outreach to local students who were "nontraditional" on the basis of age, gender, and/or educational needs had an important and immediate impact on the regular "Sem-Fems" living in Calvert Hall. Since the 1920s, St. Mary's had always had a few non-boarders —usually male commuting students, or "day-hops," as they came to be called—but the largest number of men enrolled in any year before 1955 was ten. In 1955–56 alone, however, eighteen male "day-hops" registered for the fall semester and an additional eighteen male "co-hops" enrolled for the spring term. (Co-hops were cooperative education students pursuing an engineering program in conjunction with the University of Maryland and the Patuxent River Naval Air Station.) This nucleus was large enough to form the first Men's Student Government Association and to field the first men's varsity basketball team during that academic year. The first full-time male faculty members in St. Mary's history had arrived in 1954–55 to accommodate the growing numbers of men students. These new professors, all of whom had previous teaching experience at four-year colleges, were: B. Elwood Fahl (M.S., University of North Dakota), chemistry and physics; Arthur Whitman (M.A., Iowa State University), speech and theatre arts; Kenneth W. Wood (M.A., University of Kentucky), modern languages; and Kemp P. Yarborough (M.A., University of South Carolina, LL.B., Wake Forest College Law School, Ph.D. candidate, Columbia University), social sciences. The sudden influx of males quickly became *the* topic of campus conversation and debate, and the 6 March 1956 issue of the *Signal News* contained four articles on the new phenomenon of coeducation. Some Sem-Fems saw the confusing array of "regular day-hops, special day-hops, co-ops, and special co-ops" as destructive of the nostalgic Seminary sisterhood that had attracted them to St. Mary's in the first place. As early as 1955, many students predicted that coeducation would eventually transform the school into a vastly altered senior college, and they saw themselves as the last traditional Seminarians who would know the

The close sisterhood of the old Seminary would be challenged by the influx of males on campus in the mid-1950s. The "beanie" tacked to the bulletin board was used in the traditional hazing period for freshmen.

special female heritage that had existed at St. Mary's for a century.

The administrative commitment to coeducation and the growing male enrollments that resulted were essential to the future development of St. Mary's as either a junior or a senior college. Although much of the traditional Seminary would be sacrificed to progress, the school would have faced ultimate extinction if President Russell and the Board of Trustees had not acted decisively to bolster enrollments in the early 1950s. Most of the Sem-Fems did not realize the degree to which school officials were being scrutinized for their flexibility and creativity in meeting the new educational challenges of the postwar era. Evaluators from the Middle States Association returned to campus in April 1958 and were pleasantly surprised that the total enrollment had risen from 84 to 310 students in only seven years. Although they described St. Mary's as an "admirable junior college," they would not recommend accreditation until school officials dealt with the issue of the Evening Division. Ironically, the "night school" had solved the enrollment deficiencies too well, with almost four times the number of full-time boarders (53), and the Middle States Association was concerned that St. Mary's would quickly lose its "unity of educational aims and spirit" in trying to accommodate such different, and often incompatible, constituencies. A preliminary

The May Queen of 1964, Kathi McKenna, and the princesses of her court. Rear Admiral James Lee of the Naval Air Station officiates at the crowning ceremonies in the Garden of Remembrance. The May Day Festival reflected the glamour that May Russell brought to the lives of the Sem-Fems even as she was assuring the rapid extinction of such activities in the move to senior college status.

Middle States report issued in November 1958 praised St. Mary's for having "come through a critical and trying period with credit," but warned that "the next twelve months will show whether [school officials] . . . have the strength and wisdom to consolidate their gains and regenerate the invigorating intellectual atmosphere which is the . . . one difference between a dull and an exciting college."

President Russell and the trustees used those twelve months in which accreditation was in limbo to make some crucial decisions on the future of St. Mary's. The Evening Division, which diverted "about three hundred man hours . . . each week" from the regular Seminary curriculum, would be retained but modified to emphasize quality over quantity in both the course offerings and student body. The "intelligence and maturity" of nontraditional students had been amply demonstrated, and the school would continue to be enriched by adult commuters down to the present. However, academic excellence in the liberal arts would not be compromised, and purely vocational subjects were eliminated in order to preserve the special character of the institution. In abandoning the very popular engineering courses because they were "educationally

unsound," the St. Mary's administrators made a courageous decision to uphold high academic standards despite a substantial loss of revenue.

St. Mary's left the crossroads in 1959, rejecting the route of a community college and keeping to its traditional path as a residential school of the liberal arts. It was now clear to all, including the Middle States Association, that the Seminary had a future clearly charted by accomplished leaders. After three additional progress reports by President Russell and yet another visit by a new team of outside evaluators, the Middle States Association of Colleges and Secondary Schools finally accredited St. Mary's Seminary Junior College on 28 November 1959. The final evaluation, entitled "Point of No Return," praised school officials for refocusing the Seminary's "fine old tradition" on "the new needs of a changing society." Convinced of the "continuity of progress" at St. Mary's, the evaluators wrote: "The trustees, administration, and faculty are aware that these excellent beginnings only clear the way for the college's real future. It is a sound educational institution now, giving its students good value for their time and money, but even more than most colleges, St. Mary's has *entrancing possibilities* for becoming as fine an institution of higher education as it really wants to . . . [at an] *"increasingly advantageous* [time]." The Middle States, however, specifically "caution[ed] against expansion into a four-year program" before "the achievement of excellence as a junior college." Noting that excellence costs more than competence, the educational experts warned of "two temptations: complacency . . . and expansion into a four–year program, which would be fatal to quality in the foreseeable future. The thing to do now is to win an unchallengeable reputation for St. Mary's as an absolutely first-rate junior college. There could be no finer goal."

A Decade of Explosive Change: 1960–1969

That advice was not heeded, as a "finer goal" was in fact realized in the rapid evolution of St. Mary's to senior college status. Receiving national accreditation after thirty-three years of operation, the Junior College existed for only eight more years. A remarkable convergence of favorable factors—the unprecedented generosity of state funding, the unprecedented availability of land for campus expansion, and the unprecedented student demand for collegiate education—precluded the slow and cautious development that the Middle States Association had deemed desirable. Few American colleges have experienced such explosive, convulsive, and significant changes within a single decade—a decade that began with the ending of the Seminary high school after 113 years and ended with the beginning of St. Mary's College of Maryland as a baccalaureate institution. Grasping opportunities that were indeed "increasingly advantageous" during the 1960s, St. Mary's became like a boom-town in a gold rush, making the most of its "entrancing possibilities" and vast potential while it had the chance.

The dizzying decade of change opened with one of the most memorable years in the history of St. Mary's. In 1960, the Seminary graduated its final class of high school seniors in June, and the reorganized, two-year Junior College admitted its first freshman class in September. A new era had dawned. During the 1960–61 academic year, John F. Kennedy's election and inauguration as America's first Roman Catholic president was the ultimate vindication of the Calverts' legacy of religious

The end of an era—Commencement Day, 5 June 1960. This is the last high school class to graduate from St. Mary's after more than a century of Seminary operation. In alphabetical order the members of this milestone class were: Marion August Blunt, Donna Lee Doeller, Janice Louise Endrizzi, Lelia Eleanora Gardiner, Pamela Price Jones, Barbara Wynne Laughead, Shirley Lockwood Moore, Rebecca Irene Murray, Gail Hamblen Naylor, Patricia Lyn Ottomeyer, Patricia Diane Parker, Patricia Louise Stellwagon, Nancy Priest Stevens, Frances Mae Turner, Priscilla Yvonne Whittaker, Leila Kathryn Willis, and Elizabeth Stuart Wilkinson.

toleration. On campus, expectations for the rejuvenated Junior College seemed as refreshingly optimistic as those for Kennedy's "Camelot." St. Mary's now had seven permanent administrators (president, registrar, director of admissions, librarian, assistant librarian, dean of women, and director of public relations) and fifteen full-time faculty members, holding four doctorates and seventeen M.A.s as terminal degrees. The school's annual operating budget, counting salaries, was $323,382, and its tangible assets of $1,116,650 included land and improvements appraised at $93,397, buildings worth $848,907, equipment valued at $158,346, and endowment funds of almost $16,000. The academic year began with 141 full-time students in the Day Division, including 98 female boarders in Calvert Hall (60 of them freshmen) and 31 male commuters, with another 113 enrolled in the Evening Division (69 men, 44 women). The Junior College now charged $250 for in-state tuition, $450 for out-of-state students, and $750 for a year's room and board.

The progressive spirit of the "new" St. Mary's Seminary Junior College was even more obvious in the dramatic expansion of the campus. The school, which had acquired only eleven acres of land during its first 110 years, added another 274 acres between 1956 and 1969 alone. Emerging from the constricting cocoon of the old campus boundaries (the river and Route 5), St. Mary's was like a maturing butterfly that needed room to spread its wings. In May 1956, the school paid $18,000 for 119.63 acres along the bend of Route 5 north of Chancellors Creek (also known as Wherrits or Fishermans Pond) from the original holdings of the defunct Slavic Farmers Association of Maryland. This was the largest single tract ever acquired by St. Mary's, and its placement, more than a half-mile from the original campus, dictated the development of a separate "North Campus." In 1959–60, the firm of Olmsted Brothers, landscape architects of Brookline, Massachusetts, designed a master plan of development that advised the use of the old "South Campus" for instructional purposes, while reserving the new "North Campus" for student residences and recreation. The plan called for the construction of a student union-dining facility, up to four additional dormitories, a new auditorium, a fieldhouse, athletic fields, an infirmary, and a library—at a projected cost of $4.5 million. (Fortunately, the Board rejected one of the consultants' proposals—to remove the "architecturally unimportant" Alumni Lodge, where May Russell lived throughout her tenure as president.)

In 1959, with accreditation imminent and the need for expansion verified, President Russell and the trustees took their "Ten-Year Development Plan" to state officials for approval and funding. Although they made their requests in modest stages, beginning with a $170,000 proposal for new faculty housing, neither Governor J. Millard Tawes, nor the State Planning Commission, nor the recently formed Commission on Higher Education, displayed much interest in supporting the College's expansion. In 1961, after two fruitless years of lobbying, during which a governor's aide even intimated that St. Mary's "might . . . have to fold in a few years anyway," frustrated but resolute school officials upped the ante. If state officials were reluctant to spend so much money on the Junior College, perhaps large expenditures would be more justified for a new *four-year college* in Southern Maryland. Disregarding the "go-slow" advice of the Middle States Association, the Board of Trustees on 31 August 1961 announced its determination to "have a four-year college in our section of the state"—the only area in Maryland without one. President Russell's thirty-five-page "Progress Report to the Middle States Commission on Institutions of Higher Education," dated 1 October 1961, defended the proposal by emphasizing the rapid growth of St. Mary's County and its increasingly critical need for enhanced educational opportunities.

The radical idea that seemed so far-fetched just a decade earlier, and that had to be deferred until after Junior College accreditation was attained, now received united and dedicated support throughout Southern Maryland. In July 1961, Board Chairman R. Bascom Broun, Jr., appointed a Legislative Committee from the trustee membership, chaired by Mrs. Felix E. Wathen Boone. Together, Bascom Broun and Geneva Boone enlisted the assistance of influential alumni, ex-Governor McKeldin, and State Comptroller Louis L. Goldstein of Calvert County. Goldstein hosted a meeting of the entire Southern Maryland legislative delegation in his office on 22 September—a preliminary step to Dr. Russell's inspired political maneuver a few weeks later. On Friday, 3 November 1961, the president and trustees hosted the College's first "Governor's Day," a luncheon-conference at which 100 state and county politicians came to honor Governor Tawes and to discuss the future of St. Mary's. Following a Southern Maryland feast of oysters and country ham in the crowded basement dining room of Calvert Hall, Tawes rose to speak, reportedly "deeply moved" to be the first chief executive so honored by the school. "Possibly the State hasn't done as much as it should have done in the past for St. Mary's," he said. "There will be some funds forthcoming, [because] there is a great need today at St. Mary's for some unusual help, beyond the ordinary aid it has

The first "Governor's Day," Friday, 3 November 1961. Left to right on the steps of Calvert Hall are: Board of Trustees Chairman R. Bascom Broun, Jr., State Comptroller Louis L. Goldstein, Mrs. Helen A. Gibson Tawes, Governor J. Millard Tawes, and President Russell.

been receiving." The remarks of the next speaker, Comptroller Goldstein, were more specifically committal. He declared that "right here on the hallowed and sacred ground of St. Mary's we can establish a great four-year college," boldly estimating that $5,000,000 in state funds might be required. "No matter how much our educational system costs today, it is worth every penny," Goldstein said, convinced that "the greatest force in making the American dream come true . . . has been free education for the youth of our citizenry." Before President Russell presented a set of commemorative plates to Mrs. Tawes and costumed students took guests on tours of the historic campus and ancient capital, Trustee George L. Radcliffe, a former United States Senator and now president of the Maryland Historical Society, offered a toast to the "Spirit of St. Mary's—let us hope that it will continue throughout the ages."

The successful "Governor's Day" celebration in 1961 was a turning point in the creation of St. Mary's College of Maryland and helped give reality to the sentiments of that toast. As had happened so many times before, reflections on the memorable past of the Monument School again helped pave the way for an even brighter future of distinguished service to the state. After two

and a half years of indifferent support for the school, the Tawes administration suddenly allocated $890,000 to St. Mary's in the supplemental state budget of January 1962 (approved by the General Assembly on 6 March) for site development on the North Campus and the construction of a dormitory there. But before these funds became available in June 1963, there was an equally startling revelation: Jeannette Brome Howard, granddaughter of Trustee Brome and widow of Trustee J. Spence Howard, offered the College a critical thirty-eight-acre tract of land bordering St. John's Pond and Route 5, including almost a full acre of St. Mary's River beachfront. The acquisition of that strategic parcel in July 1963 necessitated the immediate amendment of the current funding legislation to permit land purchase, site development, and construction on a completely new and previously unanticipated "East Campus," located midway between the South and North campuses. With the support of Governor Tawes, Comptroller Goldstein, St. Mary's County Delegates Frank A. Combs and Henry J. Fowler, and State Senator Walter B. Dorsey, the General Assembly wholeheartedly approved this crucial change, retroactive to 1 June 1963, thereby permitting the concentration of most new construction adjoining the original campus instead of at the more distant North Campus.

These key developments in the summer of 1963 signaled the close and invaluable ties that would exist be-

The "South Campus," showing the mini-building boom of the early 1950s (Margaret Brent Hall and Anne Arundel Hall) and, in the foreground, part of the key Brome-Howard lands on which the major building boom of the 1960s would focus.

tween St. Mary's and Governor Tawes throughout his second term (1962–1966). The governor became increasingly important to the Junior College at an auspicious time for educational development in Maryland and across the nation. Citing "the advancement in public education . . . as the greatest single achievement" of his administration, Tawes enlarged the University of Maryland into the tenth largest in the country, reorganized the old normal schools into five regional state colleges, and centralized their governance through a single board of trustees and the new Advisory Council for Higher Education (while leaving the St. Mary's Board of Trustees independent as before). At the second "Governor's Day" in October 1963, Tawes explained that St.

Mary's "enjoys a singular status . . . [as] the only [junior college] operated exclusively by the state," and that he was "solidly behind the efforts that are being made here." Tawes's support for the Junior College was as significant as Governor Albert C. Ritchie's had been for the Female Seminary forty years earlier, and he will always be remembered for signing, on 7 April 1964, the legislation that changed the name of the institution to the present St. Mary's College of Maryland (effective 1 June 1964). It must be noted, however, that Governor Tawes was ambivalent about whether the "bright future" he envisioned for St. Mary's was as a junior or a senior college.

Not even Tawes's approval of the name change in

"Thoughts on a College Name"

When those in charge of things in 1839–1840 chose to incorporate the name "St. Mary's" into the name of the educational institution, they no doubt wished to honor the name of the first permanent Maryland settlement much more than the Virgin Mary. Yet "St. Mary's" is a possessive noun, and it "possesses" all that follows it. "St. Mary's College" to the uninitiate can only mean a religiously oriented institution, probably under Roman Catholic auspices. It cannot be otherwise when all four colleges of this name are Roman Catholic institutions. There are at least an additional sixteen colleges . . . that have "St. Mary" or "St. Mary's" as an integral part of their names; of these, fifteen are Roman Catholic and one is Protestant Episcopal.

. . .

The insertion of the word "State" to form "St. Mary's State College" prevents this misconception. This name is unique; it is euphonious. It preserves the "St. Mary's" as a link with the past while indicating the true orientation and support of the college.

. . .

The objection has been raised that the use of the word "State" might in some way cause our college to come under the same control as the other colleges with "State" as part of their name. . . . Our college, it is true, may in the future resemble other state-supported colleges more and more closely, whatever its name, for working toward similar goals (as we shall be doing) may well produce certain likenesses. . . . The risks involved here seem overshadowed by the alternative—a continued, constant, erroneous conviction in the public mind that this is a church-related institution.

—Source: Mimeographed sheet, "Thoughts on a College Name," attributed to May Russell in 1963.

A new beginning—7 April 1964. Governor Tawes signs the legislation that changed the school's name to the present St. Mary's College of Maryland. Witnessing this historic moment for the institution that has had so many different names are alumni representatives, from left to right: Mrs. Hal D. Tracy, Alumni President Mrs. Arthur G. Turner, Mrs. Manley Miller, and Miss Lucy F. Spedden '16. President Russell had proposed some name change in April 1963, but it was the St. Mary's alumni who suggested the present name for the College.

Spring 1964 gave official state authorization for St. Mary's to become a four-year college, although school administrators proceeded with their plans for expansion as if it had. As construction commenced on Queen Anne Hall, the first building erected on the new East Campus, the trustees created a Development Committee from their membership that included William Aleck Loker of Leonardtown (the chairman); Board Chairman Broun; Mrs. Boone of the Legislative Committee; Senator Radcliffe; Vice-Admiral Felix Johnson, USN (Ret.); Kent R. Mullikin, regional vice president of The Equitable Life Assurance Society; and Mrs. William S. Morsell, Jr., of Baltimore. This committee, working closely with President Russell and local politicians, was instrumental in obtaining an additional ninety-three acres of land on the East and North campuses in the summer of 1965. Whether or not the state had given formal approval for elevating St. Mary's to senior college status, the public recognized the profound growth that was transforming the old school. A 20 May 1964 *Baltimore Sun* article, entitled "St. Mary's College—Always Prepared for Change," interpreted the evolution of the Monument School to a four-year curriculum as "still another metamorphosis in its development . . . to keep pace with the times."

The important land acquisitions of 1963 and 1965, coming so close together, created a dynamic momentum that helped make May Russell's dream a reality. Generous state funding and the availability of key properties converged, until the school had bought enough, built enough, and grown enough to be seriously considered for senior college status. Another $932,000 was appropriated for capital improvements in 1965—the same year that St. Mary's had male residents for the first time in its history (76 in Calvert Hall) and Queen Anne Hall opened as a women's dormitory, with all 150 beds filled. The resident population in 1965–66 had doubled in one year, and mushrooming enrollments caused impatient trustees to criticize the "foot dragging" of the state's construction schedule. Soon, however, new buildings appeared so fast that the Board had little choice but to name them after Maryland's twenty-six counties: Queen Anne Hall (women's dormitory), 1965; Dorchester Hall (men's dormitory), 1966; Charles Hall (student center and dining room), 1966; Talbot Hall (infirmary), 1968; Baltimore Hall (library), 1969; Somerset Hall (gymnasium), 1969; Prince George's Hall (coed dormitory), 1970, and Caroline Hall (coed dormitory), 1970. The Cobb residence was purchased in July 1969 to serve as the President's House, and the Chapman property (now the Admissions Office) was procured in August 1974. These were the last major land acquisitions that

expanded the St. Mary's campus to its present size.

What is often overlooked in focusing on the frantic pace of expansion and construction during the 1960s is that St. Mary's did not receive formal state approval to become a senior college until 8 July 1966. Only then did the Maryland State Board of Education authorize the procedures that would result in the first conferral of bachelor's degrees in June 1971. Until that approval was granted, neither the support from Governor Tawes and Comptroller Goldstein, nor the huge appropriations in the mid-1960s, nor the name-change in 1964, officially committed Annapolis to anything but a larger *junior* college. The state's cautious strategy helped ensure that St. Mary's College of Maryland would be as academically prepared for four-year status as it was physically.

Although the building boom was the most tangible evidence of a maturing institution, school administrators, trustees, faculty, and students spent long hours in the mid-1960s planning new academic programs and policies for a senior college. Dr. Jeremiah Finch, dean of the faculty at Princeton University, was appointed as a

The start of a new era—September 1965. The first male students ever to live on the St. Mary's campus take up residence in Calvert Hall.

The new Queen Anne Hall (women's dormitory) reflected in St. John's Pond. The opening of this residence hall in September 1965 helped stimulate a major increase in student enrollment.

consultant and made several key recommendations after his initial campus visit on 11–13 May 1965. (He was later a member of the Academic Council of outside consultants, along with Dr. Winton Tolles and Dr. J. Renwick Jackson, Jr., who met in 1968–1969 to discuss the new College's educational mission.) Once the campus community had devised academic policies and designed the first majors in art, biology, English, history, and mathematics, state officials in 1966 were convinced that St. Mary's was mature enough to become a baccalaureate institution. The St. Mary's faculty was officially informed of the State Board of Education's long-sought authorization on 28 September 1966; statewide newspapers did not report the elevation to senior college status until the summer of 1967; and the St. Mary's catalog for 1967–68 was the first to announce the new program to students.

It seems incredible that an institution with a high school division as late as 1960 could become a senior college in less than a decade. Doubtless the fine academic reputation of St. Mary's and the timely restructuring of Maryland's public colleges contributed greatly to the creation of the four-year school, but such explanations will not satisfy the cynics seeking the "real," underlying political motivations for change. Dr. Russell was personally convinced that her persuasive charm, glamorous clothes, and stylish hats (her trademark) had bedazzled legislators into granting massive appropriations to St. Mary's. In a 1986 interview with English Professor Andrea Hammer, she explained: "I used to buy special hats when I went to Annapolis because I knew those guys noticed them. . . . They'd be looking at the hats, and I just thought about the buildings. When I'd get back to St. Mary's [after a successful budget hearing], students would be waiting for me, and we'd celebrate. They would make me wear a fictitious hat." President Russell all-too-obviously manipulated Governor Tawes with the "Governor's Day" celebrations in 1961, 1963, and especially in 1965, when the school commissioned a portrait of his wife and named Somerset Hall in honor of his home county. But was the Democratic governor really so impressed with this staunchly Republican college president as to give her a four-year institution out of gratitude? An equally cynical counter-theory contends that Tawes was a very shrewd politician who gave a senior college to Southern Maryland in exchange for the abolition of slot machines there. (Gambling was a thorny issue that plagued him from 1963 to the end of his term.) Of course, whether or not St. Mary's College of Maryland was "built on a bluff" as a political payoff has little relevance to the institution of today, for however created, the school has certainly demonstrated its true educational value to the region and state in the years since 1967.

Final Challenges

It was sadly ironic that May Russell's triumphant accomplishment of her far-sighted goal for St. Mary's was somewhat overshadowed by controversy in her last two years as president. Like Moses, she was destined to glimpse the "promised land" she had long pursued but would not lead the school into its glory days as a senior college. The enormous energy required to create that institution and its new campus exacted a heavy toll from Dr. Russell, and she became a victim of the complex problems that inevitably accompany such accelerated growth and change.

Controversy erupted at St. Mary's in 1967–68, the first academic year of operation for the senior College. The 4 March 1968 issue of *The Point News* announced that the "Campus Reeks With Discontent–President Sued for $3,000,000 & Charged With Unethical Conduct." Actually, as the next issue explained on 16 April, *three* civil suits had been filed seeking multi-million-dollar judgments against Dr. Russell and her supportive Board of Trustees, two brought by faculty members and one by a former student. Dr. Richard W. Griffin, professor of history and president of the Faculty Senate, sought $3,000,000 for defamation of character, alleging that President Russell had disclosed harmful and unsubstantiated rumors about him to his colleagues; accused him of giving alcoholic beverages to students; and declared him an "insidious influence" with "ulterior motives" for giving a faculty seminar on "The American Revolution as a Social Movement." Charles K. Henley, assistant professor of English, charged in his $1,000,000 suit that Dr. Russell had "falsely and maliciously" accused him of "smoking pot with students" at Dr. Griffin's house; publicly characterized him as "a bad influ-

Historic St. Mary's City

Since its creation as the Monument School in 1840, St. Mary's College has venerated and popularized the site of Maryland's first settlement and seventeenth-century capital. In those 150 years, several plans were proposed for preserving or restoring the original "Citty of St. Maries," with few results until the past two decades. The 1930s produced the pioneering archaeological research of Dr. Henry Chandlee Forman (author of *Jamestown and St. Mary's: Buried Cities of Romance,* 1938) and renewed popular interest in the site because of Maryland's Tercentenary Celebration. In the early 1950s, the St. Mary's County Historical Society, of which May Russell was vice-chairman, gave added impetus to local restorationists. The radio commentator, Fulton Lewis, Jr., of Hollywood, Maryland, announced in his national broadcast on Christmas Eve, 1951, "that Old St. Mary's City should be rebuilt, with the buildings serving as dormitories, classrooms and laboratories for St. Mary's Seminary." Lewis's appeal to make the ancient capital a national shrine to toleration, funded by all Americans, was restated by Maryland Senator Daniel B. Brewster in August 1963. He introduced a bill (S. 2089) in the 88th Congress "to establish the Saint Mary's City National Memorial Commission," which would determine the feasibility of operating a restored site by the National Park Service. That was the apparent catalyst for the Maryland General Assembly in 1966 to create the present St. Mary's City Commission "to preserve, develop, and maintain" the first settlement as a state, not a federal, monument. Certified as a National Historic Landmark in 1969, the revered capital of the Calverts has assumed new life in the last two decades as a significant site for archaeological and historical research and interpretation. The programs and personnel of this outdoor museum provide unique benefits for St. Mary's students, and, like the Seminary, enhance the aesthetic and educational value of this historic region of rural beauty.

ence on students" (because he was divorced); and denied him a salary increase "while threaten[ing] . . . further reprisal." The civil suit brought by the former student alleged that Dr. Russell had summarily expelled her in 1965 without proper adjudication under the provisions of the honor code and charged that the president had "falsely and maliciously invaded her privacy by publicly stating . . . that she was a 'proven cheat and liar.' "

The filing of these lawsuits coincided with the growing unrest on college campuses across the nation following the January 1968 Tet Offensive in the Vietnam War. Although St. Mary's was as yet "non-activist" with regard to anti-war demonstrations, the move to senior college status stimulated both faculty and students to demand a greater participation in campus governance and institutional development. The Griffin case, in particular, involved a struggle for power and respect between the new Faculty Senate and the traditionally paternalistic administration of the veteran president and Board of Trustees. On 31 January 1968, the Faculty Senate circulated a memorandum to the full faculty that accused Dr. Russell of duplicity and bad faith, and on the same day, the campus chapter of the American Association of University Professors (A.A.U.P.) voted 20-0-2 to request from that national professional organization an investigation of administrative practices at St. Mary's. President Russell responded on 1 February by canceling the next day's meeting with the Faculty Senate, "in view of the content of the statement issued . . . on January 31." While the trustees ultimately admonished Dr. Russell for her handling of Griffin's Senate, they were not about to surrender their authority over the fragile, young institution that they had so carefully nurtured—certainly not to new teachers and transient students seeking as radical a goal as self-governance. The first priority of the trustees in this critical period was to remain independent and strong while avoiding public controversy, because officials in Annapolis were still trying to disband the Board and bring St. Mary's under the centralized governance of the other state colleges. (Legislation that would have ended the traditional independent Board of Trustees was defeated by a narrow margin of 21 to 19 in the Maryland Senate in early 1969.)

President Russell's once-amiable relations with staff and students suffered in the late 1960s, because she was admittedly preoccupied with the expansion of the school's physical plant and had less time to deal effectively with "people problems" before they mushroomed into crises. Like so many other college presidents in this era of campus unrest, Dr. Russell had trouble relating to the radically different culture of that vocal, some-

The end of an era—Commencement Day, 8 June 1968—as the last of 39 classes graduates from the Junior College. To signal the transition from associate to bachelor's degrees, St. Mary's held no commencements in 1969 or 1970.

times hostile undergraduate generation. In April 1967, for example, she summarily suspended a bearded student for "excessive abuse of dress standards" (wearing a sweatshirt and cut-off jeans to dinner) and then re-suspended him for "insubordination to a member of the administrative staff" after he refused to apologize upon his return to campus. In response, a majority of the 400 students at St. Mary's (70 to 90 percent) boycotted classes for two days to protest the president's actions. The traditional dress code, which required men to be clean-shaven and attired in coat and tie for most campus functions, was liberalized as a result of this massive protest. But the central, unresolved issue that aroused most students (and even some sympathetic professors) was Dr. Russell's seemingly "arbitrary" suspensions without adjudication by the Student Senate.

A year later, during the nation's "revolutionary spring" of 1968, student discontent again reached a fever pitch. Coinciding with the height of faculty criticism and the filing of the lawsuits against President Russell, students complained that she disregarded their rights, attempted to censor their press, and mistreated the most popular teachers. The student staff and faculty advisor of *The Point News* resigned in protest, while the Women's Dormitory Council filed a grievance against the dean of women for allegedly stating in public that

"75 percent of the women in the [Queen Anne] dorm were not virgins." Dr. Russell probably would not have contested the allegation that she was trying to impose the conformist values of the early 1950s on the unruly undergraduates of the late 1960s. But the student charge of presidential authoritarianism became a self-fulfilling prophecy, as she seemed to grow ever more defensive, and even punitive, in reacting to criticism. In 1968, President Russell summoned the state police to disperse a crowd of student protesters and threatened prosecution under a new Maryland law that called for $1,000 fines and/or six months in jail for trespassing in college administration buildings. Convinced that undergraduates were too immature to regulate their own affairs, the president took a firm stand against "a very few [students] trying to run things, [which] they cannot do." Nearly twenty years later, Dr. Russell recalled this period of strained relations with students by observing that "my generation was told what to do and they did it. I suppose we were brought up differently. We dated back to a different era."

Considering how far St. Mary's College had come and the direction in which American undergraduates were going, it was not surprising that Dr. Russell announced in December 1968 that she would resign her presidency, effective 30 June 1969. Although she retained the allegiance and loyal friendship of the "old guard" trustees, several Board members doubted her ability to administer the new senior college following the many controversies of 1967 and 1968. It had been a rough beginning, and the trustees sought fresh leadership for an infant institution in changing times. In announcing her retirement, May Russell stated that "I am resigning because I have always felt that at such time as the number of men and women on campus became equal, the college should have a man president. St. Mary's is larger now and the presidency is a job which entails tremendous responsibility. I may be old-fashioned, but I think it should be coped with by a man. I'll miss St. Mary's, there's no question about that. But my way of life is looking to the future and planning for the future, and I never look back."

The Board of Trustees sponsored a day of tribute to President Russell on 24 May 1969, in recognition of her dedicated, successful service to the old school and the new college. Since there would be no commencement exercises between the granting of the last associate of arts degrees in 1968 and the first granting of bachelor of arts degrees in 1971, this festive day of tribute was the major campus event in Spring 1969. Board Chairman Loker, the other trustees, alumni, and legions of faithful friends from throughout Southern Maryland gathered to honor President Russell in Baltimore Hall, the newest of "her" buildings. The guest speaker was Dr. Jeremiah S. Finch of Princeton University, a member of the Academic Council of educational experts that had worked so closely with the retiring president in developing a four-year curriculum. Gifts were presented to Dr. Russell from the Board of Trustees and the Alumni Association, and her formal portrait, painted by Peter Egeli, was unveiled on that occasion. An "Encomium" that was published in the program for this day of tribute described President Russell as a "new founder" in the best tradition of her Maryland forebears and praised her tireless efforts on behalf of St. Mary's College—"a beautiful, graceful monument to the past," which now, more than ever, found "its meaning and fulfillment . . . in the present and future."

A Tribute to May Russell

My first meeting with May Russell was by telephone. The connection wasn't very good, but that didn't matter, because the power of her enthusiasm, the strength of her character, and the warmth of her heart came through—and the connection has been getting better ever since.

. . .

My acquaintance with May really began after my first day here, sitting on her porch and listening to her describe the College. . . . And I remember that as I listened, looking out at the fading sunlight over the river, May Russell's warmth, strength, and enthusiasm began to blend with the idea of the college she was committed to bring to reality.

. . .

Now that so much has happened, so many struggles carried on, so much accomplished, and now May is leaving the place her dreams helped to shape, I confess to a certain sadness. No—it is not sadness that she is leaving, for as an old hand in the education business I believe that there comes a point in the lives of persons, and of institutions, when change is good—for the person who has led it, and for the institution itself. . . . Colleges, I've observed, have a life of their own. No matter what the changes, controversies, the developments, a college is larger than any single person or group within it; it transcends all the internal to-and-fro; and as the years go on, it retains its character. The lasting influences are those of its people who have worked most constructively for its best interest—Mark Hopkins at Williams, Woodrow Wilson at Princeton, Gilman at Johns Hopkins, and—someday they will say here—May Russell at St. Mary's.

—Source: Speech by Dr. Jeremiah S. Finch, Princeton University, at the tribute to May Russell, 24 May 1969, as printed in the *Alumni Newsletter* (Fall 1969), 4, 12.

Baltimore Hall (the Library)—the last academic building that May Russell built and site of the day of tribute to her—as it appeared when new in 1969. An indication of the pace of change at St. Mary's is the fact that the school outgrew this modern facility in only two decades.

The Legacy of May Russell

Dr. Russell's departure ended the 120-year tradition of Maryland-born female chief executives at St. Mary's, but her dynamic, progressive leadership in modernizing both the campus and the curriculum established a new tradition that continues to invigorate the College to this day. Her legacy is truly set in stone, as the buildings she envisioned and erected will constitute the core of this campus for decades to come. When she began her presidency in 1948, St. Mary's was a combined high school and Junior College with seventy-three female students, five buildings on an eight-acre campus, a faculty and staff of sixteen, and an annual operating budget of $66,841. When she ended her presidency in 1969, St. Mary's was a four-year college with a coeducational enrollment of 630 (in which men outnumbered women), seventeen buildings on a 285-acre campus, forty-nine instructors and administrators, and an annual operating budget of $1,223,768.

In her twenty-one years as president, May Russell nurtured the strengths of Adele France's Junior College and vastly expanded the educational benefits of St.

Dr. Anna May Russell (2 October 1914–11 April 1988), "The Builder," B.S., LL.D., Western Maryland College, M.A., Teachers College, Columbia University. President of St. Mary's Seminary Junior College, 1948–1964, and first president of St. Mary's College of Maryland, 1964–1969. Portrait by Peter Egeli of Drayden, Maryland, 1969.

Mary's to future generations of students. The campus that she had enlarged by 4,000 percent and the many buildings she had constructed at a cost of some $8 million proved indispensable in addressing the needs of a growing collegiate population in Maryland. Enrollments in 1969 were 850 percent higher than they were in 1948 and had increased by 37 percent in only two years. In addition to offering students an educational alternative to large universities, May Russell increased the visibility of, and respect for, the office of president at St. Mary's, due to her work with the Maryland Higher Education Association (president), Maryland Association of County Boards of Education (secretary), American Association of Junior Colleges (chair, Commission on Student Personnel), Junior College Council of the Middle Atlantic States (executive board member), Maryland Commission for the 1964–65 New York World's Fair, Southern Regional Education Board, St. Mary's County Board of Education, and St. Mary's County Historical Society. Finally, President Russell left to her successors the seeds of a significant, independent endowment and an enthusiastic desire among state

May Russell's legacy to St. Mary's—a dozen modern buildings on a vastly expanded campus.

officials to support her fledgling College—a refurbished Monument School with a new mission—for countless thousands of future students.

Dr. Anna May Russell, pioneering president of the venerable Seminary, of the resilient Junior College, and of the infant St. Mary's College of Maryland, retired to Newport Beach, California. In 1972, she made a brief visit to campus to deliver the commencement address and to be inducted into the Order of the Ark and Dove. On 6 October 1984 (Homecoming), she returned again for "May Russell Day," at which she received an honorary doctorate of humane letters—appropriately, the first woman to be awarded an honorary degree from St. Mary's College. May Russell paid her final visit to the county of her birth and the land of her dreams on 14 April 1988, the day she was buried at Christ Episcopal Church in Chaptico.

The Changing of the Guard

In March 1969, the Board of Trustees unanimously selected Dr. J(ames) Renwick Jackson, Jr., as May Russell's successor from a field of more than sixty applicants. Dr. Jackson was already well known to the trustees for his service on the Academic Council of ad-

The Philosophy of Gentle Ren, 1968–69

Self-righteous adolescents are defining themselves over against adults—this is normal. This is the least attractive and most dysfunctional feature of the student movement. There is a new culture coming which we do not understand. . . . One of its features is a protest of the fractured nature of the university itself . . . and calls for the whole man to be thought of. It is the affirmation of the flesh—physical expression and fulfillment. The students are saying that it is not an illicit or rebellious thing, but it is a positive thing, for a man and woman to love each other aside from the marriage contract. The sharpest criticism is against those persons who verbalize, but do not live by, their ideals.

President J. Renwick Jackson, Jr., in his trademark commencement attire. His personal charm and rhetorical talents made him a charismatic leader who began to make a name for St. Mary's beyond the borders of Maryland.

. . .

American society has moved beyond representative democracy to participatory democracy. . . . If you are committed to a democratic process, then you must really be committed to it. {St. Mary's needs to} give your best minds to the development of a new model which would express participatory democracy, discovering what the appropriate roles are for each group. We need a community where there is a mutuality in dealing with the functions appropriate to a college.

. . .

The course that an individual would follow from the time he enters college until he leaves it—everything that is a part of his college experience—is the curriculum. . . . {It should be} a constellation of persons, resources, materials, times, places, and events. . . . The goals of higher education are achieved more fully if students are able to be responsible for their own education.

. . .

The incredible energy which students have needs to be channeled constructively. "Freedom is the oxygen of love and truth and learning." We have to find ways . . . for the constructive outlet of student concern.

. .

Most places are so rigid you can work twenty years and not effect much. Here {at St. Mary's} you have an opportunity and unformed potential. . . . There is a growth situation before you in a beautiful setting with excellent facilities. This is an exciting place to be. I hope you will create something that will offer experience, models, and data needed to build the new kinds of higher education.

—Source: Transcribed comments of Dr. J. Renwick Jackson, Jr., at the Council on Academic Development, 4–6 September 1968, 8, 12, and 13 January 1969, 11–12.

visors in 1968–1969, and this forty-year-old Presbyterian minister brought vast and varied experience to the office of president. After earning a bachelor of arts and a doctor of divinity degree from Westminster College in Pennsylvania, a B.D. from Princeton Theological Seminary, and a Ph.D. in history from the University of Edinburgh, Dr. Jackson had worked for *Newsweek* magazine, had been a pastor at several churches, and had taught history, philosophy, and religious studies from New York to Hawaii. His administrative experience was gained as dean of students at York College, of the City College of New York; as president of the Ecumenical Foundation for Higher Education in Metropolitan New York; and as associate director of national program development for the National Conference of Christians and Jews.

Dr. Jackson's eclectic interests and boundless energy shaped an ambitious presidential agenda. This former peace protester, cosmopolitan academic, and educational visionary was determined to make May Russell's new campus reverberate with the excitement of intellectual vitality. Committed to the liberal principles of social justice in an age of activism, President Jackson had, by his own admission, "looked all over the country for a place that was politically ripe" before accepting the post at St. Mary's. Inheriting a respectable, albeit conventional, curriculum and a modern physical plant from his predecessor, Dr. Jackson was able to focus his energies on educational experimentation and to transform the school into his vision of it as "a poor man's Swarthmore."

As President Jackson assumed his duties in September 1969, there was a noticeable changing of the guard and a transition to a new era in the history of St. Mary's College. He was the school's first male president and the only man since Mr. Meany in 1846 to be its chief executive. Dr. Jackson's high starting salary of $22,500 partially reflected the fact that he was also the first president in the school's history to bring a growing family onto the campus. He and his wife, Elizabeth Knox Jackson, and their four young children were the first "first family" to occupy the recently-acquired President's House. (The Alumni Lodge, which had served as the presidential residence for twenty-one years, again became the campus guest house.) There were also changes on the Board of Trustees, as Trustees Broun, Radcliffe, and Mullikin followed President Russell into retirement, after serving twenty-eight, twenty-one, and fourteen years, respectively. Mrs. William S. Morsell, Jr., was reappointed to a six-year term, and three new trustees—Frank J. Barley of California, Judge Philip H. Dorsey of Leonardtown, and Dr. Merriam H.

Trytten of Silver Spring—joined the Board at the beginning of President Jackson's tenure.

As the first male and first non-Marylander in an office that had had only three chief executives in the last sixty-nine years, President Jackson faced the challenge of quickly introducing change to an institution that was already experiencing the disruptiveness of lost continuity. Not since the mid-nineteenth century had St. Mary's embarked on a new mission with a new curriculum and a new chief executive all at once. Adele France's Junior College had succeeded because of the stability of the traditional Seminary high school, and May Russell built St. Mary's College of Maryland on the solid foundations of the Junior College. Now, however, there were no other divisions to fall back on, and the past reputation and long history of the Seminary could not ensure the viability of the senior College. In trying to preserve some continuity with school traditions while promoting large-scale innovations, Dr. Jackson pledged "to conserve the authentic values of the past, to be relevant to the crises of the present, and to pioneer the new higher learning of the future."

Nothing illustrated the problems that were inherent in the new institution better than Dr. Jackson's pres-

The *"St. Mary's Female Seminary"* road-marker, which still stands at the entrance to the old campus, took on a significance in the transition years of the late 1960s and early 1970s. The new College had a bright future but was still immature, retaining many programs and policies from the Junior College era. (*Cartoon from the* Alumni Newsletter, *Fall 1968.*)

idential inauguration during a weekend of festivities on 3–4 October 1970. The inauguration ceremony–the first in school history–had been postponed one year, due to more pressing concerns and the inductee's predeliction for perfection in hosting public events of this type. Student pageants would not do for this occasion, and President Jackson emphasized his ties to elite scholarly circles by inviting eminent historians to deliver the major addresses of the weekend. Two Harvard Ph.D.s– Wilcomb E. Washburn, of the Smithsonian Institution, and Robert D. Cross, president of Swarthmore College– delivered speeches on the future of liberal arts education and received honorary degrees from an institution that had yet to grant its first B.A. Although the presence of such academic "nobility" brought credibility to both the new president and the new College, there was much campus criticism about the cost, timing, and practicality of the inauguration ceremonies. Anticipating some of the difficulties that lay ahead for Dr. Jackson, criticism focused on his apparent emphasis of style over substance and of idealism over pragmatism. Faculty members, who had refused to wear academic regalia for the inauguration, feared the emergence of an "imperial presidency" at St. Mary's–a term then current in describing Richard M. Nixon. Dr. Jackson defended the inauguration as "a splendid communal event that can unite the college community in a fresh determination to develop the potentialities of this place."

Growing Pains

President Jackson's rhetoric truly reflected the kind of rare optimism that had motivated the early Maryland colonists to grasp opportunity in a frontier of chaos at seventeenth-century St. Mary's City. Chaos was back at the old capital city, as the new College faced serious problems that would sorely test the president's optimism. In September 1969, sixteen new faculty members still did not have approved contracts, several key administrative positions remained unfilled, and the College had not yet received furniture for twenty-nine offices. This school in transition did not award degrees or issue catalogs in either 1969 or 1970, and students had to consult the campus newspaper to learn of the most recent decisions on graduation requirements– many of them retroactive. Only two years away from granting its first B.A. degrees, St. Mary's continued to offer secretarial science courses that Adele France had instituted, and the home economics room in Anne Arundel Hall would not be renovated into the present physics laboratory until 1971. The library was 75,000 volumes under minimum standards, and many students, who were now paying $1,200 per year for tui-

tion, room, and board, wondered if they were getting their money's worth. The lack of adequate facilities was exacerbated by a tripling of the enrollment between 1968 and 1971. Freshmen outnumbered seniors by 500 percent, classes were grossly overcrowded with up to 200 students, and the many young, first-time faculty members faced enormous problems of adjustment. But the upperclassmen had the greatest concerns, because they would receive bachelor's degrees before St. Mary's achieved final accreditation as a four-year institution. Considering this chaos, it was not surprising that student attrition skyrocketed; of the 217 freshmen who matriculated in September 1967, 79 percent would not graduate in 1971.

Students did not hesitate to voice their complaints and challenges to the new administration–to a degree unthinkable in May Russell's day. There was some residual discontent from the former president's last two years, which now merged with the growing radicalism of Vietnam protest that reached St. Mary's following the Kent State Massacre in May 1970. But most of the student discontent grew out of the disruptive campus environment, and impatient critics demanded the beneficial results of change, instead of just the rhetoric of change. Feeling victimized by an administration that represented too much authority and not enough direction, and outraged by issues ranging from international racist conspiracies to the high cost of dormitory washing machines, a vocal minority of St. Mary's students presented the first challenges to President Jackson during the spring and fall semesters of 1970. *The Point News* accused the president–whom it called "The Messiah"–of forcing students "to conform to his way of educational thinking." The student press circulated information on drugs, drug busts, anti-war protests, and civil rights issues, and distributed a three-page mimeographed essay called "The Student as Nigger." In Fall 1970, the first of a growing number of underground newspapers appeared, satirizing the president. Coinciding with a campus strike by work-study students in the library, the state's rejection of supplemental funds for the College, and persistent rumors of alleged mismanagement in the business office, *The Clam* listed fictional Jackson budget requests for: "A white charger . . . to ride at official ceremonies," "Publishing the first 152 volumes (*Infancy*) of [his] autobiography," and "50 'I Like Gentle Ren' buttons." In an accompanying lexicon of Jackson catch-phrases, the underground student editor defined "partnership" as "a vision of all sectors of the College cooperating like a horse and rider, with the College President being symbolized by the rider," and "participatory democracy" as "a form of government in

which everyone is given the right to agree with all official policy."

Despite or because of the sometimes savage attacks by students who doubted the sincerity of his motives, Dr. Jackson did attempt to address many of their concerns during the energetic and enthusiastic early days of his presidency. St. Mary's enrolled only nine full-time black students in 1969–70 (up from one the year before), and Jackson made widespread racial integration a top priority. Consistent with his beliefs in the "mutuality" of decision-making, he appointed an All College Council and Long-Range Planning Committee com-

The vocal defiance of student activists and the genial apathy of nonconformist "flower children" were the two extremes represented in the St. Mary's undergraduate population of the early 1970s. National collegiate trends in these turbulent times exacerbated St. Mary's difficult transition into a mature senior college.

posed of faculty, students, and administrators. His commitment to off-campus and hands-on learning opportunities was expressed in plans to develop College programs in cooperation with the St. Mary's City Commission (historical archaeology), the Smithsonian Institution (history), and the Harry Lundeberg School of Seamanship (marine biology). Although administrative practices did not always correspond to stated principles, President Jackson in fact liberalized the strict and dated student regulations by terminating dormitory curfews, permitting the consumption of alcoholic beverages by those of legal age, allowing students to reside off campus, and initiating a college-wide referendum on other problems. The president and trustees also instituted a Student Bill of Rights, which stated that "the college does not stand *in loco parentis* for its members; that the rights of the individual and the institution are guaranteed; that members of the campus have the same rights and responsibilities as all citizens; that the campus is not seen as a sanctuary from the general law; and that persons have the right to be heard and considered at appropriate levels of decision making."

The faculty and the administration also addressed the curricular confusion that had provoked many stu-dents to transfer in disgust during the critical years of institutional transition. In the 1971–72 academic year, social science became the College's sixth major (joining art, biology, English, history, and mathematics) and quickly emerged as one of the most popular. This gave more balance to the course offerings, which were grouped—then and now—in innovative, integrative, and interdisciplinary "divisions," rather than in traditional and disjointed departments. Designed to give students a coherent and multi-disciplinary view of humankind's physical, social, and artistic "environments," these divisions were Natural Science and Mathematics (majors in biology and mathematics), Social Science (majors in history and social science), and Humanities (majors in art and English). In 1971–72, the fourth and final division was added—the forerunner of the present Division of Human Development. Called simply "Division Four" when created, this new division was designed to integrate "all aspects of campus life having to do with the generation of a living-learning environment which is open, creative, and developmental in character."

The early seventies proved to be an exciting period of educational experimentation and curricular flexibility, as St. Mary's partly anticipated and partly responded

Former trustees—(from left) Kent R. Mullikin, Adm. Felix Johnson, Sen. George Radcliffe, William Aleck Loker, and R. Bascom Broun, Jr.—discuss campus expansion with President Jackson in the early 1970s.

to the student demands being heard across the nation. President Jackson and the College faculty promoted curricular flexibility by instituting Independent Study tutorials, designing a new three-week Winter Term of special topic seminars in January 1971, and encouraging a high percentage of experimental classes—almost one-fifth of all courses offered in the 1971–72 school year. At the same time, traditional grading standards were relaxed in an effort to focus students more on the joy of learning than on the pressures of numerical rankings. Under the new system of the early 1970s, only A, B, C, and "Credit" grades were recorded on official transcripts, and no quality point averages were computed. St. Mary's students were permitted to elect a Credit-No Credit option for one course per semester, and they could drop classes at any time during a semester without incurring grade penalties.

The Light At the End of the Tunnel
These and other changes during the 1971–72 academic year showed that the presidency of Renwick Jackson had

emerged from its turbulent beginnings. The difficult transition to a baccalaureate institution had been accomplished, and the College finally had the essential programs and policies in place to assure its stability—at least temporarily. By the end of 1972—the high-water mark of the Jackson presidency—St. Mary's College of Maryland would achieve a significant level of institutional maturity for the first time.

One critical test of the stability and maturity of the new College was how successful it would be in producing graduates, not merely in attracting students. On Saturday, 29 May 1971, St. Mary's College of Maryland awarded its first baccalaureate degrees—thirty-five bachelor of arts and thirteen bachelor of science diplomas—and began a new, and continuing, tradition of May commencements. The ceremony was held on State House Green, and William V. Shannon of *The New York Times* was the commencement speaker. Although the small number of graduates revealed the high rates of student attrition that had resulted from the disruptive years of transition, the very fact that commencement was held

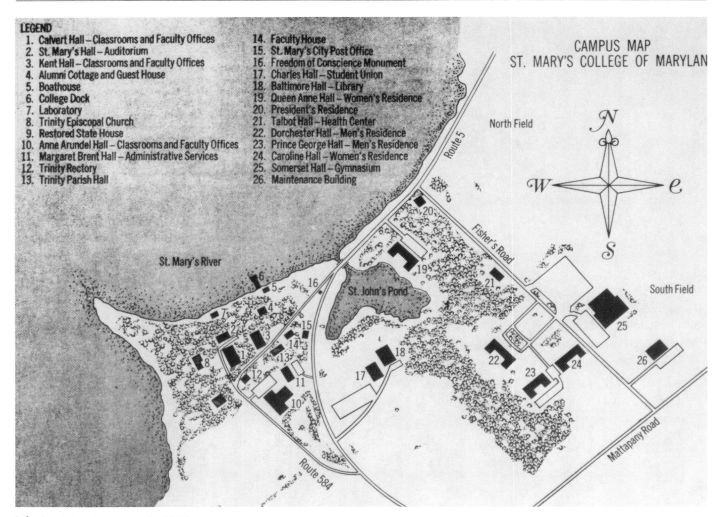

LEGEND
1. Calvert Hall – Classrooms and Faculty Offices
2. St. Mary's Hall – Auditorium
3. Kent Hall – Classrooms and Faculty Offices
4. Alumni Cottage and Guest House
5. Boathouse
6. College Dock
7. Laboratory
8. Trinity Episcopal Church
9. Restored State House
10. Anne Arundel Hall – Classrooms and Faculty Offices
11. Margaret Brent Hall – Administrative Services
12. Trinity Rectory
13. Trinity Parish Hall
14. Faculty House
15. St. Mary's City Post Office
16. Freedom of Conscience Monument
17. Charles Hall – Student Union
18. Baltimore Hall – Library
19. Queen Anne Hall – Women's Residence
20. President's Residence
21. Talbot Hall – Health Center
22. Dorchester Hall – Men's Residence
23. Prince George Hall – Men's Residence
24. Caroline Hall – Women's Residence
25. Somerset Hall – Gymnasium
26. Maintenance Building

CAMPUS MAP
ST. MARY'S COLLEGE OF MARYLAN

The St. Mary's campus in 1972.

on the earliest date in St. Mary's history signaled better relations between the administration and student body. During the previous fall, the graduating class had requested that commencement be held in May instead of the scheduled date in June, and the president and trustees agreed to accommodate the seniors, even though classes would still be in session. The rapid development of the College was reflected in its second commencement, held on Saturday, 27 May 1972. The graduating class was twice as large as the year before, with 102 students receiving their degrees (79 B.A. and 23 B.S.)—a proud moment witnessed by Dr. May Russell, the commencement speaker.

Nineteen-seventy-one and 1972 were banner years for St. Mary's in many other ways as well. The College's comprehensive, ten-year Master Plan, which would receive the unanimous approval of the Maryland Council for Higher Education on 1 March 1974, finally emerged in 1972 after years of deliberations by all segments of the campus community. The Master Plan represented continuity with the most sacred traditions of the Seminary and Junior College, in proposing that St. Mary's always remain a small and affordable liberal arts college—an educational alternative to both large universities and expensive private schools. Since excellent teaching was central to the "mission" of St. Mary's under the Master Plan, school officials sought to ensure career-long professorial productivity, vitality, and dedication by abolishing faculty tenure on 1 July 1971. According to the *Washington Post,* St. Mary's was "the nation's only college to do so successfully." Professors who had achieved tenure, here or elsewhere, before 1971 could keep it, but for increasing numbers of faculty members at St. Mary's, tenure was replaced by a contract system, which is still in operation today. Under the contract system, instructors received a two-year, then a three-year, and then a series of five-year teaching contracts, pending satisfactory performance as judged by divisional promotion and retention committees, a College-wide review committee, the dean/provost, the president, and the Board of Trustees. Yet another key development that would help make the Master Plan a reality was the creation in 1972 of the St. Mary's College of Maryland Foundation, Inc. With roots in the nineteenth-century attempts to begin a private endowment for the Seminary, "The Foundation" finally became a reality after State Senator J. Frank Raley, Jr., (a College trustee since 1966) sponsored legislation in the General Assembly that would permit such an organization at a public college. Pledged to "enhance, improve, and develop . . . St. Mary's College of Maryland and to benefit that institution, its students and faculty," this

The Mulberry Tree Papers

In the spring of 1972, President J. Renwick Jackson, Jr., inaugurated the publication of *The Mulberry Tree Papers* and even served as its first editor. Lieutenant-Governor Blair Lee III introduced the inaugural issue by writing: "These papers serve as reassuring evidence that St. Mary's will continue along the path of a liberal arts college, limited in size but unlimited in her striving for excellence. . . . I hope that *The Mulberry Tree Papers* will flourish for many years to come, providing both enlightenment for its readers and continuing proof of the vitality of the spirit of St. Mary's."

This publication, named by the historically-minded Jackson for the famous old tree that was a landmark to the first colonists at St. Mary's City, has indeed fulfilled the high expectations that the president and the lieutenant-governor had for it. Under editor Gordon Kester (1977–1986), *The Mulberry Tree Papers* won four citations for achievement in collegiate publications from the Council for Advancement and Support of Education. In 1978, the magazine was the national Grand Award winner in the Publications Improvement category. The January 1990 "Sesquicentennial Issue" was the largest and most lavish issue to date, as *The Mulberry Tree Papers* approaches its twentieth anniversary still keeping the staff, students, alumni, and friends of St. Mary's apprised of history in the making.

independent, non-profit corporation has greatly facilitated the donation and distribution of private funds in support of College programs.

Although those developments were essential to the maturation of St. Mary's College, they would have mattered little if accreditation had not been attained. The Commission on Higher Education of the Middle States Association of Colleges and Universities granted the first accreditation to the senior College in 1972. However, the accreditation was merely provisional and valid for only two years, because the visiting evaluators were disturbed by the discrepancies they found between the plans and the performance of the College's administration. After a thorough review of the ninety-page "Institutional Self-Study" and on-site inspection between 13–17 March 1972, the Middle States team reported "a situation in which the only constant is change itself." The "lack of direction and the constant shifting

Trustee J. Frank Raley, Jr., one of the last of May Russell's trustees (appointed in 1967) who is still on the Board in 1990. "J. Frank," a St. Mary's Countian with family ties to the nineteenth-century Female Seminary, continues the tradition of dedicated service to the school by local citizens. As a state senator in the mid-1960s, he sponsored the bill to change the name to St. Mary's College of Maryland and helped to generate larger budgets for the school and to preserve its independent Board of Trustees.

to the future had been accomplished in a few short years at a school still experiencing growing pains. Dr. Jackson had fashioned St. Mary's into a distinctive institution, with change and innovation as the source of its energy. The symbolic pendulum had swung far to the left, at some distance from the conformist center of the academic world. The youthfulness of the institution had allowed such radical experimentation, while in many ways the youths of the time demanded it. Change, often disruptive, would continue to rule at St. Mary's, but in a different direction. As invariably as the pendulum swings back, toward the center and the right, so, too, do educational experiments adjust to the national mood and changing times. Unfortunately for all too many committed faculty members at the College, the swinging pendulum that was the institutional mission suddenly switched direction, moving from left to right, from idealism to pragmatism after 1972, and pushed them through the swinging doors of terminated employment.

After the high-water mark of 1972, all hell broke loose at St. Mary's. Almost constant controversy reverberated on campus between 1973 and 1977, and there

of emphases and priorities," wrote the evaluators, "appear to be underlying causes for the widespread dissatisfaction among students and faculty and are, no doubt, contributory factors in the high turnover rate of faculty and the high attrition rate of students." They further observed that mere "enthusiasm" for "an exciting intellectual experience" counted for little unless it was tempered by patience and supported by consistent administrative follow-through. In their final report, the Middle States evaluators wrote that "the differences between the professed philosophy of administration and certain administrative actions has caused considerable controversy on the campus, resulting in a lack of faith and trust. . . . The President professes the principle of collegiality and tries to maintain a low profile to guide unobtrusively, but when decisions are made or actions taken by him, the authority of the office is challenged."

Swinging Pendulum, Swinging Doors

Probably both the College and President Jackson deserved better evaluations from the Middle States Association in 1972. Much that was significant and relevant

Mrs. William S. (Aurine) Morsell, Jr., member of the Board of Trustees from 1960–1982 and a Foundation board member since 1972.

were so many separate challenges to administrative decisions that they became a seamless tapestry of crisis and confusion. Most of the conflicts were precipitated by unpopular personnel decisions and all involved the erosion of campus confidence in the beliefs and behavior of the president. Looking back at that era in a February 1982 article in the *Empath,* students Barbara Shaeffer and Gretchen Sorensen wrote that "from 1972 to 1974, President Jackson attempted to alleviate some of the problems caused by the supposed excess of freedom at St. Mary's. Apparently, the progressive faculty Jackson had hired, described as a 'really freaky crew' by *Empath* editor Pat Elder, had gotten out of hand." Dr. Richard Stark, professor of mathematics and president of the Faculty Senate in the mid-1970s, likewise observed that Jackson "really brought in a group of radicals and liberals who wanted to remodel education. I think he went too far in his first attempt to establish a progressive school, and . . . [then went] too far in trying to get rid of all the progressives."

In Dr. Jackson's own view of those years, published in Jim Brady's *Washington Post* interview with him on 21 July 1982, he observed that the first phase of his presidency, through 1972, "were wonderful days of people doing their own things brilliantly." However, his innovations took on a dangerous momentum: "[I] had to dissuade a group of students from designing a class around a pregnant student who wanted to give birth in her dormitory. Then, in 1972, an advertisement appeared in *Rolling Stone* [the rock music magazine] offering a teaching job at St. Mary's. 'No degree necessary,' it read, 'just experience with The Movement.' That's when the governor called me in." Forced to abandon his early, preferred roles as "'an enabler, a recruiter, a nurturer,'" he recalled becoming a more authoritative–his enemies claimed "authoritarian"–chief executive after 1972, which helped precipitate the many conflicts and controversies that followed. Because he had brought success and momentum to the young College in transition despite his critics, this man of the pulpit was more inclined to trust his own instincts and to inflict righteous wrath on those who did not share the certitude of his visions.

The preconditions for the confrontations of the mid-1970s extended back to May Russell's presidency, for although the college had avoided legal liability in the civil suits of 1968, issues involving faculty rights, responsibilities, and job security remained largely unresolved five years later. The tensions between the administration and the faculty were exacerbated by the rapid growth of the instructional staff and the equally dramatic rates of attrition during President Jackson's first few years. The faculty grew from thirty-six in 1969–70 (average age: thirty-five) to fifty-two in 1971–72, but to obtain that net increase of sixteen teachers, a total of *forty-two* instructors had to be hired between September 1969 and September 1971 to replace the twenty-six who departed. In January 1972, twenty of the fifty-two professors were in their first teaching jobs, and the entire faculty had a mean length of service at the College of only 3.2 years. St. Mary's benefited from an academic

Campus Drug Bust, 1973

June 14, 1973

Dear Friends of St. Mary's College:

In the early morning of May 16, officials of the Maryland State Police came to the campus to serve warrants on four students who allegedly have been selling marijuana and hashish to residents of St. Mary's County. As the police were attempting to serve their warrants, an unidentified person gained access to the public address system in Prince George's Hall and began to urge residents to obstruct the officers. Subsequently, two state troopers were temporarily blocked into a student's room; a small number of students, no more than two dozen, began to throw rocks at police cars; approximately 125 other students gathered to watch developments; the police called for additional troopers and attempted to quell the destructive students with tear gas pellets.

. . .

While it is important that we take careful measures to prevent the recurrence of events of this kind on campus, it is equally important that this particular incident should be seen in proper perspective. The disturbance lasted no more than two hours; academic activities continued normally; only a very small number of students were involved; damage to College property was limited almost exclusively to broken windows; only six students were received at the College Infirmary after the incident, and those on an outpatient basis for minor eye and skin irritation; the full supervisory services of the College, including the Dean of Students and his staff, the Dean of Administration and his staff, and I, were continually on the scene well into the morning hours to ensure that events did not get out of hand. Finally, the rumor that a 'horde of hippies' would come to the campus for a 'smoke in' proved to be unfounded.

Sincerely yours,

J. Renwick Jackson, Jr. {signed}

–Source: Mimeograph on letterhead stationery; Loose Papers, College Archives.

buyer's market in which talented Ph.D.s were both available and affordable, but the very abundance of qualified professors, coupled with the abolition of tenure in 1971—the ultimate safety-net of job security—made the faculty very vulnerable to shifting administrative priorities. The dropping of tenure had produced a "predictably stormy" reaction from the St. Mary's faculty. Although the contract system can be a workable substitute for tenure (as it has generally been in the 1980s), it requires the utmost faculty confidence in, and the accountability of, top administrators, who must scrupulously adhere to the doctrines of fairness and due process.

President Jackson and the St. Mary's faculty locked horns in Spring 1974 over the real or imagined "purge" of the instructional staff, as he and his critics struggled to distinguish progressive reform from harmful change. At issue was the administration's refusal to renew the contracts of Dr. David Porter, a popular but outspoken associate professor of political science, and James H. Hayes, an instructor of humanities, despite the positive recommendations from the faculty retention committees. Whereas President Jackson said that he was "replac[ing] those he thought were impeding progress," his faculty critics, frustrated with their subordinate position and relative impotence under the contract system, found his actions abusive, arbitrary, and designed more to silence opposition than to improve instructional quality. Charging serious irregularities in due process, including allegations of presidential bullying

A stern-faced, not-so-gentle Ren.

to obtain the negative decisions on Porter and Hayes, the faculty, in what the president regarded as the "May Massacre" (15 May 1974), voted 36–14 to censure Dr. Jackson and 29–19 on a resolution of "no confidence"—in effect a request for his resignation or non-renewal of his contract. The Board of Trustees investigated the faculty complaints, and considered as well the recent criticisms of the administration in yet another report from accreditation evaluators of the Middle States Association, but a majority of the Board rewarded President Jackson with a new three-year contract.

The battle was rejoined in the fall semester of 1974, as numbers of returning students, dismayed over the

"They Won't Forget Us"

We won't forget it.

We didn't arrive together. For some, St. Mary's was the only school. For others, just the last. For some, 1975 was year four. For others, year five or even six.

We saw changes, and we changed. We ventured into an old college, but one that was new. Just recently turned a four-year school, St. Mary's was struggling with an identity crisis. It developed as we developed. Its formative years were ours.

There were events. They busted us, and we rioted. They fired our teachers, and we protested. They sold us beer on campus, and we drank it.

We saw a student government die, and be reborn. We saw a newspaper fold, and be unfolded. We saw a radio station finally emerge.

There were traditions. A bath in St. John's Pond for a

birthday. Waterfront day. A lacrosse game on a sunny afternoon.

We worked, and we played. We laughed, and we cried. We loved, and we lost. We grew.

It became a way of life. Springtime on the water. Lolling in the sun. Thursday nights. And all-nighters during finals week to compensate.

Then it was over. For some, too soon. For others, not soon enough.

We left one experience for others. We traded books and friends for paychecks and bosses. We left a leisurely stroll to class on a long path for a crowded journey through life on a hazardous road.

They wished us well, and we left in style.
They won't forget us.

Brian Murphy 1975

—Source: *The Castellan* 1974–76.

Porter case and angry about paying a new $165 instructional fee (up 650 percent from the year before), now supported the faculty in expressing deep distrust of President Jackson's leadership. Despite the fact that the extra $140 they paid in instructional fees funded faculty salary increases, students expressed solidarity with their teachers in opposition to the administration. The atmosphere of contentiousness was exacerbated by Dr. Jackson's refusal to release the full details of the Middle States accreditation report of 1 June 1974. Although St. Mary's finally received long-term accreditation, which was good news indeed, the visiting evaluators continued to have serious reservations about administrative performance—so much so that they recommended the appointment of an independent provost to serve as a buffer between the mutually mistrustful president and professors. On 7 October 1974, the faculty urged the Board of Trustees to appoint someone they trusted—Dean of the Faculty Fred S. Honkala—to the new post of provost. However, only one month later, Dr. Honkala left the College, alleging sustained conflict with, and increasing "verbal abuse" from, President Jackson, who was already on record as saying that "one of the College's

primary problems is that there are too many [faculty members] who want to be chiefs, . . . and not enough who are willing to be Indians."

Ironically, the position of provost, originally proposed as a solution to campus conflict, now exacerbated the problem. Dr. Manning M. Pattillo, Jr., an experienced, respected administrator, left the University of Rochester in late February 1975 to become the first provost at St. Mary's. Provost Pattillo helped turn faculty suspicions to full-blown paranoia when, after only three months in office, he issued negative judgments on the retention or promotion of several professors he barely knew and then abruptly resigned on 21 May to accept the presidency of Oglethorpe University in Atlanta. The administration overruled the faculty's positive recommendations on colleagues in six of twenty-five cases for retention, two of three cases for tenure (involving teachers hired before July 1971), and seven of nine cases for promotion. The student press alleged that Pattillo had already known of his imminent departure to Oglethorpe when he arrived at St. Mary's, and critics charged that President Jackson had specifically recruited Pattillo to be his designated "hatchet-man."

In the midst of campus crisis, President Jackson initiated the first Governors Cup Yacht Race in August 1974. This overnight sailboat race down Chesapeake Bay, from the present capital in Annapolis to the original capital at St. Mary's City, was the brainchild of SMC student sailors Dale Rausch '71, Pete Sarelas '74, and Russ Baker '75. Described as the largest sailing race on the East Coast and as "summer's most breathtaking sight," the Governors Cup is today an enduring tradition enjoyed by thousands—few of whom recall the controversies of 1974.

The 1975–76 academic year promised to be just as stormy, as both the Faculty Senate on 15 September and the full faculty on 24 September issued stinging rebukes of administrative decisions on personnel during the previous spring-time of discontent. Although they threatened unionization and A.A.U.P. investigations, the faculty was somewhat mollified by the appointment of Dr. Harriet D. Hudson, a well-respected dean at Randolph-Macon Women's College, as the next provost. From September 1975 to June 1978, she brought greater respect, efficiency, and stability to that office. The faculty was also pleased with the Fall 1975 reinstatement of Andrew Chovanes as assistant professor of sociology (albeit with the loss of tenure), following his 1973 conviction and incarceration for growing marijuana. A popular, effective instructor and former acting dean of students, Chovanes had become a *cause celebre* because President Jackson and Provost Pattillo had strongly opposed his reinstatement. But in this instance, the Board of Trustees supported the hundreds of students who had circulated petitions in Chovanes's behalf and the dozens of faculty colleagues who had donated funds for his legal defense.

These two positive developments, however, had to be balanced against the continuing high attrition of discontented students and staff members. Morale at all levels was becoming a serious issue, as the *Empath* reported that 328 of the 382 students who entered St. Mary's in the fall of 1971–86 percent—had not "persisted" until graduation in May 1975. Moreover, the student paper on 3 September 1976 listed fourteen *faculty* departures in a very moving "Gone . . . But Not Forgotten" feature, complete with photos of the most popular teachers who were leaving. On the inside page were the names of sixteen new faculty members and administrators who had arrived, like military replacements, to take their turn at the battlements. Continuing this theme, senior Clay Evans, Jr., presented a stinging public rebuke of the administration's personnel policies at commencement ceremonies in May 1976. The newness of the College was no longer a sufficiently valid excuse for the fact that freshmen still comprised 42 percent of the student body in 1975–76 and the faculty still suffered from constant turnover. Student Will Foreman observed that "this place is like a train station, it's constant come and go. The faculty are afraid of losing their jobs, while we're concerned with the quality of our education."

The following academic year (1976–77), there were new challenges to the administration based on old grievances of the faculty and students. It was clear to the critics that the swinging-door employment practices now stifled rather than stimulated enthusiastic and creative educational experimentation, and they sought to challenge the previously "unresponsive" Board of Trustees into taking some bold and beneficial action that would justify its independent status.

The focal point of confrontation in the spring of 1977 was the administration's decision not to renew the contract of Dr. Christopher Wilson, professor of physics and chairman of the Natural Science and Mathematics Division. Dr. Wilson was the last of the division chairs still in office who had supported the faculty's 1974 "no confidence" vote against President Jackson. The president's critics charged him with seeking retribution in a "vendetta" against Wilson—a personnel decision that was perhaps too personal and the latest in a long line of faculty ousters that collectively signaled a challenge to academic freedom. The *Empath* reported that thirty witnesses, including Provost Hudson and all but one member of the Natural Science Division, had testified on Wilson's behalf during a ten-hour session with the trustees in January—but to no avail. Faculty members collected thousands of dollars for Wilson's legal fund, but officially they rejected angry confrontation with the Board, favoring a "limited strategy" of discussing their grievances with the trustees. Student activists were in no mood for accommodation, however, and quickly

Members of the Blackistone family assemble on 31 May 1975 for the campus dedication of the "Blackistone Memorial Room" in Anne Arundel Hall, which has since become a popular meeting and reception area for a variety of College functions. The commemorative plaque reads: "In Memory of Mrs. Jennie Smith Blackistone, Class of 1892; Martha Morris Blackistone Orme, Class of 1932; Anne Woodall Blackistone Labat, Class of 1937." In this photo, the woman at the far left is Virginia ("Gina") Cross Blackistone, a Junior College graduate of 1935 and subsequently alumni editor of The Mulberry Tree Papers.

A Message from the Class of 1976

President Jackson, members of the Board of Trustees, distinguished guests, members of the faculty and administration, members of the Class of 1976 and their families, ladies and gentlemen. On behalf of the Class of 1976 I welcome you to St. Mary's College and thank you for joining us in this celebration of our academic achievement.

St. Mary's College has given us more than an education; it has given us four years of pleasant and lasting memories. In the years to come, we will become even more appreciative of the College's pastoral setting, with its broad expanses of playing fields and its proximity to the river. Perhaps this natural setting will be for many of us as Tintern Abbey was for Wordsworth, a place of natural beauty by which to measure our spiritual progress.

. . .

The most important effects of the education we have received here must be measured in personal terms. . . . The best teaching we received came from those teachers who taught not only their subjects but also their lives—those teachers who were honest enough and courageous enough to allow us into their private lives where we could see them as real people. These teachers taught us the meaning of courage and rectitude. We know because we watched them fight injustice and indifference. We learned something from them about being human; and we learned something about the world we live in when we saw them lose their jobs. The

professed aims of the College were given life through these teachers and we the students could have believed those in authority had these teachers been given places of honor. Instead, we, like the students of Socrates, are left to question the wisdom of those in authority who would rid the College of such fine teachers in a manner that indicates hypocritical disregard for the College, the students, and their own words.

We have observed those in authority at the College well, and they have taught us what to expect in the world. We will see the rules of justice bent to serve self-interest; we will be lied to; our appeals for redress will be disregarded. We will be dismissed as immature, we will be told that we do not understand. We will see those in whom we have expressed no confidence remain as leaders against our will. We will see public relations take the place of meaningful actions, and finally we will see the public agony of those who are so driven that they will not have the grace to resign.

We have learned much about how far apart words and actions can be. We take with us a knowledge of duplicity—a knowledge that hopefully in the privacy of our hearts will lead us to the opposite and contrasting knowledge of private honesty and truthfulness.

—Source: Commencement remarks by Clay Joseph Evans, Jr., Class of 1976, as excerpted from *The Empath*, IV, No. 1 (3 September 1976), 1, 6.

mounted forceful protests in an effort to convince the Board of Trustees not to renew Jackson's own contract, which was to be reviewed that spring. In late February 1977, the Student Government Association Senate unanimously voted "no confidence" in President Jackson and in March held a referendum, which registered a vote of 630–26 against renewing the president's contract. Students kept up the pressure, organizing rallies and reportedly even vandalizing the President's House. On 24 March, Dr. Sheldon Knorr, Commissioner for Higher Education in Maryland, conducted an on-campus investigation of the controversy surrounding President Jackson, reputedly at the direct request of Governor Marvin Mandel. However, Dr. Knorr was unable to report his findings, due to the governor's illness, before 23 April 1977—the day the Board of Trustees voted 9–1 to renew the president's contract until 30 June 1981. Three days later, on Tuesday, 26 April, St. Mary's students made a desperate, last-ditch effort to dissuade Dr. Jackson from *accepting* that contract, as an estimated crowd of 200 to 250 boycotted classes and

On 26 April 1977, President Jackson was called out of his office by some 200 students. This rally—the last hostile campus protest to date—failed to dissuade Jackson from accepting a new contract.

held a rally outside the president's office. This angry April "March on Calvert Hall" was reminiscent of the boycott and rally directed at May Russell a decade before, except that President Jackson did not call the police—he addressed the crowd of hostile critics! Neither rampant dissatisfaction nor Professor Wilson's subsequent moral victory (a 1980 out-of-court settlement of $32,500) could persuade President Jackson to leave office. Confident of riding out this storm as he had done with previous ones, the president accepted the new contract from the Board of Trustees on 5 May.

The Winds of Calm Conformity

Few critics of the administration doubted President Jackson's capacity for surviving the storms of controversy, but no one could have predicted the eerie but welcome calm that quickly descended over the campus following the confrontational spring of 1977. The "March on Calvert Hall" proved to be the last angry protest rally by St. Mary's students to this day, and relations between the president and faculty improved as well. In retrospect, it seems that similar national trends anticipated this sudden shift at St. Mary's, as a rising, self-interested "me generation" of undergraduates finally outnumbered the earlier student activists who knew and cared about Vietnam, Woodstock, and Watergate. Student radicalism had come late to St. Mary's and took its time leaving, but the spring revolt of 1977 was the grand finale for the politically committed "long-hairs" and "pot-heads."

Apart from national trends, there were factors unique to St. Mary's that explain the sudden calm on campus. The most committed student critics were overtaken by exhaustion, frustration, and, especially, graduation late in the spring semester, and the departure of dedicated activists like Bill Schladt and SGA President Will Foreman in the Class of 1977 left a void that would not be filled in the following academic year. Another important factor was the genial apathy of the undergraduate majority—that sizable percentage of professional partyers who had seen education as recreation and had always "done their own thing," ignoring, and

The "March on Calvert Hall," 26 April 1977—the last major student demonstration at St. Mary's College. This collage of photographs appeared in the Buford times, *which was described as "a one-time effort created and distributed by the St. Mary's College Journalism II class," on 19 May 1977. "Buford" was a much-loved dog that served as a campus mascot in this era.*

ignored by, the publicity of political protest. With improvements in dormitory life and expanded extracurricular activities, more and more students in the late 1970s and early 1980s discovered the pleasurable distractions at St. Mary's, including Spring Fairs, Waterfront Days, and the frequent, near-addictive frisbee golf tournaments sponsored by the "International Bong Association" (IBA).

The rise of recreation as a quasi-religion on this campus was no accident, as President Jackson approved of almost any diversion that would distract students from focused criticism of his administration. Although he genuinely enjoyed attending campus activities in his trademark straw hat, bartending at student affairs, and playing frisbee with dorm residents, he was now in his late forties and had disavowed his earlier idealism about educational experimentation and participatory democracy among students. His campaign to thwart undergraduate activism was illustrated in 1976–77 by his determined opposition to student representation on the Board of Trustees and his attempt (unsuccessful) to allow campus security officers to carry revolvers. Although he agreed to let the seniors select speakers for commencement in 1977, it was only with the firm assurance that the public addresses would not vilify him or condemn his administration as had been the case in 1976.

Yet another, and most significant, factor in shifting the campus mood away from radical activism was the new emphasis on academic rigor and the return of traditional grading standards. With careerism increasingly important across American campuses in the late 1970s, St. Mary's reinstituted the "D" and the "F" in the fall of 1976 and began computing cumulative quality point averages to determine which students deserved academic distinction or dismissal. Conventionality had indeed returned to this College with such potential for innovation. President Jackson himself scuttled a popular proposal for a new field studies program (the "Montana Project"); began hiring older, more experienced professors with tenure; and even tried (unsuccessfully) to reintroduce a tenure system at St. Mary's. Calm conventionality returned to the College after 1977 at some cost to educational innovation and academic creativity. The trade-off was a mixed blessing. The school became less idealistic and less exciting than it had once been, but it was also less bloodied and disrupted by constant battles.

Nineteen-seventy-seven was yet another turning point in the history of St. Mary's, after which the College reestablished continuity with its traditional strengths and adopted a skeptical view of change for

Construction sites proved undaunting to frisbee golfers.

change's sake. The school was henceforth not as progressive as it had once tried to be, but at least its maturing, experienced faculty was more focused on, and successful in attaining, dramatic results in all of the established criteria of academic excellence. Between 1977 and 1981, the stability and continuity of the faculty increased substantially; twenty-three of the current professors (about one-third of the total) were hired in this period. Many came as young Ph.D.s and progressed through the ranks under a series of contracts without ever experiencing a tenure system. They also never experienced the drastic and disillusioning swings of the pendulum, having known neither the most visionary, nor the most vindictive, side of President Jackson in earlier years. However, they did encounter a still-charismatic chief executive, who was capable of stimulating their efforts in pursuit of "the mission" to realize the old potential of the new College.

This stabilized faculty, in turn, helped stimulate the record enrollments of more accomplished students, who flocked to St. Mary's as an affordable alternative to the increasingly expensive private liberal arts colleges. Operating above normal dormitory capacity, the College in the fall of 1977 enrolled 268 freshmen, whose mean verbal score of 453 on the Scholastic Aptitude Test placed them first among Maryland's public colleges. Matriculating freshmen had a composite mean SAT score of 949 in Fall 1979 and 971 the next year; every entering class since then, with the exception of Fall 1981, has produced higher averages than previous matriculants. More importantly, despite the new grading standards St. Mary's students were actually staying to graduate—182 in 1979, 194 in 1980, 169 in 1981, 170 in 1982, and 215 in 1983. Every graduating class after 1979 had a valedictorian based on quality point average, and beginning in 1977, the College instituted an annual awards ceremony (since 1980, called the Honors Convocation) to recognize students' academic achievement and leadership.

St. Mary's College began to generate a focused momentum again after what seemed like a wild goose chase of shifting priorities earlier in the 1970s. The school was still innovative—and certainly inexpensive—enough for most students, and the professors had a renewed sense of the wonderful, albeit less idealistic, potential of this still-young College. The news media responded with favorable publicity for a change, especially regarding new extracurricular activities and community-oriented events. In the midst of crisis in April 1977,

The solitude of venerable Calvert Hall reflected the calm conventionality that returned to the St. Mary's campus after 1977.

President Jackson had observed that "in the welter of other and spicier news about campus goings-on, solid accomplishments at the College are often overlooked by the news media." However, the press could not long ignore St. Mary's consistent rankings among the nation's top ten sailing and canoe/kayak teams, or the All-American honors accorded to three students, or the popular and rewarding Tidewater Music Festival, or the new Charlotte Hall Fellowships for county high school students, or the enormously successful Governor's Cup Yacht Race inaugurated in 1974. Between 1978 and 1981, the College sponsored stimulating and popular public symposia on China, the Soviet Union, and Islam; initiated a long and still-fruitful study-abroad program with the Centre for Medieval and Renaissance Studies at Oxford; opened a $4-million fine arts center (Montgomery Hall), which has stimulated new majors in music and theater and developed into an enriching cultural resource for the surrounding community; and instituted a highly selective Honors Program that has since attracted some of Maryland's brightest students to this campus. In those same years, two distinguished scholars were members of the St. Mary's faculty—Dr. Melvin H. Jackson, former maritime curator of the Smithsonian Institution, and Professor David Beers Quinn, former chairman of the department of history at the University of Liverpool, author of more than fifty books, and considered the world's authority on the early colonization of North America. In the 1977–78 academic year, these eminent scholars collaborated on a successful College lecture series that featured internationally-known speakers and resulted in the publication of a notable collection of essays, entitled *Early Maryland in a Wider World*.

The Storm After the Calm

In August 1979, an obviously pleased President Jackson observed that "St. Mary's has completed its most successful year ever. . . . The spirit of collegiality . . . is growing—one can see and feel it—and it is this spirit that will accelerate the process of transforming our good college into an excellent one." Ironically, the spirit of collegiality that helped nurture, and was nurtured by, an atmosphere of calm, steady progress on campus did not depend on, or extend to, President Jackson himself. Only two and a half years later, he would suddenly vanish, resigning his office quickly and cleanly once the Board of Trustees rallied behind the faculty and students. But an even broader and deeper sense of collegiality survived, indeed thrived, without him, evolving into a renaissance of the spirit at St. Mary's that is with us still.

Montgomery Hall Fine Arts Center (or "Kennedy Center South"), dedicated as part of Maryland Day festivities on 23 March 1980. This $4-million building provided 34,600-square feet of floor space to the Division of Arts and Letters and quickly became a rich community resource for art exhibits, musical performances, and theatrical productions. The terra cotta frieze seen above the north portal was copied from the Parthenon of ancient Athens ("Lord Elgin's marbles") by Princeton University in 1888 and resided on that campus until Professor Jonathan Ingersoll procured them for St. Mary's in 1973.

In the fall of 1981, President Jackson seemed tired and distracted, perhaps bored with the administrative routine at a school that was progressing all too predictably toward goals that were no longer visionary or especially challenging. Like a sailboat, the College now had the wind in its sails and was moving along in smooth waters with less need for a restless, creative navigator to keep a constant watch. The president seemed incapable of pursuing objectives to their logical conclusion before losing interest. One new initiative seemed to intrigue Dr. Jackson—a unique interdisciplinary institute for seventeenth-century Chesapeake studies—but after the plan received enthusiastic support from several influential scholars, he inexplicably killed the idea by clumsily trying to circumvent its approval by the faculty. Untypically, he did not fight for passage of the proposal, and the plan was aborted. That same semester, a state auditor's report was highly critical of administrative procedures, and President Jackson successfully defended himself against a charge of driving while intoxicated. But the old fire was gone, and concern mounted across campus that something was amiss.

On 5 December 1981, President Jackson publicly declared to the Board of Trustees that the "college had had a most successful semester; . . . everyone worked well together . . . and the morale on campus was op-

timistic." But he must have known how faculty confidence had plummeted in a few short months amid unmistakable signs that the distant, distracted president was not providing strong or consistent leadership. Jackson belatedly confirmed what campus rumors had already suggested—that he had fallen in love with Dr. Alison Baker, his vice-president for academic affairs, who was in her first semester at the College. As he told the *Washington Post:* "'Facing a long relationship with Alison, there wasn't any way we could continue at St. Mary's. I had told some of the board that I was getting ready to go.'" Once the president's "pilgrim heart and mind began to dream of new challenges," as he put it, there was no shortage of faculty members, students, and even trustees most anxious to ease him out of office expeditiously, with a minimum of public controversy. Considering their scars from past personnel disputes, the faculty was especially concerned with the potential for a conflict of interest in the president's sexual relationship with the academic officer designated as the faculty's advocate and official liaison to the president.

Everything came to a head soon after the Spring 1982 semester began. On 26 January 1982, the faculty issued a nearly unanimous resolution, stating forcefully but ambiguously that the teaching staff was "concerned about the present situation at the college." The reason for this "concern" was news to some of the trustees, and the faculty selected a special committee of five to discuss matters with the Board in more detail. On Friday, 5 February, an all-campus meeting attracted about 250 people to St. Mary's Hall, where a consensus was

Ethel "Chancie" Chance retired in 1980 after thirty-two years of service to St. Mary's—originally as May Russell's secretary and later as the head nurse at the Infirmary.

reached that the time for a change in leadership had arrived. Facing restrained but persistent opposition from old enemies and former friends, most of whom were less concerned with his moral lapses than with his administrative ones, President Jackson submitted his resignation in time for the regularly scheduled meeting of the Board of Trustees on Saturday, 6 February 1982. On that bitterly cold day in Annapolis, the trustees met most of the morning with campus constituencies and unanimously accepted the resignation when it became clear that this scandal was subverting administrative efficiency and academic progress. Vice-President Baker would resign a month later (effective 15 May 1982), and both departing administrators received a large financial settlement from the College. In fact, the resignation agreement worked out between Dr. Jackson and the Board, with the advice and assistance of Derick Savage, of the Attorney General's Office, and Dr. Knorr, of the Board for Higher Education, officially placed the president on a one-and-a-half year sabbatical leave with pay ($44,683 per annum) until his contract expired on 30 June 1983.

The Legacy of Renwick Jackson

In a farewell statement following his resignation, ex-President Jackson wrote that "Elijah left the world in a chariot of fire. And there is a Viking tradition of going out to sea in a fiery boat. My years at St. Mary's have had fire and intensity. . . . My service to St. Mary's has been an act of love. It is meet and right that my departure moves on the powerful tides of the mysteries of profound love." In a 21 July 1982 interview with the *Washington Post,* Dr. Jackson said that "if the criticism [of his administration] is that I was not an implementer of dreams, the record proves that's untrue. If the criticism was that I had more dreams than I could implement, I plead guilty."

Renwick Jackson's twelve-and-a-half year presidential administration was a microcosm of the St. Mary's experience, in which change and continuity exist as equally valuable attributes. As a historian, he appreciated and continued the College's traditions as a state-owned, independently administered, affordable, nonsectarian school of the liberal arts. But he also envisioned an especially idealistic new future for the College with the optimistic certitude of a clergyman. Jackson's early dreams were daring—similar to those of former St. Mary's leaders who offered ambitious curricula when there were too few teachers, planned buildings when the funds were not there, and took it on faith that students would come. But dreams are extremely disillusioning without administrative consistency. It was hard

to reconcile Jackson's words with his deeds; some good dreams were never implemented for lack of administrative follow-through, while others that became reality were later disavowed. Where did he stand on issues? Although his presidency was the shortest of this century up to that time, there were three distinct and contradictory periods in Jackson's twelve and a half years. The idealistic intensity of 1969–1972 produced laudable creativity at St. Mary's, but the subsequent period of retrenchment between 1973–1977 engendered a mean-spirited atmosphere of repression and retribution that sapped vital energy from the institution at a critical time. In the third phase of the Jackson presidency (1978–1981), the College found the mid-point between the extremes of radical idealism and reactionary pragmatism and made notable progress according to most of the accepted benchmarks of academic respectability. The president's final flirtation with unorthodox behavior, however, proved unsettling for a campus community that was by then fond of stability, conformity, and conventionality.

In the end, President Jackson brought stability and continuity to this campus—and he was destroyed by his own creation. It was ironic that in the same month that Jackson resigned, St. Mary's College was listed among the 265 "best and most interesting four-year institutions in the country" in *The New York Times Selective Guide to Colleges* by Edward B. Fiske (who had been the commencement speaker in 1976). That recognition brought the College one step closer to fulfilling Dr. Jackson's belief that it could become "the poor man's Swarthmore." Equally ironic is the fact that the school's subsequent progress has resulted largely from the talented faculty that the former president recruited and did not purge. In 1988–89, forty-five of the ninety-eight staff members with faculty rank came to St. Mary's during President Jackson's tenure.

Years earlier, at the beginning of the Jackson presidency, Dr. Ralph C. Baxter, then chairman of the Division of Humanities, wrote, with pun definitely intended, that "it takes an eagle's eye to see ahead and a wren's cunning to get there." Ren Jackson certainly had cunning, and he relished its use to generate chaos—which he asserted, was the "proper temper for creative endeavor." The chaos of the seventeenth century had indeed produced opportunity for the strong and the lucky in old St. Mary's City. But was Ren's cunning chaos necessary to maximize opportunities for the struggling new College, or was it a costly distraction from more consistent development? Did he grow unpopular because of his radical innovations, or did academic experimentation become unpopular because of him? Would

Dr. Jackson's Official Statement

Released, 8 February 1982

I am grateful for the adventure we have shared in the development of a public college that embodies the finest qualities of the best private liberal arts institutions.

I am grateful, too, for the confidence of the Board of Trustees and the support it has given to my leadership since 1969. The strong personal bonds of love and understanding which we have established have infused this mission with an extraordinary quality of friendship that is rare in public institutions.

That quality of friendship has characterized relationships with colleagues and students as well. A spirit of celebration and laughter and shared commitment has given grace and elan to our daily activities.

When it became clear that we had accomplished our primary goals at St. Mary's—the building of a distinctive institutional model in public higher education and an effective utilization of the democratic process to establish idealistic public policies and to implement them—my pilgrim heart and mind began to dream of new challenges. For more than a year, I have thought my time at St. Mary's was drawing to a close.

Next week, as I begin my sabbatical, I will take on a new task as senior consultant with the American Association of State Colleges and Universities in Washington, D.C. My project will be to design, in radically new forms, a curriculum of the 21st century.

I trust that what we've accomplished at St. Mary's will be confirmed in the future, and that the quest for excellence will continue to go forward. I extend my best wishes to all of my colleagues in that endeavor.

Dr. J. Renwick Jackson, Jr., first male president of St. Mary's College of Maryland, 1 July 1969–6 February 1982; B.A., D.D., Westminster College (Pennsylvania), B.D., Princeton Theological Seminary, Ph.D., history, University of Edinburgh. Portrait by Peter Egeli, 1981.

this College be more daringly progressive and creative today if the rhetoric of participatory democracy had been allowed to become reality? Did St. Mary's prosper because of, *or despite,* Renwick Jackson's leadership? These are significant questions that another historian will be better able to answer on the 200th anniversary of St. Mary's College of Maryland. That this institution will surely have a 200th anniversary to celebrate is in part owing to that zestful, vengeful, charismatic, and complex president who was once so committed to making the Monument School a great college of the future.

Pragmatic Idealism: 1982–1990

After the temporary interruption caused by President Jackson's last crisis, the St. Mary's campus returned to an atmosphere of calm, competent conventionality under the interim presidency of Dr. Richard D. Weigle. The sixty-nine-year-old former president of St. John's College (1949–1980) and a St. Mary's trustee since

1976 stepped down from the Board on 6 February 1982 and served as the institution's first interim president until 30 June 1983. This internationally respected educator came out of retirement to restore stability and respectability to St. Mary's. Dr. Weigle virtually volunteered his invaluable services (earning only $6,000 annually, the maximum allowed under the Social Security laws) to assist staff and students in putting negative publicity behind them and in refocusing their energies on concrete, achievable goals for this College. President Weigle's administrative experience and ability brought the school through the latest of its transitions with ease and contributed to the College's maturity and enhanced reputation as it prepared to select a new, permanent chief executive. St. Mary's had come far in a turbulent decade and was finally ready to reap the benefits of a long-promised but much-deferred bright future.

On 1 July 1983, a new era began at St. Mary's College of Maryland when Dr. Edward T. (Ted) Lewis became its third president. Selected from 200 applicants after the most extensive and intensive executive search in the College's history, Dr. Lewis represented, in the words of Dr. Weigle, "a rare combination of teacher, humanist, administrator and effective advocate." The forty-nine-year-old father of two teenage sons had obtained his B.A. from Union College (New York), an M.A. from Boston University, and a Ph.D. in English literature (Shakespeare studies) from the University of Denver. His credentials in the humanities were well established by teaching literature, writing poetry, and editing journals, but his diversified career also took him to

the Graduate School of Business and Public Administration at Cornell University, where he served as associate dean for nine years. As an administrator at that prestigious university, Dr. Lewis played an influential role in fund-raising and curriculum development—both of which St. Mary's desperately needed in 1983.

When he arrived on campus, Dr. Lewis accurately deciphered the mixed legacies of the two immediate past presidents and quickly determined that he would have to combine the strengths of the pragmatic builder, May Russell, with those of the idealistic innovator, Renwick Jackson, in order to prepare St. Mary's College

Dr. Weigle on the Liberal Arts

As president of St. John's College, Annapolis, and overseer of that school's unique "Great Books" curriculum, Dr. Richard D. Weigle had impeccable qualifications for assessing a liberal arts education. In his commencement address to the St. Mary's Class of 1975 he said:

Liberal arts are skills, liberal or liberating skills, skills of the mind. . . . A liberal arts education is a broad and versatile education which should enable students to successfully tackle anything she/he comes in contact with.

. . .

Knowledge advances and the fundamental outlook of man may change over the centuries, but these liberal arts of understanding remain in one form or another indispensable. They enable men to win knowledge of the world around them and knowledge of themselves in this world and to use that knowledge with wisdom. Under the guidance {of the liberal arts}, men can free themselves from the wantonness of prejudice and the narrowness of beaten paths. Under their discipline, men can acquire the habit of listening to reason. A genuinely conceived liberal arts curriculum cannot avoid aiming at these most far-reaching of all human goals.

. . .

Whether each of you has succeeded in these four years is not attested to by the diploma you are about to receive, but rather by your own quiet assessment of how well you meet certain criteria which seem to me to measure a liberal education. . . . Do you respect reason and do you have confidence that dialectic-reasonable conversation and communication between rational men and women can arrive at solutions to problems and can approach the attainment of truth?

I hope your four years at St. Mary's College of Maryland enable you to share my conviction that the liberal arts

college is hardly archaic and my faith that it can and will provide a paradigm for the future.

–Source: *The Mulberry Tree Papers*, Vol. II, No. 1 (Fall 1975), 10.

Dr. Richard D. Weigle, the first interim president in the history of St. Mary's, 6 February 1982–30 June 1983; B.A., M.A., Ph.D., Yale University, plus ten honorary doctorates. President Emeritus of St. John's College, Annapolis and Santa Fe, and a member of the St. Mary's Board of Trustees, 1976–present.

Changing Times

{F}or some elusive yet quintessential reason, I am still very attached to the quiet beauty of Southern Maryland and the close-knit community that is St. Mary's College. . . . I came here in a typically freshman daze that lasted two years. Going to college and socializing became synonymous. Rather than books, I concentrated on saying "hi" to everyone I met on the path, talking until four in the morning, . . . joining every club on campus, drinking five cups of coffee after dinner, . . . attending sideline lacrosse parties right on the field, playing frisbee golf, listening to . . . Marshall Tucker—and, oh yeah, 16 credits a semester. Fall semesters featured . . . Halloween, bonfires on Church Point, and the Winter Formal. Springtime meant Spring Fair Weekend, swimming and sailing in the river, and being thrown in the pond.

. . .

Being back at St. Mary's after just a year's absence {at the Centre for Medieval and Renaissance Studies, Oxford}, I found what seemed to me a myriad of differences. More students, at earlier ages, seemed to be finding interest in their studies as well as their parties. The library had begun to draw larger crowds than the Snack Bar. . . . The campus as a whole seems a lot less noisy, a bit more conservative. Occupational drinkers have left campus for the glamorous two-bar strip in downtown Park Hall. . . . No longer is there a proliferation of sweat pants; people dress up more often. Lacrosse games are now held in the stadium, where spirited fans are kept a safe distance from the game.

The dorms are being carpeted. The drinking age has gone up. And in the past two years I have not seen one person thrown into the pond.

. . .

I have found myself in the paradoxical position of longing for the spontaneity of old, casual St. Mary's, while simultaneously helping to create a more structured environment. . . . Until lately many of the school's policies and procedures have been fluid, written in sand so to speak. . . . The past year and a half {December 1981—May 1983} has seen the emergence of more stability throughout the College{:} . . . the adoption of a new faculty governance document, a new Student Government Constitution, and a Code of Student Rights and Responsibilities.

Having been at least peripherally involved in all these changes, I have learned to deeply appreciate St. Mary's and what it has to offer. . . . My experience in Oxford was, again, invaluable. But a truly liberal education allows one to learn how to learn in a way that a more narrowly-focused education cannot. Our liberal arts mission as a small, public college, the history of our setting, the heritage of our "Woodstock South" years, and the beauty of the river all add up to the "quintessential reason" that St. Mary's College is such a special place for so many of us.

—Source: Mary Beth Brady '83, "Reflections of a Senior," *The Mulberry Tree Papers*, Vol. X, No. 2 (Fall 1983), 16–17. (Ms. Brady graduated with honors as a dual major in English and mathematics.)

for the multi-faceted challenges of the twenty-first century. President Lewis's varied academic and administrative experiences prepared him to do both, and on his first weekend as a campus resident, he previewed the pragmatic idealism that has come to characterize his administration. Addressing the Alumni Association on 11 June 1983, the president-elect emphasized the need to spread the gospel that a liberal arts education was "the most practical of educations" for the modern world. His genuine enthusiasm for one of the College's most enduring traditions surpassed that of his predecessors, as he proceeded to change the public's perceptions of the liberal arts rather than altering the school's curriculum to offer faddish vocational courses. Dr. Lewis's other major priority was fund-raising, especially from private sources, to supplement state support for critical campus needs. If the public were to accept St. Mary's as an excellent alternative to private liberal arts colleges, the facilities and the faculty had to be first-rate. The College

had to offer an equivalent educational experience that was affordable, not cheap, and private funding was essential for providing new scholarships and academic programs as well as improving the physical plant.

The new president proved to be a quick study with regard to the political realities and business climate in Maryland, and his emphasis on practicality and efficiency was apparent when he held a series of statewide public receptions instead of an expensive, formal inauguration ceremony. Dr. Lewis's sobering predictions of tighter budgets and hard decisions reflected the pragmatism of the planner, while his confident conviction that St. Mary's could achieve national prominence in public liberal arts education reflected the idealism of the dreamer. Planners and dreamers would have to co-exist, indeed cooperate, at every level if St. Mary's were to revitalize its physical plant, revise its curriculum, and recruit superior faculty and students.

Although the president set the agenda and estab-

"1984"

Nineteen-eighty-four did not fulfill the chilling prophecy of George Orwell's novel; rather, as the year of Maryland's 350th anniversary, it became the source of celebration for the freedoms so long enjoyed at St. Mary's City. Tens of thousands of citizens came to this birthplace of toleration to enjoy pageants, fireworks, historical exhibits, and the ceremonial visit of the Duke and Duchess of Kent. But this state birthday party was unlike any previous ones. Since the 1934 tercentennial, American society had extended the liberal Calvert legacy to more citizens than ever before in finally addressing racial, cultural, religious, and sexual discrimination.

Recent decades had also produced invaluable new research on seventeenth-century social history, so that scholars appreciated the past pioneers of the Maryland legacy better than ever before. With the old capital now a focal point for researchers from around the world, St. Mary's College and the St. Mary's City Commission hosted an international scholarly conference of unprecedented scope and significance—"Maryland: A Product of Two Worlds." Between 17–20 May 1984, several hundred historians, archaeologists, archivists, and interested citizens gathered on campus to learn of the latest research on the early Chesapeake. The distinguished list of participants included James Axtell (William and Mary), Bernard Bailyn (Harvard), T. H. Breen (Northwestern), Nicholas Canny (Galway), Lois Carr (St. Mary's City Commission), Cary Carson (Colonial Williamsburg Foundation), Peter Clark (Leicester), James Deetz (Berkeley), Richard Dunn (Pennsylvania), Jack P. Greene (Johns Hopkins), Allan Kulikoff (Princeton), Russell Menard (Minnesota), Edmund Morgan (Yale), Edward Papenfuse (Maryland Hall of Records), David Quinn (St. Mary's), Joan Thirsk (Oxford), and Wilcomb Washburn (Smithsonian). Selected papers from this conference have been published in Lois Green Carr et al., eds., *Colonial Chesapeake Society* (Chapel Hill, 1988).

lished the goals, all segments of the campus community were involved in implementing his initiatives. In annual addresses to the faculty, President Lewis promised an administration that would be frank, fair, and open, and his repeated emphasis on the essential role that the faculty would play in the development of the College accorded long-overdue respect to the professors, thus helping to heal the wounds of past controversies. He also recruited experienced administrative specialists to deal with budgeting, fund-raising, campus planning, curriculum development, student recruitment, public relations, and other highly technical tasks in an increasingly complex institution. This delegation of authority and the building of continuity in certain key staff positions prevented President Lewis from trying to do everything himself, as his predecessors had attempted to do, and allowed his administration to move forward on several fronts at once.

In his six years at St. Mary's, President Lewis has established ambitious expectations and demanding standards of performance for all members of the campus community. He has emphasized a new image for St. Mary's, but it is an ideal image with a surprising amount of substance behind it. He has observed that when he assumed the presidency, "St. Mary's was undoubtedly better than its reputation; today {September 1988} the opposite may be true." By setting goals that seem impossible to fulfill and providing incentives to the campus community for surpassing the most optimistic expectations, President Lewis has replaced mediocrity with productivity and dispelled complacency with a refreshing new spirit of momentum that is infectious.

In 1983, the number one priority for President Lewis and the Board of Trustees was curriculum reform.

President Ted Lewis gives a warm greeting to President Emerita May Russell on "May Russell Day," Homecoming Weekend, 6 October 1984.

Reaffirming St. Mary's 143-year commitment to liberal arts education, the new president wrote that "the curriculum identifies and defines the institution . . . [and] will determine, in fact, how we survive, or if we survive." After two years of dedicated effort by faculty, administrators, and trustees, the Board on 16 March 1985 unanimously approved a new General Studies curriculum that the faculty had developed. It was described as a positive change for the future because it re-established continuity with a traditional past, requiring students to complete a sequence of interrelated core courses in the humanities (Western Legacy I and II, Introduction to Literature, and Philosophical Inquiry) and to fulfill other specific requirements in English, mathematics, arts history, creative expression, and the physical, biological, behavioral, and policy sciences. Several major field programs were revised as a result of these changes, but four features of Ren Jackson's old curriculum have been retained at St. Mary's—the unique grouping of academic disciplines into four divisions, the unique four-credit courses, independent studies (tutorials), and internships in off-campus learning.

Dr. Robert Strider, past president of Colby College and a consultant with the Association of American Colleges, observed that the new curriculum brought St. Mary's "into the mainstream of American education" by providing more structure, coherence, and focus in the liberal arts coursework required of its students. He said he "wouldn't be at all surprised if . . . other colleges look at St. Mary's when they decide to review their programs." The "giant step" that curriculum reform represented was recognized in 1987 when the National Endowment for the Humanities awarded the College a grant of $171,000 to develop its humanities sequence in more depth and breadth. At the same time, the Board of Trustees authorized new majors in philosophy and chemistry and approved a five-year plan for curricular enrichment, to include the funding of endowed chairs, increases in scholarship and faculty development support, and a $2-million endowment for library materials. Most recent curricular developments include the Board's approval of a self-designed major for exceptionally motivated students and the state's sponsorship of an eminent scholar's program, beginning with the appointment of poet Lucille Clifton as distinguished professor of literature for the 1989–1991 academic years.

A revised curriculum would be only as effective as the professors who gave it life in the classrooms, and sweeping reforms soon addressed faculty morale, attrition, and compensation. When President Lewis arrived in 1983, the St. Mary's faculty was the lowest paid in

The Poets of St. Mary's

The peaceful charm and idyllic beauty of the St. Mary's campus have always proved conducive to the writing of poetry. Mrs. Maria Briscoe Croker, a Seminarian in 1891, was named the first official "Poet Laureate" of Maryland by Governor J. Millard Tawes in 1959. Combining her love of poetry and history, this St. Mary's County native published her first poem, "Mt. Vernon," in the *Baltimore Sun* and wrote "Land of the Singing Rivers" to commemorate Maryland's tercentennial in 1934. Mrs. Croker served as associate editor of *The Spinners,* a New York magazine, and was a member of the Poetry Society of America and Penwomen. Other Seminary poets were Henrietta ("Etta") Coston Lockner '92, author of the 1895 "Alma Mater," and Eleanor B. North, who wrote the "Daughters of St. Mary's" in 1944.

More recently, Professor Michael Glaser has placed St. Mary's in the forefront of regional poetry during his twenty years at the College. He organized the Festival of Poets and Poetry, which has convened annually here since 1979, and has run the annual Ebenezer Cooke Poetry Festival since 1977. Glaser has published two volumes of poetry: *A Lover's Eye* (1989) and (editor) *A Cooke Book: A Seasoning of Poets* (1987), containing selections from the Ebenezer Cooke Poetry Festival. Professor Glaser has inspired students for two decades by attracting notable poets to this campus. In 1981, one of America's leading poets, William Meredith, came to St. Mary's as a Woodrow Wilson Visiting Fellow. He shared his inspiration with the College community and allowed *The Mulberry Tree Papers* to publish three of his poems.

St. Mary's rich poetic tradition was stimulated anew with the recent appointment of Lucille Clifton as visiting distinguished professor of literature for the 1989–90 and 1990–91 academic years. Ms. Clifton's volumes of poetry have thrice been praised in Pulitzer Prize citations, and in 1979, she was named the state's "Poet Laureate." Formerly a Woodrow Wilson Visiting Fellow on campus, she is the first Eminent Scholar appointed at St. Mary's under a new state program.

the state system, but in only three years' time, it became the highest paid among public colleges in Maryland. Between 1983 and 1989, the mean salaries for all ranks increased by 70 percent, and in that latter year, the average compensation for all ranks rose to $44,600. The General Assembly supported large annual increases in merit pay because the St. Mary's professors, rated as "the finest teaching faculty in the State system" by the State Board for Higher Education, had also demonstrated an enormous burst of creative energy in research and scholarly publications. In a five-year period, nine of the seventy-five full-time faculty members had received prestigious Fulbright Fellowships for foreign study (four in 1984 alone). In addition, the faculty received several National Endowment for the Humanities fellowships, a $250,000 research grant from the National Institute of Child Health and Development, and other awards. A dramatic increase in faculty development funds, supplied almost entirely by the St. Mary's College of Maryland Foundation, Inc., supported the research of many professors, several of whom have attained regional, national, and even international recognition as leading scholars in their disciplines. In 1985,

Dr. Norton T. Dodge, professor of economics and a former trustee (1966–1979), established awards through the Foundation to honor faculty members for outstanding accomplishments in scholarship, teaching, and service to the College.

The encouragement and support that the administration gave to the teaching staff helped end the high faculty attrition that had been endemic since the nineteenth century and of epidemic proportions in the mid-1970s. By 1988, the mean length of service at St. Mary's was 7.4 years for all ranks, with full professors averaging 13 years and associate professors 10 years at the College. Today, the experienced full-time faculty, 93 percent of whom hold the highest academic degree in their fields, is still youthful by collegiate standards, averaging 42 years of age for all ranks and only about 50 years of age for full professors. Tenure has not returned, and increasing numbers of talented young Ph.D.s have found that the contract system is no impediment to their advancement.

One important factor in maintaining faculty continuity and longevity has been the significant improvement in the students they teach. Since President Lewis

Alive with the Sound of Music

Although the evolution of a music major at St. Mary's College did not reach fruition until 1975, musical expression has long enriched the campus and surrounding community. The Seminary Junior College Choir achieved a strong regional following throughout the 1950s and 1960s and in March 1949 appeared on an early television broadcast (WBAL-TV Baltimore). President Renwick Jackson encouraged the formation of the now-famous St. Mary's College Jazz Ensemble in 1971, under the inspired leadership of Professor Bob Levy, who remained its director until 1979. Because the College lacked a music major, the first Jazz Ensemble supplemented its eight student members with eleven community players, including a middle-aged Navy officer and an eighth-grade saxophonist (John Long) who later became a professional musician. The Jazz Ensemble frequently played at national invitational music festivals and was the catalyst for campus visits by artists like Count Basie, Maynard Ferguson, and Stan Kenton. Ensemble alumni have presented reunion concerts at Homecoming twice in the past ten years.

In 1972, the St. Mary's music faculty instituted

The Tidewater Music Festival and Summer Music Camp, which has given talented adolescent musicians the opportunity to study and perform with great American composers like Aaron Copland and Alec Wilder. This program stimulated the development of a music major at the College in 1975. In November 1980, the new major achieved the rare distinction of being accredited by, and earning associate membership in, the National Association of Schools of Music on its very first application. Acclaimed for the quality of its faculty over the years, the music program reached a new pinnacle of achievement in December 1989 when Brian Ganz, musician in residence and head of the piano faculty, was named co-winner of the prestigious Marguerite Long International Piano Competition in Paris. The musicians of St. Mary's also added a special dimension to the 150th anniversary on 9 July 1989, when the St. Mary's Tidewater Chamber Players premiered William Thomas McKinley's "When the Moon is Full," a composition commissioned by the College in celebration of its sesquicentennial, at the Baltimore Museum of Art.

St. Mary's, as Seminary, Junior College, and College, has regarded sports as recreation, an important adjunct to studies, but only an adjunct. Although the school offers intercollegiate competition in several varsity sports, it awards no athletic scholarships and continues to emphasize intramural activities.

In competition with other schools, the teams of St. Mary's—known over the years as the "Retrievers," the "Saints," and since 1984 as the "Seahawks"—have, not surprisingly, fared best in the water sports. As the unique feature of this campus, the St. Mary's River has accommodated generations of Seminarians and collegians in the enjoyment of swimming, rowing, sailing, and most recently, windsurfing along its tranquil shores. The College waterfront took on added importance in the life of this school with the building of The Boathouse, a gift of the Alumni Association in 1964, and the inauguration of the Governor's Cup Yacht Race in 1974. The annual August yacht race stimulated a growing interest in competitive sailing at St. Mary's and inspired generous supporters to donate a veritable fleet of boats to the school. The sailing team has been consistently ranked as one of the nation's top ten for the past fifteen years, and St. Mary's varsity sailors have received coveted All-American honors four times—Monte Spindler and Scott Steele in 1979, Steele again in 1981, and Pete McChesney in 1986. Steele also won the silver medal in board sailing (wind-surfing) at the 1984 Summer Olympic Games in Los Angeles.

The women of St. Mary's, true to the school's origins, have likewise distinguished themselves in competition. The swimming team has won the Chesapeake Women's Athletic Conference championship in each of its three years of competition. Even more notable was the performance of Julie Croteau, who became a national media celebrity in Spring 1989 as the first woman to play NCAA varsity baseball. She earned All-Conference Honorable Mention as a first "baseman" and was honored as "Sportsman of the Week" on the 20 March 1989 *Today Show* broadcast.

assumed office, the mean composite Scholastic Aptitude Test scores of entering freshmen have risen nearly 180 points (956 to 1132), giving St. Mary's the highest scores among all Maryland public institutions for five consecutive years. In the same period, mean SAT scores for Honors Program freshmen rose from 1180 to 1350, including a one-year increase of 60 points for the entering class in Fall 1989. That tenth anniversary Honors class of fourteen contains eleven students who received National Merit commendations, indicative of their ranking in the top 5 percent of all American students taking the SAT, and five of them were also designated as Maryland Distinguished Scholars on the basis of exceptionally high grade point averages.

Early in his administration, Dr. Lewis observed that "one of the objectives of the College is to become a meritocracy and to attract the best students in the State of Maryland." The school in general and the Honors Program in particular have taken great strides in accomplishing that goal. But St. Mary's aims to have an excellent student body with a difference—one that blends diversity with quality—by offering educational advantages to undergraduates of all cultures, colors, creeds, and economic conditions. The College can achieve that goal because it still embraces a long heritage of affordability and continues its traditional commitment to providing generous merit scholarships. Of the $1.6 million in total financial assistance that the College awarded in 1989–90, 36 percent was in the category of merit scholarships—contrary to the prevalent national trends. Merit scholarships include, among others, the Margaret Brent-Leonard Calvert Fellowships for Honors students ($210,000 annually) and the Mathias de Sousa Fellowships for minorities ($210,000 annually), both of which awarded between $2,000 and $5,900 to each successful applicant in 1989–90. The Monument School of the People still serves the people well, keeping Maryland's talented youth in state for their educations and providing many first-generation college students of modest means with a true alternative to elite, expensive liberal arts institutions. Despite necessary increases in tuition, room, board, and fee charges for in-state students, from $4,185 in 1983–84 to $6,300 in 1989–90, St. Mary's remains a bargain in higher education today, especially considering that comparable private colleges cost two to three times as much.

Impressive progress has been made in both student recruitment and student retention as the reputation of St. Mary's finally caught up with its momentum. The Admissions Office reported a significant increase in the number of inquiries from interested students, from 6,500 in 1983 to 12,000 in 1988. Applications and enrollments have risen correspondingly, as the number of full-time students grew from 1,110 to 1,310 in those years (1,585 counting part-time students). At the same time, however, St. Mary's became much more selective in the students it accepted for admission. The College accepted 554 (or 79.3 percent) of 699 freshman applicants in 1983 and 616 (61.5 percent) of 1,002 freshman applicants in 1988, but only 507 (39.7 percent) of 1,277 freshman applicants in 1989. Minority enrollment for all class years increased to 10.1 percent of the total full-time student body in Fall 1989, with twenty-nine black freshmen comprising 12.8 percent of their entering class. Only two decades after the matriculation of the first full-time black baccalaureate student in 1968, there were ninety-one full-time black students at St. Mary's. Retention rates for all students have also improved dramatically since the disruptive transitions of the 1970s. More than 80 percent of full-time freshmen now regularly return for their sophomore year, and the

College has graduated record numbers of students since 1983, despite an increasingly rigorous curriculum. Between 1983 and 1988, an average of 209 students graduated each May (some 6 percent with dual degrees), and the 246 recipients of bachelor's degrees at the nineteenth baccalaureate commencement in 1989 constituted the largest class in St. Mary's history. (Altogether, 3,291 students have graduated since St. Mary's became a four-year institution.)

Higher levels of student retention, as well as student surveys that rate St. Mary's above all other public colleges in Maryland, have been directly related to vast improvements in campus life. In 1986, the State Board for Higher Education and the Department of State Planning approved the College's five-year, $29-million Master Facilities Plan, which called for the construction of townhouse dormitory units, a new science building, and an auditorium, and the renovation of Calvert, Kent, and Anne Arundel halls. The overcrowding in the residence halls that once greeted every entering class was alleviated in 1987 with the completion of forty

The Townhouse Complex and Daughterty-Palmer Commons, dedicated on 23 April 1988. The townhouses provide housing for 160 students in forty apartment-style suites, and the Townhouse Green is now the site of commencement. The Commons serves as a focal point for campus meetings, concerts, and receptions.

The old Library in Calvert Hall, 1925, a gift of Miss Bessie Kibbie of Washington, D.C., and the new Library as it will appear when completed in 1990.

The Growth of the Library

Unlike lavishly endowed private institutions, St. Mary's has suffered an endemic shortage of library collections and facilities throughout most of its history. The Seminary principal in 1848 "felt [a] great need of books to read to the pupils—I do not think I can continue to furnish them at my own expense." A century later, the school was still spending an average of only $82 per year on new library acquisitions. When the State Department of Education reviewed the Seminary's collections in 1947, it reported that "about half of the [approximately 2,500] books now in the Library . . . have no reason for use in the school" and advised that all science books more than ten years old should be discarded (some dated to 1911). This prompted the trustees to request an immediate $5,000 in state funds for the Library, which was granted, and to budget $500 "for books only" for each of several subsequent years.

In 1958, the Middle States Association was severely critical of the inadequate library, which, although it had moved into more spacious quarters in Anne Arundel Hall, still contained only 5,000 volumes—about half of the minimum required for an accredited junior college. The only positive note was the Maryland Room, which outside evaluators described as "a most noteworthy special collection" and "indeed an asset to St. Mary's."

Although progress was made in acquiring more books, when the new Library (Baltimore Hall) opened in 1969, St. Mary's still had only 25,000 volumes—far short of the minimum 100,000 required for a four-year college. The school had not yet reached that standard ten years later, when the 1978–79 catalog listed collections of 85,000 books and 1,100 current periodicals. Substantial improvement has been made in recent years, however, with the College collections growing to 104,000 in 1984 and to 120,000 in 1989. The new Library addition will provide the space and the incentive to increase holdings to 175,000 by 1994.

apartment-style suites in the $4.5-million Townhouse Complex. This new approach to campus living was funded by a special Department of Education loan that only eleven colleges in the United States received. But the centerpiece of the complex—Daugherty-Palmer Commons—was built through the generosity of former Trustee Jack Daugherty (served 1964–1966), his wife, Kay Palmer Daugherty, and the employees of Maryland Bank and Trust Company. In Fall 1989, a striking new addition to the Library opened as the first phase of a $7-million expansion that will double the space formerly

available in Baltimore Hall. When the project is completed in 1990, the new Library will house a vastly improved book collection, which has grown from about 25,000 to almost 125,000 volumes in two decades, as well as centralized data processing facilities, an expanded audio-visual department, a new learning skills laboratory, the College's first computerized card catalog system, and the venerable "Maryland Room" collection of historical materials, as mandated by the Monument School's founding legislation in 1840.

The quality of life at St. Mary's dramatically improved

in the decade of the 1980s, thanks to the generous support of private and corporate donors. Successful urban entrepreneurs like Meredith Capper and Joseph A. Waldschmitt retired to the solitude of St. Mary's County, recognized the vast potential of its College, and actively served the school as directors of "The Foundation." The St. Mary's College of Maryland Foundation has helped fulfill one of President Lewis's primary objectives—to increase annual giving and to create a large endowment that would facilitate and accelerate the attainment of institutional excellence. Annual giving, which totaled only $85,120 in 1985, increased almost 500 percent to $409,168 in 1988. Contributions of all types, including gifts of personal computers from the Epson Corporation, bequests, and donations of sailboats and artwork, exceeded $1 million in the 1988–89 academic year, nearly a five-fold increase since 1982–83. Less than two decades ago, the largest single endowment at St. Mary's was the Martha ("Mattie") Maddox Key Legacy—$12,200 that had been willed to the school in 1944 by a Seminary alumna whose father (George Frederick Maddox) and husband (Joseph Harris Key) had both been trustees. Since the creation of the Foundation in 1972, however, the College has received substantial and on-going financial support from the Zachariah D. Blackistone Trust (the largest bequest in

school history), the Cremona Foundation, the France Foundation, the Philip L. Graham Fund, Maryland National Bank, and many other institutional and corporate contributors.

In this sesquicentennial year, the College has initiated a $10.75 million Capital Campaign—the first in its history. To raise those funds for vital projects in the second half of its second century, St. Mary's College will have to enlarge its "extended family" of alumni and parents and reach out to the vast numbers of local citizens who have benefited from the school's sponsorship of continuing education programs, summer courses, theatrical productions, learning vacations, scholarly symposia, music festivals, and other special activities. Critical, too, will be the support from the President's Council—the twenty-seven prominent advisers who have given freely of their time, expertise, and financial resources to assist the College since 1986. Of course, the College's own trustees, who have been so critical to the dramatic progress in all areas, remain its most steadfast supporters. Remaining independent after yet another challenge to disband it in 1988–89, the Board of Trustees has been a valuable resource for fund-raising and policy-making under the recent chairmanships of Eleanor Digges Harrington of Cambridge (1981–1986), the first chairlady in history; Rupert G. Curry of

The Science Building Controversy

After two years of preparing a new master plan for campus expansion with the apparent support of the St. Mary's City Commission and local citizens, College officials in the summer of 1989 were confronted by a sudden and united opposition to the proposed location of the new $12-million science building. According to architect Jacquelin Robertson's plan for an academic "tidewater village," the new science center was designed to occupy the hill adjoining Charles Hall and Baltimore Hall (Library) as a key component of a more cohesive and centralized campus. But site selection was criticized as being destructive of the important archaeological, historical, environmental, and aesthetic features of that location, known as "Gallows Green" in the seventeenth century capital. The College commissioned a more intensive archaeological analysis of the site, and its Board of Trustees appointed an ad hoc committee to arrive at a recommendation. This committee sponsored several meetings and public forums with critics, most notably the Historic St. Mary's City

Rescue Coalition, directed by Michael Lynch, a 1981 St. Mary's graduate. After learning that the proposed construction site may contain the remains of the first Protestant church in Maryland, and following some three hours of testimony critical of College plans on 20 July, St. Mary's President Edward T. Lewis decided to choose another location for the science center. In January 1990, it was announced that the present Somerset Hall parking lot along Fisher's Road would most likely be the new site for the building. Although the alteration of the architect's master plan and the delay in breaking ground for the much-needed new facility had proven costly, the Monument School had fulfilled its duty to preserve the "sacred precincts" of the ancient capital. "As a college committed to the preservation of this special place," observed President Lewis, "we can do nothing less." St. Mary's College can be proud of the local alumni from three generations who challenged its decisions and conscientiously upheld enduring principles they learned as students.

Rockville (1986–1988), the first black trustee; and Edward O. Clarke, Jr., of Baltimore (1988–present).

Forever Young—The Magic of St. Mary's

A certain magical vitality has returned to the old school and new College as it celebrates its 150th anniversary. The over-crowded parking lots and the bustle at construction sites contrast greatly with the solitude of the campus woodlands and the broad, quiet waters of the St. Mary's River. The past six years have been a period of unparalleled achievements that may well be regarded as a golden age by subsequent generations. In 1984, the Middle States Association of Colleges and Secondary Schools expressed no reservations in reaccrediting St. Mary's, observing that it had become a "more cohesive, vital, and on-the-move college community that is, in a sense, a new college." A year later, the Maryland Department of Budget and Fiscal Planning agreed with College officials that St. Mary's was "a distinctive college, with a distinctive student body and an outstanding faculty." Large funding increases have been the result of the state's new pride in its oldest educational institution, and bigger budgets have, in turn, helped generate more momentum than ever. As this book went to press, it was announced that the state was planning to increase the College's operating budget by $3.4 million over the next three fiscal years (on top of an 8.6 percent annual increase to $9.7 million for the 1990–91 academic year), which will allow St. Mary's to expand its faculty dramatically.

Few colleges are fortunate enough to celebrate a major anniversary just when things are going well. However, this sesquicentennial, in its sweeping look at the past, reminds us that the present success of St. Mary's is no accident, but rather the product of people, policies, and programs over the course of five generations. The infectious spirit of progressive change has been present before at this special school, with its uncanny capacity to survive adversity and to exceed the most ambitious expectations. President Lewis deserves considerable praise for bringing St. Mary's to 1990 in such excellent shape, but the momentum he has generated and the glowing image of the school that he has nurtured still draw inspiration from Lucy Maddox's traditional Seminary, Adele France's Junior College, May Russell's beautiful buildings, and Renwick Jackson's idealistic visions. To his credit, Dr. Lewis has appreciated the varied legacies of this old school and identified the best of them for preservation and promotion in the College of the future.

Those who have observed St. Mary's College over the past four decades realize that the school of today is the result of evolution, not revolution. However, many outside observers, with little knowledge of the school's long heritage, imply that the College recently burst forth, fully developed, out of nowhere to serve as a valuable model of an alternative, affordable liberal arts education for the twenty-first century. In addition to Edward Fiske's *Selective Guide to Colleges* (1982) and his even more laudatory *Best Buys in College Education,* published three years later, Dr. Martin Nemko issued high praise to St. Mary's based on his experience as an admissions director and nationwide research on colleges. His book, *How to Get An Ivy League Education at a State University* (1988), advised that "if you want a decent copy of an elite New England private liberal arts college that will cost $50,000 less than the original, SMC is worth remembering." The 26 October 1987 *U.S. News and World Report* special issue on "America's Best Colleges" ranked St. Mary's sixth among regional liberal arts colleges in the northeast, based upon a survey of university presidents and observed that it "fills a special niche . . . offering an intimacy not found in most taxpayer-supported schools." Two years later, the *U.S. News and World Report 1990 College Guide* issue of 16 October 1989 ranked St. Mary's *first* among the seventy-four regional liberal arts colleges it surveyed in the northeast, based on academic reputation, student selectivity, retention patterns, faculty quality, and financial resources. The magazine's evaluators wrote: "By remaining small and devoting itself exclusively to the liberal arts, St. Mary's manages to achieve the look and feel of a more elite private institution. . . . And because it is a state school, St. Mary's does all of this at bargain prices."

St. Mary's College of Maryland was not the beneficiary of such laudatory national publicity before 1982; indeed, it struggled to be known within the borders of Maryland as a four-year, coeducational, *public college* of the liberal arts. Now the goals and expectations are boundless, as President Lewis has promised a continuation of the frantic pace of progress until St. Mary's is regarded as "one of the best colleges—not simply in Maryland, or in the mid-Atlantic, but in the entire country." To attain goals that so recently seemed unattainable, all members of the College community "will have to hold ourselves to even greater expectations and higher standards."

But that has always been the case at St. Mary's. Complacency has rarely characterized this College, where constant change and the quest for ever-greater challenges *are traditions.* This new College with the old school ties has appreciated the excitement, energy, and expectations of adventuresome pioneers generation after generation. St. Mary's has always been the *living* monu-

Ever Forward

We have reason to be pleased with what we have accomplished. We have established significantly higher standards across every sector of the College—from the curriculum to academic and administrative planning, from fiscal management to plant development, from fund-raising to student activities. Because of . . . what you {the faculty} have done, we are a much better College. There is, in fact, reason to celebrate the 150th anniversary of St. Mary's College in 1990 because we have a lot to celebrate. And, no doubt, a major part of this cause for celebration is the work of the faculty.

. . .

{But} the work before us is even more difficult and perhaps more pressing. Whereas several years ago St. Mary's was undoubtedly better than its reputation, today the opposite may be true. Having achieved so much in the past several years and having been acclaimed so much for our achievements, the public's perception of the College is, I believe, larger than life.

. . .

All this is to say that St. Mary's is—as we all so well know—an institution in transition. The acceptable levels of performance of several years ago are no longer good enough. We are, in brief, now driven by our own success, by our enhanced reputation. It is a given in higher education that if we do not ask more of ourselves, we give less; that if we do not, as a college, move forward, we will fall behind. That is why we have worked so hard during the past several years to improve the curriculum, to attract better students, to construct new facilities, to build a better Board, and to increase faculty support and salaries in order to recruit and retain the best in our profession.

So when I describe this new imperative, I certainly do not mean to sound an ominous note. Because I think, in fact,

that we should freely celebrate what we have accomplished and be glad that momentum . . . drives us toward greater achievement and a reputation solidly founded on substance and worth. I can think of no better way to celebrate the founding anniversary of this special College.

—Source: Excerpts from an address to the faculty and staff by President Edward T. Lewis, 1 November 1988.

Dr. Edward T. (Ted) Lewis, president of St. Mary's College of Maryland, 1 July 1983—present.

ment it was originally intended to be, kept alive and forever young by the process of nurturing, and being nurtured by, youth. *Ageless vitality* epitomizes this place. The seventeenth-century bricks in the walls of the Alumni Lodge once reverberated with the voices of colonial legislators in Maryland's old capitol building. But those bricks were not discarded due to age; they were reused time and again because they were needed to serve the present and future—in the carriage house of the Female Seminary of the 1800s, in the alumnae guest house of the 1920s, in the home economics cottage of the 1930s–1940s, in the president's residence of the 1950s–1960s, and in the current alumni guest house. Ageless vitality also epitomizes the people who have embraced St. Mary's and been embraced by it. One of these people was Annie ("Lizzie") Thomas Lilburn, who arrived on campus as a girl of thirteen, graduated at seventeen, became principal at twenty-one, retired at thirty-five, and continued to live in the shadow of Calvert Hall, still serving her alma mater, until her death at age seventy-six. Another of those vital, ageless people was Virginia ("Gina") Cross Blackistone Leopard, who graduated from Miss France's new Junior College in 1935 and received her B.A. from St. Mary's College

The St. Mary's alumni did not wait long to string this congratulatory banner across Route 5 following the 16 October 1989 publication of the U.S. News and World Report 1990 College Guide.

of Maryland in 1980—in between serving as the alumni director and unofficial cheerleader for a special school of two eras.

Ageless vitality has brought St. Mary's to this special anniversary. Amid countless crises and challenges, the school refused to abandon its founding principles for the mere sake of survival or to preserve the less relevant elements of its heritage if it meant certain extinction. It is this institution's special, successful *blending* of continuity and change, tradition and innovation, that we celebrate and applaud in this sesquicentennial year. Recently, the chorus of praise for the innovativeness of St. Mary's has grown larger and louder. To be an excellent but affordable, small and personable, state-owned liberal arts college might be recent developments at some schools, now called "public ivys," but that unique combination of characteristics has existed here for 150 years. If St. Mary's College of Maryland is worthy of praise in 1990, it is because the radical, seemingly fanciful dreams of 1840 were profoundly valid and exceptionally vital. The Monument School of the People has reached the milestone of 150 years *younger than ever,* because it has kept faith with its unique heritage and founding philosophy on its original, historic campus—a significant site of constant reminders that the past is present for the future.

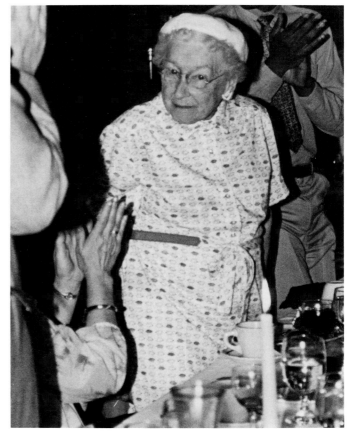

Miss Lucy Franklin Spedden, Seminary Class of 1916—the epitome of ageless vitality.

From a bend in the road we first saw the river
Where we would sunbathe, study, learn to wait
For crabs to grab the bait

Ideas to grab our minds. Sailboats point always
To the wind, the river gives us strength, renews,
We begin and then begin again.
. . .
Here at this place of beginnings, we leave
Shadows on the nurturing shore,
This bend in our lives, St. Mary's

The river, the nurturing shore.

–"The Nurturing Shore" copyrighted © 1983 by Professor
Michael Glaser of St. Mary's College.

Despite the lack of footnotes or endnotes, *Monument School of the People* is a factually accurate account based on extensive primary and secondary sources. A fully annotated copy of the book will permanently reside in the Special Collections of the St. Mary's College Library for consultation by future generations of researchers.

The most complete and essential primary source for this book was the Board of Trustees Minutes. The first five volumes (I: 27 October 1845–17 May 1854; II: 24 March 1870–December 1898; III: 20 March 1899–16 October 1916; IV: June 1918–September 1941; V: September 1941–September 1956) are deposited in the Maryland State Archives, Annapolis, cataloged under "St. Mary's Female Seminary." The College Library has microfilm and photocopies of these, and the original Board Minutes since 6 October 1956 remain on campus, in the keeping of the President's Office. The only significant gap in this 145-year record is unfortunately for the critical decade of the 1860s, which hampers our understanding of the Civil War in Southern Maryland. Sadly, too, the Board of Trustees Minutes never mentioned graduates prior to the first official commencement in 1874, and that omission, coupled with the destruction of old student files in the Calvert Hall fire of 1924, has obscured the identity of the earliest Seminarians. The best sources of information on alumnae prior to 1900 are the listings of graduates in catalogs and commencement programs, the *St. Mary's Seminary Junior College Newsletter,* published in Spring 1950 and quickly superceded by the *Alumni Newsletter* (1950–   ), and *The Mulberry Tree Papers* (1972–   ).

The late nineteenth- and twentieth-century newspapers of Southern Maryland give valuable perspectives on the growth of St. Mary's, and an incomparable view of campus life is contained in the several collections of student newspapers—*The Seminary Signal* (October 1923–1940), *The Signal News* (October 1940–1948), *The Ripples/Tidal Wave* (September 1948–June 1949), *Signal News* (September 1949–June 1959), *Point News* (September 1959/September 1970–May 1973), *St. Mary's College Empath* (October 1973–January 1982), *The Empath* (15 February/28 September 1982–4 December 1984), and *The Point News* (29 January 1985–   ). This history was also enriched by reference to a large collection of St. Mary's catalogs—one dating to 1858 and the rest forming an almost unbroken sequence since 1895. Despite such extensive printed materials, this book could not have been written without the many rare manuscripts, photographs, clippings, files, artifacts, scrapbooks, and student memorabilia that were loaned to the project by generations of alumni. Those former students and their descendants are truly too numerous to mention individually, but they all have my inestimable gratitude for showing such devotion to their alma mater.

The other major sources for *Monument School of the People* include:

Chapter I

Matthew Page Andrews, *The Founding of Maryland* (New York, 1933).

William Hand Browne, ed., *Archives of Maryland,* 72 vols. (Baltimore, 1883–   ).

Lois Green Carr and David W. Jordan, *Maryland's Revolution of Government, 1689–1692* (Ithaca, 1973).

Lois Green Carr and Russell R. Menard, guest editors, "St. Mary's City Commission Special Issue," *Maryland Historical Magazine,* LXIX, No. 2 (Summer 1974).

Lois Green Carr, Philip D. Morgan, Jean B. Russo, eds., *Colonial Chesapeake Society,* Institute of Early American History and Culture (Chapel Hill, 1988).

J. Frederick Fausz, guest editor, "Fresh Perspectives on Maryland's Past: The Seventeenth-Century Experience," 350th Anniversary Issue of *Maryland Historical Magazine,* LXXIX, No. 1 (Spring 1984).

J. Frederick Fausz, "The Secular Context of Religious Toleration in Mary-

land," *Maryland 350th Anniversary Lectures* (Baltimore: Loyola College, 1984).

Captain Henry Fleet, "A Breife Journal of A voyage made . . . to Virginia and other partes of the Continent of America Anno 1631," 22 February 1631/32, MS 688/19, Lambeth Palace Library, London.

Henry Chandlee Forman, *Jamestown and St. Mary's: Buried Cities of Romance* (Baltimore, 1938).

Clayton Colman Hall, ed., *Narratives of Early Maryland, 1633–1684* (New York, 1910).

J. A. Leo Lemay, *Men of Letters in Colonial Maryland* (Knoxville, 1972).

Henry M. Miller, *Discovering Maryland's First City: A Summary Report On the 1981–1984 Archaeological Excavations in St. Mary's City, Maryland,* Archaeology Series No. 2 (St. Mary's City Commission, 1986).

Henry M. Miller and Julia A. King, guest editors, "Exploring a 'Splendid and Delightsome' Land," special Southern Maryland issue of *Historical Archaeology: Journal of the Society for Historical Archaeology,* XXII, No. 2 (1988).

Edward C. Papenfuse, ed., *A Biographical Dictionary of the Maryland Legislature, 1635–1789,* 2 vols. (Baltimore, 1979, 1985).

Chapters II–IV

Edwin W. Beitzell, "Early Schools of Southern Maryland," *Chronicles of St. Mary's: Monthly Bulletin of the St. Mary's County Historical Society,* V, No. 3 (March 1957), 29–38.

John S. Brubacher and Willis Rudy, *Higher Education in Transition* (New York, 1958).

Robert J. Brugger, *Maryland: A Middle Temperament, 1634–1980* (Baltimore, 1988).

George H. Callcott, *A History of the University of Maryland* (Baltimore, 1966).

Clippings File, "St. Mary's Female Seminary," Maryland Room, The Enoch Pratt Free Library, Baltimore.

Clippings File, "St. Mary's Female Seminary," Library Reading Room, The Maryland Historical Society, Baltimore.

Lawrence A. Cremin, *American Education: The Colonial Experience, 1607–1783* (New York, 1970); *American Education: The National Experience, 1783–1876* (New York, 1980); *Traditions of American Education* (New York, 1977).

Charles A. Doub, "The History of Education in Saint Mary's County, Maryland, Prior to 1900" (unpublished M.A. Thesis, University of Maryland, 1939), chap. VI.

R. S. Fisher, *Gazeteer of the State of Maryland, 1852* (Baltimore, 1852).

Eleanor Flexner, *Century of Struggle: The Woman's Rights Movement in the United States* (Cambridge, Mass., 1959, 1975).

Family/Genealogy Files, St. Mary's County Historical Society, Leonardtown.

Regina Combs Hammett, *History of St. Mary's County, Maryland* (Ridge, 1977).

Helen Lefkowitz Horowitz, *Alma Mater: Design and Experience in the Women's Colleges from Their Nineteenth-Century Beginnings to the 1930s* (Boston, 1984).

[Jeremiah L. Hughes], *Maryland Pocket Annual for 1839; for 1840; for 1841; for 1842* (Annapolis).

Emily Regina Jones, *The City of St. Maries, Maryland: A Story and Personal Recollections,* ed. Eugene and Jean G. Rea (St. Mary's City, 1982).

John P. Kennedy, *Rob of the Bowl: A Legend of St. Inigoe's,* ed. William S. Osborne, Masterworks of Literature Series (New Haven, 1965).

Edgar W. Knight, ed., *A Documentary History of Education in the South Before 1860,* 5 vols. (Chapel Hill, 1950).

Laws of the General Assembly of Maryland, Maryland State Library, Annapolis.

Jeanne Payne Murphy, "St. Mary's Junior College: Education in an Unsurpassed Setting" (typescript, The Johns Hopkins University, May 1960).

Philodemic Society of Georgetown College, *Oration Delivered at the First Commemoration of the Landing of the Pilgrims of Maryland, Celebrated May 10, 1842* (Baltimore, 1842); *Oration Delivered at the Second Commemoration of the Landing of the Pilgrims of Maryland, Celebrated May 15, 1849* . . . (Baltimore, 1849)—in the collections of The Enoch Pratt Free Library, Baltimore.

Morris L. Radoff, ed., *The Old Line State: A History of Maryland* (Annapolis, 1971).

Beverly Redman, "'Nothing Abashed Me!'," *The Mulberry Tree Papers,* XIV, No. 1 (Winter 1988–89), 10–17.

Whitman H. Ridgway, *Community Leadership in Maryland, 1790–1840* (Chapel Hill, 1979).

David H. Wallace, "Alumni Album: M. Adele France," *Washington College Alumnus & Bulletin* (May–Aug. 1948), 7.

Frank F. White, Jr., *The Governors of Maryland, 1777–1970* (Annapolis, 1970).

John M. Whitmore, "Trial By Fire," *The Mulberry Tree Papers* (Spring 1981), 8–11.

Thomas Woody, *A History of Women's Education in the United States,* 2 vols. (New York, 1929, repr. 1974).

Photo Credits:

Baltimore Sun, p. 86; A. Aubrey Bodine, pp. 38, 97; Christine C. Cihlar, p. 147; Frank Entrekin Studio, pp. 10, 22; Dave Roche–Shutterbug, pp. 48, 50, 95, 116, 135, 146; Clifton Smith, pp. 115, 117, 121, 124, 126, 127, 131, 132, 133; Marion E. Warren, pp. 17, 31, 53, 71, 88, 102–105; Chris Witzgall, p. 15, 20, 136. Front cover: Matthew Anable. 150th Logo: Angela R. Costa.

Appendix A:
The Principals and Presidents of St. Mary's, 1846–1990

Principals of St. Mary's Female Seminary

Edward J. Meany	2 April 1846–14 December 1846	fired
Eliza M. Ohr with Rebecca R. Hough–one year as co-principal	March 1847–8 May 1851	fired
Margaret Nealy	September 1851–August 1852	–
Eliza Gillespie	4 August 1852 (elected, did not serve)	–
Mary Blades	21 September 1852–July 1853	resigned
Ellen Green	10 August 1853–1 August 1854	resigned
"The Hiatus"–School probably closed, September 1854-late 1857		
Mary Blades, co-principal with Madame Despommiers (probably did not serve)	September 1858–August ? 1860	resigned?
Lottie Leigh [Gardiner?]	1860–1862?	–
Mrs. Trimble, Treble, or Trible	April 1862–August 1862	–
Lucy L. Gardiner	August 1862–August 1869	died in office
Mary Gardiner	August 1869–August 1870	–
Lottie L. Gardiner and Henrietta K. Tilghman	September 1870–August 1872	resigned
Mrs. James R. (Jeannette) Thomas	September 1872–November 1881	died in office
Annie Elizabeth Thomas (after 1894, Mrs. John G. Lilburn)	November 1881–30 June 1895	resigned
Laurel Richardson Langley	August 1895–August 1900	resigned
Mrs. Lucy Virginia Maddox	August 1900–June 1923	resigned
Mary Adele France	30 June 1923–May 1937	continued

Presidents of St. Mary's Female Seminary-Junior College

Mary Adele France	May 1937–30 June 1948	resigned
Louise K. Rotha (acting)	February–30 June 1948	resigned
Dr. Anna May Russell	1 July 1948–30 May 1964	continued

Presidents of St. Mary's College of Maryland

Dr. Anna May Russell	1 June 1964–30 June 1969	resigned
Dr. J. Renwick Jackson, Jr.	1 July 1969–6 February 1982	resigned
Dr. Richard D. Weigle (Interim President)	6 February 1982–30 June 1983	resigned
Dr. Edward T. Lewis	1 July 1983–Present	

Appendix C:
Graduates of the "Missing Years," 1874–1904

1874–Sallie Brome Morsell
1876–Harriet Dallam Webster
1877–Annie E. Thomas
   Vallie S. Weagley
1878–Mattie L. Carson
1880–Maggie A. Andrews
   Mamie Meddars
   Victoria Roe
   Jeannette Brome Thomas
1881–Lizzie Blackistone
   Clare Thomas
1882–Ruth Carey
   Lillie Staplefort
1883–Nellie Bourne
   Julia Hayden
   Hortense deBeauharnais Mellier
   Ida Millinder
   Mamie Belle Rizer
1884–Emma Estelle Marshall
1885–Emma Jane Griffith
   Mary Elizabeth Revell
1886–Edith E. Black
   Harriet Anne Blackistone
   Carrie Chamberlaine
   Adelia E. Ellis
   Addie Hammond
   Sadie Hollingsworth
   Katie Polk
1887–Lola Wood Garner
1889–Delia Burch
   Annie Harwell
   Lulu Martin
   Maggie Smith
   Nannie Wallis

   Bessie Waring
   Elba Harris Wright
1890–Annie Dare Wilson
   Katherine Spencer Crane
1891–Olive Bohanan
   Catherine Ripley Watson
1892–Elizabeth Nairn Broughton
   Henrietta Porter Coston
   Roberta Long Dickey
   Clara Virginia Jones
   Miriam Poe
   Alice Belle Reid
   Jennie Maria Smith
1893–Julia Elise Keating
1894–Mary Blanche Hayward
   Margaret Elizabeth Turner
1895–Beulah Rebecca Arnold
   Virginia Fletcher Brewer
   Alice Anna Deckman
   Belle Xenia Gatch
   Angie May Hayward
   Ellen Ewell McGregor
   Minnie Lee Penington
   Alice Talmage Robertson
1897–Susie LaRoche
   May Eva Walters
1898–Sara Elizabeth Cruikshank
   Esther Schilling
   Clara Frances Ward
1900–Emily Clayton Bishop
   Ella Carter Hodgson
   Ruth Jourdan

1901–Florence Crawford Bounds
   Sadie B. Bridges
   Clara Blanche Coppersmith
   Sue Edgerton Davis
   Grace Linwood Gibson
   Nina Virgina Marriot
   Gertrude Elizabeth Moxey
   Helen Blakford Shermantine
1902–Mary Brighton Dougherty
   Grace Sweeney McKenny
   Élla Rochbrume Perry
   Edith May Stevens
   Anna Allen Stevenson
1903–May Peterson Broome
   Anna Elizabeth Butler
   Mary Remington Coppage
   Mary Lillia Dent
   Hettie McFarland
   Florence Amy Mellor
   Lula Conway Price
   Ella Mae Rheburger
   Mary McIntyre Wilson
1904–Grace Steele Allen
   Geneva E. Blair
   Ruth Burnside
   Virginia A. Carver
   Lula Clark
   Margaret C. Eagle
   Mary E. Miller
   Frances Reichard Mumma
   Jeanette Dossy Peterson
   Margaret Elizabeth White

* * * * * * * * * * * *

Appendix D:
Significant Dates in St. Mary's History

21 March 1840 (Enactment Day)	Gov. William Grason signs into law the "Act to Authorize the Drawing of a Lottery to Establish a Female Seminary . . . on the Site of the Ancient City of Saint Marys" (Legislative Session of 1839, Chapter 190)
3 August 1844	The cornerstone of the Seminary Building is laid
24 August 1844	The six-acre campus is deeded to the state
13 November 1845	The first meeting of the full Board of Trustees is held
14 January 1846	In a historic session, the Board of Trustees establishes the core characteristics of St. Mary's—creating an affordable, nonsectarian institution committed to academic excellence in liberal arts education—that have consistently identified this institution ever since
26 February 1846	The Maryland General Assembly makes the Board of Trustees "a body politic and corporate" in "An Act to Incorporate the St. Mary's Female Seminary" (Legislative Session of 1845, Chapter 257)
[12?] May 1846	The first students begin classes at the Seminary
October 1847 to June 1848	The first full academic year is conducted at the Seminary
24 February 1858	The State of Maryland saves the Seminary by reconstituting the Board of Trustees in "An Act to Preserve the Existence of the St. Mary's Female Seminary" (Legislative Session of 1857, Chapter 101)
28 March 1868	The General Assembly guarantees the financial solvency of the Seminary by beginning regular annual appropriations for state scholarships (Legislative Session of 1867, Chapter 193)

June 1874	St. Mary's Female Seminary issues its first "Certificate of Graduation" (diploma) to Miss Sallie Brome Morsell
10 June 1908	Music Hall (now, St. Mary's Hall)—the oldest extant building on campus—is finished in time for commencement ceremonies
1 July 1923	Mary Adele France becomes principal of the Female Seminary, beginning the longest tenure of any chief executive in St. Mary's history
5 January 1924	Fire guts the old Seminary Building of 1844–45 (the first Calvert Hall)
3 August 1924	The cornerstone for the new and present Calvert Hall is laid on the original foundations, eighty years to the day from the first cornerstone laying ceremony. The guest of honor is Mrs. Cecelia Coad Roberts, last surviving member of the first entering class, who attended the first ceremony in 1844
23 April 1926	St. Mary's becomes the first junior college in Maryland upon the recommendation of the Board of Trustees
11 June 1929	Edwin Tyler Burch becomes the first male to graduate from St. Mary's Female Seminary
12 June 1930	Katherine M. Bowdle, Dorothy Connor, Irma K. Mumford, and Virginia Dare Sollers become the first graduates of the Junior College Division
29 December 1930	St. Mary's receives national accreditation as a high school for the first time in its history; in 1931 the State of Maryland recognizes it as a "First Class, First Group High School"
15–16 June 1934	St. Mary's Female Seminary-Junior College is the host institution for the State of Maryland's Tercentenary Celebration
10 June 1935	Charles Birch becomes the first male graduate of the Junior College
May 1937	Adele France is named the first president of St. Mary's and the school is included as a regular item in the state budget for the first time
1937–1938	In this academic year, St. Mary's becomes a four-year Junior College (high school grades 11 and 12, college years 1 and 2)
21 March 1941	The Gymnasium and Recreation Building (now Kent Hall) is dedicated, a gift of the state in recognition of the centennial anniversary of the institution
17 April 1941	The four-year Junior College receives accreditation by the Maryland State Department of Education
3 June 1941	The Board of Trustees, as constituted by the state in 1858, meets for the last time before reorganization
23 September 1941	The reconstituted Board of Trustees meets for the first time and features the first members who are women, alumnae, and non-residents of St. Mary's County
1 December 1948	The Maryland General Assembly renews the state's commitment to St. Mary's, rejecting the 1 February 1947 recommendation of the Maryland Commission on Higher Education to close the institution
1 July 1948	Anna May Russell becomes the new president of St. Mary's Female Seminary Junior College, beginning a successful tenure of 21 years
1 July 1949	"Female" is dropped from the name of the institution
28 November 1959	St. Mary's Seminary Junior College receives its first accreditation from the Middle States Association of Colleges and Secondary Schools
5 June 1960	St. Mary's graduates its last high school class
7 April 1964	Gov. J. Millard Tawes signs legislation changing the name of the institution to the present St. Mary's College of Maryland
September 1965	The first resident male students arrive on campus
28 September 1966	The State Board of Higher Education approves the elevation of St. Mary's to senior college status, and the school will initiate a baccalaureate curriculum beginning in the 1967–68 academic year
8 June 1968	The last Junior College class graduates from St. Mary's
29 May 1971	St. Mary's College of Maryland awards its first baccalaureate degrees
1 June 1974	St. Mary's receives its first unconditional accreditation as a senior college from the Middle States Association of Colleges and Secondary Schools
16 October 1989	St. Mary's is ranked the no. 1 regional liberal arts college in the northeast by *U.S. News and World Report 1990 College Guide*

12/89B2043Z